THE

INSIDER'S

GUIDE

TO

SAN MIGUEL®

Compiled and written
by
Archie Dean

First Edition, January 1995
Second Edition, March 1995
Third Edition, January 1996
Fourth Edition, August 1996
Fifth Edition, February 1997
Sixth Edition, September 1997
Seventh Edition, February 1998
Eighth Edition, January 1999
Ninth Edition, January 2000
Tenth Edition, October 2000
Eleventh Edition, September 2001
Twelfth Edition, June 2002
Thirteenth Edition, June 2003
Fourteenth Edition, April 2004
Fifteenth Edition, March 2005

Laura & Jerry Frye
Sharon & Ray Giamant
Feb 1 - March 2
2006

Casa de la Vista
29B Oja de Agua

Library of Congress Catalog Card Number: 96-142573

ISBN #970-91505-0-2

Published in México

Tip 140

About the book . . .

We have the "Who are they?" (*Juarde* — the popular resident directory) and now the "Where are they?" This is a comprehensive ready reference of where to find places or things in San Miguel, designed for the traveler as well as residents. Keep in mind that this is not intended to be a directory including every doctor, lawyer, hotel or tortilla factory. Because of limitations of space, only the best known or conveniently located places in a particular category are listed. Special care is taken to produce an accurate guide. Prices, quality of service, location and hours of business were verified at the time of publication. As one quickly learns in México, things can and do change!

Any omission or oversight is not intentional. Should you wish to recommend additional places, names, etc., or make corrections and updates, or just make comments for a future edition, please bring to the attention of the author by writing to:

APDO # 1063   BC-2323
San Miguel de Allende, Gto   (or)   413 Interamerica Blvd #1
37700 México   Laredo, TX 78045-8285

This book is dedicated to my parents who first introduced me to this part of the world. They were winter residents for several years in the early 1970s. This edition is also dedicated to the memory of some men and women who have made San Miguel the very special place that we know today. Regretfully, they all passed away during the last few years. They will be missed as friends and for their contributions to the community. They are; Alan Pollard, Josh Kligerman, Bill Hunt, Walter Davies, Doña Carmina, Ivan Alten, George McGann, Norman Kruk, Dr. Bill Hall, Victor Cuevas, Don Griffin and my pal, Louise McCarthy, who contributed in so many ways to the success of this book. *Descansen en paz.*

For technical help and editing, thanks to Juan Antonio Ruiz, Robert Brown and Elizabeth Denkinger. Cover photographs were graciously donated by Dixon Adams and the late Jack Cooper. The centerfold Jardín sketch was created by a friend and winter resident, Hal Josephs. The web page colored pictures of San Miguel (**http://insidersma.tripod.com**) were taken by photographer Dixon Adams. Also, I'd like to thank my good friend, Bill Gibbons, for continuing support and counsel, as well as my son, Anil, and the many others who gave me the inspiration to press on.

¡BUENA SUERTE Y BUEN VIAJE!

San Miguel de Allende

Welcome to magical San Miguel de Allende! A town rich in culture, heritage and history, it is well known as the home of heroes of the Mexican independence movement and as a center for the arts. There are several San Miguels in México, but only one San Miguel de Allende. San Miguel de Allende is old, having celebrated its 450th anniversary in 1992. It was founded in 1542 by Fray Juan de San Miguel, a Franciscan missionary, who was born in Spain. The first settlement was made near the former railroad station. An open chapel was built and this Indian mission was named San Miguel in honor of Fray Juan's own patron saint. The area is now known as San Miguel Viejo.

Later Fray Juan's companion, Fray Bernardo Cossin, moved the small settlement to a place near the springs of Izcuinapan, known today as El Chorro. During the balance of the 16th and 17th centuries, the settlement flourished as more Spaniards and Indians made their homes there. Cattle grazing and farming grew and later tanneries were built. Silver deposits had been discovered in Zacatecas and Guanajuato. At this time the mission town was renamed San Miguel el Grande. During the 18th century San Miguel became an important commercial center.

Late in this era it was here that the heroes of the independence movement were born and educated. One, Ignacio de Allende y Unzaga, was born in San Miguel on January 21, 1769. As a young man he became a brave fighter for independence and with other revolutionaries joined forces with Father Don Miguel Hidalgo, a parish priest of the town Dolores. When their plan was discovered, he consulted with Father Hidalgo, who then delivered the famous Cry of Independence speech on September 16, 1810 in Dolores. The revolt was led by an army of insurgents fighting for independence. Unfortunately, the Spanish government was still strong and the patriots were defeated. Hidalgo and Allende together with Jiménez and Aldama were executed and their heads hung in cages outside a Guanajuato granary. In recognition of General Allende's heroic efforts, the state government of Guanajuato changed the name of San Miguel el Grande to San Miguel de Allende on March 8, 1826.

In 1926 San Miguel de Allende was declared a National Monument, preserving the historical nature of the town, the reason today the town is free of traffic lights, neon signs, fire hydrants and fast food establishments.

With the opening of Instituto Allende Art School in the late 1930s, the foreign population began to grow. The growth was noticeable in the 1950s when a flood of US ex-servicemen arrived who were able to stretch their GI Bill benefits.

Today retired Americans and Canadians make up much of the foreign community, which numbers between 2,500-4,000 depending on the season. The peak tourist season is January-March with the arrival of the "snowbirds," escaping the cold and snow up north. The second season is July & August when "sunbirds," mostly from Texas, join teachers and students. The Mexican population is also growing. Today it is estimated that some 80,000 people live within the town, out of some 135,000 who live in the municipio (10 mile radius). A comfortable life can be found in San Miguel considering the reasonable cost of living as compared with other retirement or vacation options.

San Miguel de Allende lies in the highlands of central México in the state of Guanajuato. The area is called The Bajío, a vast plateau of fertile soil and rolling hills. San Miguel is one of México's prettiest colonial towns with cobblestone streets, 16th and 17th century architecture, pastel colors and beautiful old churches. A ring of foot hills in the distance provides an ideal backdrop for some of the best sunsets you will ever see anywhere. A bronze equestrian statue of General Allende that used to overlook the Mirador now stands on a high pedestal in the middle of the traffic circle at the entrance to town (across from Gigante). In July, 2000, the Mayor designated some streets around the Jardín to be pedestrian walkways and free of cars, trucks and buses.

Another lure is the pleasant year-round spring-like climate with warm, sunny days and cool nights. San Miguel sits at 6,400 feet which keeps both the humidity and temperature down and the air crisp and clear. Below note a monthly average high/low temperature range (degrees Fahrenheit) plus a monthly average precipitation table (in inches) for the San Miguel area.

Jan	Feb	Mar	Apr
71	74	78	81
46	48	50	54
0.5	0.1	0.2	0.8

May	Jun	Jul	Aug
83	80	78	78
57	58	58	58
1.3	5.0	4.7	4.6

Sep	Oct	Nov.	Dec
76	76	74	71
57	54	49	47
4.7	1.7	0.6	0.4

During the winter season, the mid-day temperature is usually in the high 70s. Nights and early mornings can become cool requiring sweaters and fireplace fires. The rainy season is between June and September when you may experience late afternoon or evening showers. A metric temperature chart will help you convert the Fahrenheit degrees into Celsius as indicated below:

60°F — 16°C	75°F — 24°C
65°F — 18°C	80°F — 27°C
70°F — 21°C	85°F — 29°C

For a town its size, San Miguel offers a remarkably diverse list of activities. It has been said that people retire to Florida to die but retirees move to San Miguel to live! Spanish and art are taught at a number of first rate schools. Concerts, plays, lectures, readings and art openings are scheduled on a regular basis. Recreation opportunities are unlimited with golf, tennis, swimming and horseback riding available. The town does draw an interesting mix of expatriates, making it one of the friendliest places on earth. It would be difficult to be bored in San Miguel.

Another plus is the town's unique public library (the Biblioteca), an important cultural center for the community with one of the largest bilingual (Spanish and English) collections of any public library in México. In addition, an English local newspaper (ATENCIóN) is published weekly.

There is a wide variety of opportunities for public service in San Miguel. Check the **Volunteer Organizations** chapter in this book or ask at the Biblioteca English room to see the "Community Services" booklet (published 1994). Volunteers for the many non-profit community organizations need your help for either a short or long term. Foreigners do get involved and have a genuine concern for the people of San Miguel, one of the reasons for the excellent relationship. Don't be surprised to see many local Mexicans, young and old alike, wearing tee-shirts and ball caps with "Dallas Cowboys," "LA Dodgers" or "Chicago Bulls" on them. Another sign of the special connection between México and the USA is the sister city relationship with St. Augustine, Florida and La Habra, California.

As you will see after reading this publication, the town does have so much to offer. For those who are already here, take time to enjoy it all. For those who are thinking about staying, perhaps you might want to discover and see for yourself.

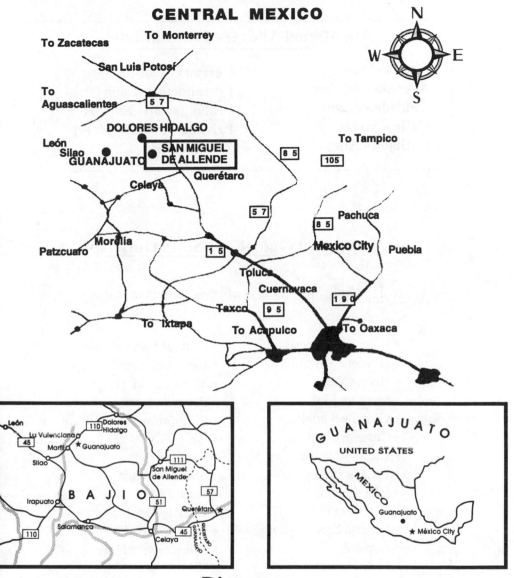

CENTRAL MEXICO

Distances

San Miguel to:

Mexico City	274 kms.	171 miles
San Luis Potosí	200 "	125 "
León Airport (Silao)	105 "	65 "
Guanajuato	90 "	56 "
Querétaro	64 "	40 "
Celaya	50 "	31 "
Dolores Hidalgo	43 "	27 "

Source: State Tourist Office

San Miguel Address Translations:

Ancha - Way
Avenida - Avenue
Calzada - Road
Calle - Street
Callejón - Alley

Cerrada - Cul-de-Sac
Libramiento - Loop Road
Prolongación - Extension
Privada - Private Street
Salida - Exit

<u>Authorized Guidebook Sales Outlets:</u>

📖 Indicates location of book outlets in text

- Allende Properties
- Border Crossings
- Buena Vida
- Casa de Liza
- Casa de Papel
- Casas Elegantes
- Casa Granada
- Casa Schuck
- Clandestino
- La Conexión
- Galería San Miguel
- Girasol
- Instituto Allende
- Lagundi

- Leather Shop
- Libros el Tecolote
- Mansión del Bosque
- Posada Carmina
- Promotion Mex Culture
- RE/MAX
- Sazón
- Sierra Nevada
- Solutions
- Tinta y Papel
- Villa Mirasol
- Villa Rivera Hotel
- Villa Santa Mónica

In order to remain completely unbiased in my recommendations, I accept no advertising. I also neither solicit nor accept commissions, gratuities or kickbacks from any establishment listed in this book.

– The Author

TABLE OF CONTENTS

American Consul/Canadian Consulate 1
Antique Shops 2
Apartments 4
Architecture 9
Art Galleries 10
Art Schools 13
Art Studios 15
Art Supplies/Framing 19
Bakeries 21
Banks/Investment Broker 23
Bars 26
Bed & Breakfast Places 29
Biking 34
Book Stores 35
Bull Fighting 36
Cafes 37
Carpets/Carpet Cleaning 40
Car/Bike Rental 42
Car Maintenance 42
Cemetery 44
Churches 45
Cinemas 48
Clothing Shops 49
Communication Centers/Message Delivery Services 53
Community Bulletin Boards 56
Computers/Internet/Web Page Design 56
Cooking Classes/Catering 62
Copy Places 64
Country Club 65
Dancing/Night Clubs 65
Delis 67
Dentists 68
Doctors/Physical and Massage Therapists 69
Drugstores 73
Electrical Shops 74
Government Offices 75
Grocery Stores/Candy Stores 79
Gyms/Aerobics/Aquatics/Pilates/Meditation/Yoga 82
Hair Salons/Barbershops 87
Hardware Stores/Locksmiths 89
Hat Shops 91
Health Salons 91
Holidays 93
Horseback Riding 96
Hospitals/Red Cross/Medical Equipment 97

Hotels 100
Ice Cream/Yogurt Shops 114
Labs (Clinical) 115
Laundromats/Dry Cleaning 116
Lawyers 117
Library 119
Liquor Stores 121
Meat & Poultry Stores 122
Medical Insurance 124
Money Changers 125
Museums 127
Music 127
Newspapers 128
Nurseries/Flower Shops 129
Optical Stores 130
Photo Shops 131
Post Office 132
Radio/TV Repair 133
Real Estate Offices 134
Rentals (Appliances, etc.) 141
Restaurants 141
Rest Places 165
Schools 166
Sewing/Seamstress/Supplies 167
Shippers 168
Shoe Stores/Shoe Repair 169
Shopping 171
Spanish Schools/Tutors/Conversation Class 196
Stationery Stores/Card Shops 200
Storage 201
Supermarket/Markets 202
Telephone 203
Tennis Courts 207
Theater 208
Things to Do 208
Tortilla Factories 215
Transportation 215
Travel Agencies 227
Utility Companies 229
Veterinarians/S.P.A./Grooming 231
Video Rentals 234
Volunteer Organizations 234
Watch Repair 237
Water (Bottled) 238

Addendum
   Dolores Hidalgo 241
   Guanajuato 247
Index 260

American Consul

American Consular Agency
Hernández Macías #72 (Int #6) across from Bellas Artes
Tel: 152-2357   Fax: 152-1588
    (after hours — emergencies only Tel: 152-0068 and 152-0653)
E-mail: coromar@unisono.net.mx
HOURS: Mon-Fri 9am-1pm
    Closed weekends and American and Mexican holidays
Consular Agent: Col. Philip Maher (USAF) (Ret)
Office opened in 1985 and moved to present location in 1988
Paula Ramírez is the efficient bilingual secretary

> **Americans, upon arrival, should register and complete an information form**

Help given to Americans in trouble with the Mexican law
Passport renewals, notarize documents, translations (for a fee)
Copy machine

American Embassy
Reforma 305
México City
Tel: 01(55)5080-2000

The Consular Section:
    Room 101
    Tel: 01(55)5080-2000 or 5533-5692
    Hrs: Mon-Fri 9am-5pm, closed 2-3pm
        Also closed Mexican and American holidays

1. American Citizen Services
    Passports/citizenship
    Death/estates
    Arrest/detention
    Welfare/whereabouts
    Property

For Mexican immigration matters check Delegación Regional de Servicios Migratorios under the *Government Offices* section.

American Consulate
Progreso 1715
Guadalajara
Tel: 01(33)3825-2998 or (33)3825-2700

Canadian Consulate
San Miguel
Closed August 1998

Canadian Embassy
Schiller 529
Col. Polanco, México City
Tel: 01(55)5724-7900 and 01-800-706-2900 (toll free)
    Fax: 01(55)5724-7980
E-mail: www.canada.org.mx
Hrs: Mon-Fri 9am-1pm and 2-5pm
    Closed all weekends and holidays
Canadian citizens are invited to register by mail or in person

Antique Shops

1. El Atico Antígüedades
Correo #24 (Showroom now faces courtyard)
Tel: 152-0667 (*casa* after 3pm)
E-mail: rlascoutx@hotmail.com
Web page: www.el-atico.com
Hrs: Daily 11am-7pm, Sun 12-3pm
Owner: Ruth Lascoutx (from New England) and son Carlos
First class place with interesting collection
Antiques from everywhere
Appraisals done

2. Border Antiques
Prol. Cuesta de San José #4 (*casa*)
Col. Balcones
Tel: 152-3482 (call for appointment first)
E-mail: vernonkostohryz@cybermatsa.com.mx
Web page: http://kostohryz.tripod.com
Owner: Vernon Kostohryz
High quality authentic Mexican antiques
Specializing in religious art and Spanish colonial
Also good selection of masks
Since 1992

3. Bazar Unicornio
Hernández Macías #80
Tel: 152-1306
Hrs: Daily 10am-2pm and 4-8pm
Very large store — good selection of *retablos*
Antique furniture, art, bric-a-brac, rugs, etc.
Accepts consignments.
Since 1974

4. La Diligencia
Hernández Macías #118 (at the bend)
Tel: 152-1626
E-mail: la_diligencia18@hotmail.com
Hrs: Mon-Sat 10:30am-2:30pm and 5-8pm, Sun 11am-3pm
Owners: José Guadalupe and Enrique Hernández
Antiques from México—good prices
Some custom reproductions
Six full rooms

5. Bazar el Viejo Oeste (Bazaar of the Old West)
Hernández Macías #121 and #126
Tel: 152-7571
Hrs: Mon-Sat 10am-8pm, closed Sunday
Many wooden antiques
Three brothers: Ramón, Enrique and Mario are partners
Large warehouse located in San Luis Potosí

6. Arte Antique
Hernández Macías #83 (near Umarán)
Tel: 152-5049 (*casa*)
Hrs: Daily 10:30am-2:30pm and 4:30-8pm
Owner: Sra. Lucrecia Ramos
Authentic colonial antiques from throughout México
Reasonable prices
Opened 1994

7. Bazar La Hormiga (the ant)
Hernández Macías #57 (just north of Sautto Hotel)
Tel: 152-0088
Hrs: Mon-Sat 10am-2:30pm and 4:30-8pm, Sun 10am-3pm
Check a second store across the street
Antiques from all over central México
Opened August 1996

8. Cantadora
Formerly El Sabino Bazar
Fábrica La Aurora
Calzada de la Aurora s/n (north of town)
Tel: 154-8302
E-mail: cantadora8@hotmail.com
Web page: www.cantadorasma.com
Hrs: Mon - Sat 10am-5pm, closed Sunday
Owner: Rocío Rodríguez (bilingual)
Indoor/outdoor space
Antiques from México
Wooden doors, limestone door frames, ceramics, saints and more
Good selection of *cantera* stone
Opened 1995, relocated Jan'04

Also: **Tiempos**, Correo #71, Tel: 152-5057
    Casa Armida, Ancha de SA (next to Instituto), Tel: 152-2505
    Josefa, Canal #16, Tel: 152-0216
    Colección Cuatro Vientos, Barranca #17, Tel: 154-9132
    La Buhardilla, Fábrica La Aurora, Tel: 154-9911
    Cos-Az, Recreo 5-B, Tel: 152-6417

Apartments

As time goes on, finding suitable housing has become a considerable effort, especially when location, condition and price must be considered. Many people liken the task to a full-time occupation. The listings in this section will provide you with a starting point for your search. Good luck!

1. Carmina Suites/Apartments
Salida a Querétaro #100 (Mirador area)
Tel: 154-9390   or   152-8888
E-mail: suites@carminasuites.com
Web page: www.carminasuites.com
14 units (some with views of the town)
Daily, weekly or monthly rates (US$700), longer stays discounted
2 bedroom, 1 bathroom, kitchen, living/dining room & fireplace
Furnished including cable TV, bedding and dishes
Maid service
Parking —also bus route
New management (Posada Carmina) Sept'03

2. Villa Xichú
Camino a Xichú #9 (off Ojo de Agua)
Tel: 152-4913   044-415-103-0225 (cell)
E-mail: info@villa-xichu.com
Web page: www.villa-xichu.com
Owner: Gloria Belendez-Ramírez (bilingual)
Manager: Flor Zepeda (bilingual)
Six beautiful villas on two acres above the city
Located in a safe, gated compound-15 minute walk to centro
All include TV, VCR, microwave and fireplaces
Nicely furnished with complete kitchens
Heated pools, jacuzzi and steam room
Large garden/walking area—ample parking
Rent daily, weekly or monthly
Opened Dec'02

3. Tres Casitas
Sollano #34 (short walk to Jardín)
Tel: 152-8128
E-mail: nanciclosson3@yahoo.com
Web page: www.infosma.com/trescasitas
Owner: Nanci Closson (designer artist)
Three deluxe one-bedroom apartments
Exquisitely furnished with Mexican crafts
Fully equipped kitchen, fireplace, telephone and cable TV
Private roof garden terrace
Includes maid service
Three day minimum
      US$60—$100 per/day, US$350—$500 per/week
Monthly discount during off-season

4. Las Terrazas San Miguel
Santo Domingo #3 (go east up Correo to Atascadero)
Tel/Fax: 152-5028
      In USA/Canada: (707) 534-1833 (rings in San Miguel)
E-mail: contact@terrazassanmiguel.com
Web page: www.terrazassanmiguel.com
Owners/hosts: Greg Johnson and Murray Friedman (from Napa,CA)
Complex of four very comfortable private furnished *casitas*
Each unit has its own patio with fountain, a full kitchen, cable TV,
      telephone and answering machine, internet access and
      purified water throughout

Laundry facilities free of charge
Fresh flowers and a chilled bottle of wine await your arrival
A copy of The Insider's Guide to San Miguel in each unit
Available by the week or month
New ownership June'03

5. Santo Domingo #16 (Atascadero)
8 units
Most are one bedroom with basic furniture
US$400 per month includes utilities plus 5-day maid service
Owner: Teresa Engelbrecht de González (bilingual)
Tel: 152-0120
E-mail: engel16@prodigy.net.mx
Web page: http://geocities.com/casaengelbrecht
Short term or long term
Central courtyard with common telephone
Inside parking
Some units have views

6. Casa Cervantes
Recreo #102 (near El Chorro)
8 Furnished garden apartments-each with fully equipped kitchen,
     fireplace and private patio
Owner: Federico Cervantes (bilingual)
Tel: 152-0928 and 152-4558
E-mail: casascervantes@hotmail.com
One bedroom— US$600 per/mo or US$350 per/week
     Long term rentals available at discounted prices
Includes all utilities and daily maid service
Central telephone for all tenants

7. Aldama #4 (across from La Conexión)
5 Units-upstairs/downstairs
1, 2 or 3 bedrooms — US$500-US$800 per month
Tel: 152-2524
Great Centro location
Furnished — some have microwave oven
Includes utilities and weekly maid service
Common telephone for local calls
Owner: Hope Harmon (bilingual)
Also owns other rentals in Atascadero area

8. Las Casitas
Tenerías #31 (between Instituto and the Jardín)
Tel: 152-0385
E-mail: luisfeqro@infosel.net.mx
Owner: Dr. Luis Sánchez (lives in Querétaro)
5 units – four are two bedroom, one three bedroom
US$1,100 (includes gas, water and general cleaning once a week)
Quiet and enclosed secure area
Furnished with fireplace and kitchen appliances
Cable TV and telephone access
Indoor parking

9. Manantial #7-A (off Cinco de Mayo)
Col. Allende
9 units
One and two bedrooms
Fully furnished, include fireplace, telephone and cable TV
US$400-$700 per month plus utilities
Tel: 154-4689, 150-0120   or   044-415-153-3897 (cell)
E-mail: beasanmiguel2002@hotmail.com
Web page: www.sanmigueldepartamentos.com
Owner: Beatriz Orvañanos (speaks four languages)
Common areas: Roof terraces and large garden area with ponds
        and many flowers and fruit trees
Opened in 2000

10. Correo #61 (up the hill past Chiquitos)
9 units — one or two bedroom with furnished kitchen
US$285-US$390 per month, includes utilities
Tel: 152-2637 (or check with Adriana at jewelry store by Pueblo Viejo Rest)

11. Posada "Villa Martha"
Recreo #72 and Huertas #5
24 Furnished apartments
Manager: Sr. Francisco Martínez
Tel: 152-0644 or 152-2055
1 or 2 bedroom (includes kitchen and bathroom)
US$300-US$550 per month, utilities included
Large parking area inside compound
Office Hrs: Mon-Fri 10:30am-2pm and 5-8pm
        Saturday 10:30am-1pm

12. Zacateros #17 (near Umarán)
5 units
One bedroom (1 or 2 beds) — US$300 per month
Furnished, including small kitchen and bathroom
Tel: 152-0050
Owner: Sra. García — speaks some English

13. Sollano #77-A (near Parque Juárez)
6 Units
1 and 2 bedroom — $375 and up, includes utilities
Owners: "Pepe" and Maruja Garay
Tel: 152-0786
Inside parking (costs extra)
Near Parque Juárez

14. Ancha de San Antonio #81 (faces Hotel Real de Minas)
20 units (18 single bedroom, 2 double bedroom)
Opened for occupancy Jan'95
Furnished US$300 per month (includes utilities)
Owner: Chelo Agundis
Tel: 152-1198 (speak to Chelo)
Also owns other rentals around town

15. Recreo #10 (near Correo)
7 Units
Tel: 152-0151
Beautiful courtyard garden
Most are one bedroom, all are furnished
US$275-US$350 per month, including utilities and twice a week
     maid service
Owner: Barbara Dobarganes
Usually long-term tenants

16. Orizaba #20 (SW of Centro)
11 Units
Owner: Chelo Agundis (Botica Agundis Farmacia)
2 bedroom, furnished apartments
US$300 per month (plus utilities)
Tel: 152-1198 (speak to Chelo)
Little turnover, long-term tenants

17. Sollano (2nd block from Calle Correo)
5 Units in a secure compound, nicely flowered courtyard
Good location, easy walk to Centro
Owner: Ruth Hyba
Tel: 152-0277 (La Mansión del Bosque)
One bedroom—US$450 per month
All have kitchens and fireplaces
Includes all utilities, weekly maid service
Laundry is extra
Mostly long-term tenants

Many more single unit apartments are available, depending on the
season, etc. Check the **Real Estate** section of this book, classifieds
in the weekly **ATENCIóN**, community bulletin board notices, the local
real estate agencies or just ask around the Jardín. Home stays may be
arranged for students at Academia and the Instituto. Rooms in homes
(with or without kitchen privileges) are another possibility.

Architecture

San Miguel has many interesting colonial historical buildings
built in the 18th and 19th centuries. Be on the lookout for the
intricately designed wooden doors, stone work, carvings, fountains,
balconies, wrought iron work and decorative metal door knockers.
There are many examples of this colonial architecture in the Centro
area, the reason San Miguel was declared a national historic site in
1926. A few examples are:

1. Casa del Mayorazgo de la Canal
Mansion is located at Canal #4
Note large wooden door carved in intricate detail and the arch
        keystone inscribed with an eagle
Beautiful courtyard
Today it is the home of BANAMEX

2. Casa de los Perros (house of the dogs)
Calle Umarán #3
Mid-18th century mansion
Note several carved dogs that support balcony above main entrance
Also interesting balconies and wrought iron railings
Now location of Casa Maxwell store

3. "House of the Inquisitor"
Calle Cuadrante #36
Judge of the Inquisition Don Victorino de las Fuentes lived here in 1815
Finely carved stone front shows French influence
Second level elaborate wrought iron balconies
Finished in June 1780

4. "El Pípila" (Juan José de los Reyes Martínez home)
Calle Barranca #44
Historical interest only
Birthplace (1782) and home of local independence hero
Plaque on front of house

5. Casa Cohen
Calle Reloj #12-22
Middle of the first block on west side of the street
Interesting landmark most people pass without noticing
Building reconstructed in 1942 by Isaac Cohen, a Syrian businessman
Called it "Arca de Noe" (Noah's Ark)
Completed for the town's 400th anniversary
Today family business continues selling brass items
Look up to see the many animals on the facade supporting the
    balconies as well as larger animals on the top of the building
Also note the Stars of David

Art Galleries

1. Galería San Miguel
Plaza Principal #14
Tel: 152-0454 and Tel/Fax: 152-1046
Hrs: Mon-Fri 9am-2pm and 4-7pm, Sat 10am-2pm and 4-8pm,
    Sun 11am-2pm
Credit cards accepted
Sylvia Samuelson is the American owner — since 1962
María Mendoza is the long-time English-speaking salesperson
Good location facing the Jardín
Contemporary Mexican art from all over México
Also a second floor loft

2. Galería Pérgola
Ancha de San Antonio #20
(Inside Instituto Allende- to the left and in the back)

Tel: 154-5595
E-mail: don@galeriademexico.com
Web page: www.galeriademexico.com/pergola (on-line gallery)
Hrs: Tues-Sat 10am-6pm, Sunday 12 noon-5pm
Director: Don Sibley
Large attractive open gallery
Fine Mexican art—Mexican masters and rising talents
Exhibitions change every eight weeks or so
Opened Dec'04

3. Galería Atenea
Jesús #2
Tel: 152-0785   Fax: 152-2647
E-mail: atenea@unisono.net.mx
Hrs: Daily 10am-2pm and 4-8pm, Sun 10am-2pm
     Closed Thursdays
Located in a 19th century colonial home
Owners: Isaac Uribe and Carlos Acuña (bilingual)
One of the leading galleries in San Miguel
Contemporary artists from around México and North America
Also sculpture, graphics and jewelry
Impressive collection by artist Sergio Bustamante
Look for art openings throughout the year
First opened in 1985, relocated Dec'97

4. Galería Dos Culturas
Zacateros #83-A (across from Espinos)
Tel/Fax: 154-7962
E-mail: luzrandy@prodigy.net.mx
Hrs: Mon-Sat 10am-6pm, closed Sunday
Owner: Luz Elena Barrera de Browning
Represent Mexican, American and European artists
Traditional or contemporary
Opened March'01

5. Galería de Cerámica
Pila Seca #3 (near H. Macías)
Tel: 154-5203
Hrs: Mon-Fri 10am-2pm and 4-7pm, Sat 10am-2pm, closed Tues & Sun
Owners: Bob Kays and Marjorie Heady
Large, attractive gallery displaying the work of most major local
     ceramic artists

11

Traditional functional pottery as well as a range of sculptural and
    raku forms
All work is unique and hand-crafted
Opened Aug'04
Also offers studio space at:
    Clay Art Center, Guadiana, Tel: 154-6825

6. Galería de Arte Fotográfico
Reloj #46 (near Insurgentes)
Tel: 152-7172   Tel/Fax: 152-2483
Hrs: Mon-Sat 11am-2pm and 4-7pm, closed Sunday
E-mail: acdfoto@unisono.net.mx
Web page: www.acdphoto.com
Director: Jo Brenzo
Attractive former stable and carriage house with stone arches
San Miguel's only photographic gallery
New exhibitions every six weeks
Opened Feb'99, relocated March'00
Connected with:
    (a) **Art Focus Studio**
        Same location (interior)
        Mixed media – changing exhibitions
    (b) **Academia de Fotografía**
        Cinco de Mayo #10 (corner of 16 de Septiembre) – Col Allende
        Tel: 152-2816 (*casa*) and 152-2246
        Specialized workshops by visiting and staff instructors
        Small classes (all levels) – English and Spanish
        Two year certificate program–travel workshops within México
        Monthly lab rental available
        Opened Sept'98
Check out www.classesunlimited.com
    Offers a variety of art and photography classes
    El Centro classroom, Mesones #57, Tel: 154-5366

7. Zacateros 81-B
Zacateros #81-B
Tel:154-8375
Hrs: Daily 11am-7pm, closed Sunday
Owned by four well known San Miguel artists
    Mary Breneman, Gerry Gill, Barbara Roberts and Delphine Scott
Opened April'03

Other Galleries:
 Artes México, Zacateros #81-A, Tel: 154-8531
 Indigo Galería, Mesones #76, Tel:152-2749
 Galería de la O, Portal de Allende #4, Tel: 152-2468
 Galería Izamal, Mesones #80, Tel: 152-6171
 Museo/Galería Pedro Friedberg, Recreo #48, Tel: 152-0885
 Toller Cranston, Sollano #84, Tel: 154-5093
 Mai Ono Kestenbaum Gallery, Quebrada #113, Tel: 152-1224
 Kunsthaus Santa Fé, Santa Fé #22-A (Col. Allende), Tel: 152-5608

Art openings are also scheduled on a regular basis at Bellas Artes and the Instituto (see the ATENCIóN for schedule). In addition, some shows can be seen at the Allende Museum. Check out the local artist exhibits every Sat/Sun 10am-4pm at "El Chorro" at the end of Recreo.

Art Schools

1. "El Nigromante" (Bellas Artes)
Calle Hernández Macías #75 (just north of Canal)
Tel: 152-0289
E-mail: cceninba@prodigy.net.mx
Office Hrs: Mon-Fri 10am-2pm and 4:30-7:30pm
　　　Sat 10am-1pm, closed Sunday and public holidays
Named after Ignacio Ramírez, a San Miguel intellectual (1818-1879),
　　　whose nickname means "sorcerer." Note a metal bust at the
　　　entrance of the courtyard.
Government cultural center
Beautiful 18th century former convent with large courtyard
Director: Francisco Vidargas (Aug'02)
Classrooms and two galleries (including Sala de Arte Mexicano with
　　　museum-quality exhibitions of Mexican contemporary artists),
　　　bookstore, theater and café
Arts and crafts courses all year
Monthly courses offered, such as drawing, painting, sculpture, en-
　　　graving, lithography, silk screening, photography, stained glass,
　　　ceramics, weaving, papermaking, music, ballet and dance
Foreign student tuition: US$100 per month (classes begin 1st of month)
　　　(children half price) plus lab fee according to course
Check out "Mural Siqueiros" in a room located in the far corner
　　　on the ground floor. The mural, painted by David Alfaro

Siqueiros, one of México's great artists in 1948, although never finished, has been completely restored (Nov'97) in commemoration of the 50th anniversary of the project.

2. Instituto Allende
Ancha de San Antonio #20
Tel: 152-0190   Fax: 152-4538
E-mail: iallende@instituto-allende.edu.mx
Web page: http://www.instituto-allende.edu.mx
Office Hrs: Mon-Fri 8am-5pm, Sat 9am-1pm
        Closed Sunday and holidays
Credit cards: Master and Visa
Director Academic Programs: Rodolfo (Rudy) Fernández Martínez Harris
Art school was founded in 1938; Stirling Dickinson was the Director
The original art school was incorporated into the new school on
        the present campus in 1951—golden jubilee in Jan'01
Incorporated with the University of Guanajuato
Large, beautiful colonial building and campus
Rufino Tamayo artist-in-residence during the 50's and 60's
Offers academic credit and awards MFA and BVA degrees
Painting, drawing, sculpture, jewelry, ceramics, batik, weaving,
        art history and more
Its students and teachers have founded many of the cottage
        industries in town
Classes year around—check out nice city view from back patio
Bilingual children's summer program (six weeks starting in late
        June) for ages 5-11
Make sure you check out the David Leonardo mural on the east
        wall overlooking the central courtyard (finished May'99)
Located on the premises is: **L'Invito** restaurant, **Galería Pérgola**,
        a small book store and a café.

3. Keith Keller's La Escuela
Ancha de San Antonio #27 (next to La Vida)
Tel: 152-0637
E-mail: keithkellerart@yahoo.com
Painting and drawing
Classes Mon, Wed, Fri 10am-1pm
US$180 per month (special price for Mexicans & FM3 holders)
La Escuela Gallery—also includes student's work
Unlimited studio time and keys available for all students
Stop in to see Fanny, "the queen of the street dogs"

14

Keith moved to San Miguel in 1985, relocated school Sept'03
Casa de Sueños guest house (2 rooms with bath and patio)
    Artist retreat available for students

4. Edina Sagert Studio
Fábrica La Aurora
Calzada de la Aurora s/n (north of town)
Tel: 120-8088 (*casa*)
E-mail: edinasagert@yahoo.com
Web page: www.edinasagert.com
Water color classes
Beginner to advanced students, 3 hour class (US$20)
Work indoor and outdoor–easy technique
Studied in Germany and USA
Moved April'04

Also: **Academia de Fotografía**, Cinco de Mayo #10, Tel:152-2246

Art Studios

1. Galería Sollano 50
Daniel Rueffert—painter of México
Sollano #50 (near Terraplén)
Tel: 152-2478
E-mail: refugio@unisono.net.mx
Hrs: Mon-Sat 9am-6pm, closed Sunday
Colorful Mexican life and landscapes (oil and acrylic)
Group landscape classes by arrangement—US$10 per hour
Gallery manager: Luz María Espinosa
New location Nov'03
Also: San Francisco #1 (entrance to Cappuccino's)
Third location: **Arte Studio**, Pozos (Hidalgo #10-B),
   Tel: 01(442)293-0112

2. Jack Hayes
Mesones #38 (interior)
Tel: 044-415-151-8050 (cell)
E-mail: jackhayesart@hotmail.com
Web page: www.sanmiguelartists.com/jackhayes
Hrs: Daily 11am-3pm
Life-long artist—painting in San Miguel since 1993
Known for his "Dove" paintings—works in oils

Successful portrait artist (children and adults)
Trained in arts schools in New York City
Lived and painted "down east" in Maine many years
Can arrange shipping
Moved to Norman's Plaza (outdoor courtyard)-Jan'04

3. Estudio Gardner
Frank Gardner Studio/Gallery
Zacateros #75 (no outside sign)
Tel: 152-2926
E-mail: frank@unisono.net.mx
Web page: www.frankgardner.com
Hrs: Mon-Sat 10am-2pm and 4-6:30pm, closed Sunday
Colorful oil paintings of San Miguel scenes
Artist from upstate New York
Since 1990 artist has established a loyal following

4. Estudio 46
Cooperative Studio/Gallery
Zacateros #46
Tel: 152-6459
E-mail: lisasimms@unisono.net.mx
Hrs: Tues-Sat 11am-2pm, closed Sunday and Monday
Owner: Lisa Simms
Sculptural jewelry, *papier mâché* puppets, masks and sculpture
Classes in *papier mâché* techniques
　　　Mon and Wed 2-6pm, adults-all levels
Special group workshops and summer programs for children
Artists who share space and display work:
　　　Keith Keller (paintings), Joan Goldberg (ceramics)
　　　Ute Wilson (glass jewelry), María Ayala (paintings)
　　　Luis Buenrostro (contemporary furnishings/accessories)
Opened Nov'95, cooperative since June'03

5. Estudio Victor Heady
Victor Heady
Pila Seca #3 (near H. Macías)
Tel: 154-5203
E-mail: heady@unisono.net.mx
Web page: www.heady-arts.com
Hrs: Mon-Fri 10am-2pm and 4-7pm, Sat 10am-2pm, closed Tues & Sun

Oils—should see to appreciate
Visitors welcome
Relocated Aug'04

6. Estudio de Pintura
Ed Osman
Cuna de Allende #11 (upstairs in back)
Tel: 152-0078
Hrs: Mon -Sat 9am-1pm and 5-8pm, Sun 10am-2pm
Working studio and gallery
Artist has been painting in San Miguel since 1962
Often visiting artists rent space
Students are welcome

7. Studio Galería Mallory
Zacateros #73
Tel: 154-8455 (*casa*)   044-415-101-3710 (cell)
E-mail: davmal@unisono.net.mx
Web page: www.davidmallory.com
Hrs: Daily 9am-10pm, closed Tuesday
Impressionism in oils: Mexican themes, North American
        landscapes and florals
David Mallory–over 400 paintings in public/private collections
        5-day painting classes in impressionist oils once a month
Also **Restaurant 73** serving drinks and food
Relocated May'04

8. La Aurora Artists
Fábrica La Aurora
Calzada de la Aurora s/n (north of town, just past bridge on right)
Large open studios in newly reopened *manta* factory
Merry Calderoni, Mary Rapp, Peter Leventhal, Brian Care, Edina
        Sagert and Juan Ezcurdia
Studios open Thursdays from 10am-4pm, other days by appointment

9. Margarette Dawit & José Ignacio Maldonado
Gallery/Studio
Calzada de la Aurora #51 (north of town, just past Artes de México)
Tel: 154-5238
Hrs: Monday-Friday 10am-5pm
        Drawing from a model: Thurs and Fri 10am-1pm
Margarette studied at The School of The Art Instituto of Chicago (SAIC)
Large working area

10. Ana Thiel
Working studio and showroom
Col. Guadalupe
Tel: 152-3979 (appointment only)
E-mail: anathiel@yahoo.com
Web page: www.fcnv.es/artistas/anathiel
Sculpture in glass and mixed media
Architectural commissions in glass
Also one-of-a-kind prints and jewelry
Working with glass since 1980, moved to SMA 1992
Exhibiting in museums and collections worldwide
Gives occasional workshops

Also: **Alejandro Rivera,** Los Frailes, Tel: 152-3358

11. Rangel Gómez
Sculpture in bronze
Huertas #18
Tel: 152-0647
Hrs: Mon-Sat 10am-6pm
Visitors welcome to see showroom and studio
Two surviving brothers, Gustavo and Mario have been working
over 30 years—English spoken
Commissioned work in New York and Toronto

12. Enrique López Larrea
Studio—classroom—showroom for silver jewelry
San Pedro #27 (blue door) (turn left two blks past Monjas Hotel)
Tel: 152-1737
Professor of silversmithing at Instituto Allende for 49 years
Retired 1995
Mon-Fri morning or afternoon classes (three hours per day)
Limited to ten students per class
Reasonable fees
No experience necessary
Assisted by son, Antonio
English spoken

13. Estudio Aparicio #4
Ceramic co-operative
Aparicio #4 (just east of Mesones and Núñez)
Tel: 152-1866 or 152-0497
E-mail: marlene_johansing@yahoo.com

Hrs: Mon-Fri 10am-4pm
Artists: Blanca García, Marlene Johansing, Bob Smith, Luis
    Helpert, Rebecca Romero and Rita Torlen
A well equipped clay studio with electric, gas, raku and smoke kilns
Clay artists are welcome to rent space
Host workshops and offer classes

A number of other established artists either live in San Miguel or come for the summer or winter. Be on the lookout as their shows are announced in the local ATENCIóN newspaper. Also check *Art Schools* chapter for additional studios.

Art Supplies

1. Lagundi (means the place where good friends meet)
Umarán #17
Tel: 152-0830
Hrs: Mon-Sat 10am-2pm and 4-8pm, Sun 11am-3pm
Colonial building— atrium with sunlight and a live tree!
Bilingual owners Fernando and Rocío Ruiz
Good selection of art supplies
Framing service

2. El Pato
Material de arte
Margarito Ledesma #19 (two blocks from Calz. de la Luz on Calz.
    Aurora. Turn left and after 1 block, left again) Col. Guadalupe
Tel/Fax: 152-1543
Hrs: Mon-Sat 9am-8pm, Closed 3-4pm and Sunday
Owner: David Salgado Arana
Good supply of art material
    Brushes, oil, wood stains, art paper, acrylics, mat materials
    and canvas frames
Less expensive than Centro stores—10% discount for students
Opened 1999

3. Tinta y Papel ("ink and paper")
Ancha de San Antonio #6
Tel: 152-5938
Hrs: Mon-Sat 10am-2pm and 4:30-8pm, Sunday 10am-2pm
Some art supplies

4. El Colibrí ("the hummingbird")
Sollano #30
Tel: 152-0751
Hrs: Mon-Sat 10am-2pm and 4-7pm, closed Sunday
Owner: Carmen (bilingual)

Framing:

1. Lagundi (art supply and book store)
Umarán #17 (corner of H. Macías)
Tel: 152-0830
Hrs: Mon-Sat 10am-2pm and 4-8pm, Sun 11am-3pm
Bilingual owners, Fernando and Rocío Ruiz, do all the custom
    framing work on the premises
Professional work, materials are excellent quality

2. Marabu Framing
Hernández Macías #43-B
Tel: 152-1300
Hrs: Mon-Fri 9:30am-3pm, closed weekends
Owner is Hector Romay (bilingual)
Clients mostly professionals—high quality work
Some basic art supplies for sale
Since 1985

3. Fortuna
Pila Seca #3 (inside courtyard)
Tel: 152-7782
Hrs: Mon-Fri 10am-2pm and 4-6pm, Sat 10am-2pm
Owner: Karen Clement (life-long artist)
Comfortable store
Good selection of imported and domestic frames
    Renaissance, classic and gold leaf
Specialist in conservation and preservation of fine art
    100% acid free materials
Opened Aug'04

4. Lavinia's Framing
Refugio Sur #35, Col. San Antonio
Tel: 154-5344
E-mail: laviniaj@prodigy.net.mx
Hrs: Mon-Fri 9am-2pm and 4-7pm, Sat 9am-1pm

Owner: Lavinia Ruiz (bilingual)—20 years experience
Custom matting and framing
Gold leaf—also shadowboxes and special installations
Pick-up and delivery—expedited service available
Also packing

5. "Boni" Marcos y Molduras (frames and mouldings)
Mesones #5 (across the street from Academia Spanish school)
Pasaje Allende (inside arcade)
Tel: None
Hrs: Mon-Sat 9:30am-2pm and 4-8pm
Owner: Bonifacio Juárez (speaks some English)
Handmade wood and metal frames (brass, copper and tin)
Reasonable prices

6. Vidriería La Muñeca de San Miguel (glass store)
Hidalgo #52
Tel: None   152-0353 (*taller*)
Hrs: Mon-Fri 9am-5:30pm, Sat 9am-2pm, closed Sunday
Custom framing
Framer: Victor Guerrero—30 years experience
Also sells clear plexiglass
Since 1985, relocated Jan'00

Also: **Marc Obras,** Zacateros #48, Tel: 154-7680

Bakeries

1. La Buena Vida (the good life)
Hernández Macías #72 (across from Bellas Artes)
Plaza Golondrinas (Int #5), across from American Consular Agency
Tel: 152-2211
Hrs: Mon-Sat 8am-5pm, closed Sunday
Owners: Melissa, Ismael and Alfonso are bilingual
Whole grain breads, muffins, rolls, donuts and cookies
Bakery is very popular with locals
Also sells locally made jams and chocolates
French bread (daily at 12:30pm) — specialty breads on different
     days; must try *pan de la mañana*
Wholesale to quality restaurants and retail stores
Accepts special orders
Since 1989

"El Cafecito" (coffee shop — entrance to bakery)
    Small patio with tables and chairs plus potted flowers
    Serve coffee, juice, *licuados* and fresh baked goods
    Note the colorful "Diego Rivera" like Mexican landscape
    mural painted June'96 by Melinda Carwile
Expanded indoor cafeteria next door to American Consul
    Complete breakfast and light lunch
    Good place for hot oatmeal with healthy toppings
    Baguettes, sandwiches, soups—also daily Mexican specials
    Hrs: Mon-Sat 8am-5pm, closed Sunday

2. La Casita Feliz
Guadiana #15-B (two blocks south of Instituto)
Tel: 152-6555
Hrs: Mon-Sat 10am- 8pm, Sunday 10am - 6pm
Owner: Hortensia Mendoza (bilingual)
Some of the best cake and cookies in town
    Also will take special orders
Second location: Plaza Real del Conde (near Gigante exit)

3. Antares Pastelería (a star constellation)
Ancha de San Antonio #28-A (near Instituto Allende)
Tel: 154-8910
Hrs: Daily 10am-8:30pm, Sunday 11am-5pm
All pastries; cheesecake, tarts, breakfast rolls, cakes and cookies
Four bakeries in Querétaro
Opened July'04

4. La Colmena Panadería (aka the "blue door" bakery)
Reloj #21
Tel: 152-1422
Hrs: Mon 8:30am-2pm and 5-9pm, Tues-Sat 6am-2pm
    and 5-9pm, Sunday 6-9am
Self service—just pick up a metal tray and tongs and make your
    selections. A clerk will total your purchase and write price on
    the bag. Before exiting, pay the cashier. Cashier is usually the
    husband or wife owner (speak some English)—a fun experience!
Good location—½ block from the Jardín—since 1901
Well-known place among tourists and locals
Good selection of rolls, cookies, cupcakes, donuts, bread (whole
    wheat or soya), *empanadas* and *bolillos*

5. Petit Four
Mesones #99 (between H. Macías and Hidalgo)
Tel: 154-4010

Hrs: Tues-Sat 10am-8 pm, Sun 10am-6pm, closed Monday
Owner: Francisco – formerly worked at Marriott Hotel pastry
    department in México City
Scrumptious European delights not found elsewhere in town
Cakes, cookies, croissants plus hand-dipped Belgian chocolates
Custom orders and catering
Also a small café and bar serving coffee, cold drinks and alcohol
Opened April'98

Other Bakeries:
  Bagel Cafe, Correo #19, Tel: 154-6524
      Freshly baked breads and bagels
  Panadería la Purísima, Hernández Macías #120, Tel: 152-1843
  Panadería la Espiga, Insurgentes #119, Tel: 152-1580
  Panadería Malena, Salida a Celaya #57, Tel: 152-1595
  Tenorio, Calzada de la Aurora #28, Tel: 152-3818
  Panadería El Maple, Salida a Celaya #51, Tel: None

Banks

1. BANAMEX (Banco Nacional de México)
Casa de los Condes de la Canal (purchased building in 1982)
Canal #4 (entrance Portal de Allende)
Tel: 152-1040 and 152-1004   Fax: 152-3732
Web page: www.banamex.com
Hrs: Mon-Fri 9am-4pm, Sat 10am-2pm, closed Sunday
Dollar exchange during normal business hours (travelers' checks
    until 2:30pm)
Manager: Cristóbal Delgado Ramírez
Founded 1884, privatized 1992
More than 1000 branches
Often long lines at cashier counters, especially on Mon.and Fri.
    (customers now take a number)
BANAMEX Accival (Brokerage Division-largest in México)
Also a Cultural Department
Two ATM's (24 hours)— CIRRUS and PLUS systems
    —unfortunately they don't always work so shop around
Can receive Western Union money transfers
Inquire about a US$ direct deposit account with Banamex's
    California Commerce Bank
Merged with US giant, CitiGroup, August'01

Branch
- (a) Inside Gigante (near checkout)
  Plaza Real del Conde
  Tel: 152-7328
  Hrs: Mon-Sat 10am-8pm, Sunday/holidays 10am-5pm
  Dollar exchange and check cashing
  One ATM Machine – CIRRUS and PLUS systems
  Opened April'97.
- (b) ATM only
  Presidencia Municipal-Ground floor
- (c) ATM only
  Plaza Golondrinas (near American Consul office)
  Hernández Macías #72

2. BBVA-BANCOMER
Juárez #11
Tel: 152-0847, 152-0665 and 152-2124   Fax: 152-3196
Hrs: Mon-Fri 8:30am-4pm, closed weekends
Exchange: same hours as above
Largest bank in México
Two ATM'S (24 hours)—PLUS system only
Copy machine
New location as of April'95, Merged with BBVA-June'00

3. BANORTE (formerly BANCEN)
San Francisco #17
Tel: 152-0019, 152-7950 and 152-8099   Fax: 152-2202
Hrs: Mon-Fri 9am-5pm
Exchange hours: Mon-Fri 9am-1:30pm
Headquarters: Monterrey
Large bank, nice lobby and lounge area
Changed name Nov'97
One ATM (24 hours) -CIRRUS and PLUS systems
  Sweep card in machine
  Only local bank which allows cash withdrawals in US$'s or
    pesos when using a Mexican bank card

4. SERFIN-SANTANDER
San Francisco #32
Tel: 152-1161, 152-1162 and 152-1168   Fax: 152-3092
Hrs: Mon-Fri 9am-3pm
Exchange 9am-1pm
Merged with Banco Santander Sept'00
One ATM (24 hours)—CIRRUS and PLUS systems

5. HSBC (Hong Kong & Shanghai Banking Corp)
Formerly BITAL
San Francisco #31 (next to Lloyd's)
Tel/Fax: 152-6299, 152-7042 and 152-7318
Hrs: Mon-Sat 8am-7pm
Headquarters in México City (more than 1,400 branches)
    5th largest in México
Old colonial home—lobby has a water fountain and orange tree
Often no waiting time
Opened October'96
Always has change for large bills
New ownership (Aug'02)
One ATM (24 hours) — CIRRUS and PLUS systems
Second ATM (24 hours), Plaza Real del Conde

Insider's Tip: Banco Azteca, inside Elektra appliance store, Zacateros #36, Tel: 152-6930, is open daily 9am-9pm, 365 days a year.

Investment Broker:

1. Allen W. Lloyd (Lloyd's)
Plaza Lloyd
San Francisco #33
Tel: 152-4100
        Tel: 01-800-573-2000 Call Center (M-F 8am-8pm)
            01-800-570-2000 automatic info service
Web page: http://www.lloyd.com.mx
Hrs: Mon-Fri 9am-5pm
Exchange 9am-3pm (now have four teller windows)
Area Manager: Rafael Gonzáles (bilingual)
Office Manager: Sra. Inés Zavala (bilingual)
Customer service:
        Yvonne Jankord (bilingual)—very helpful
        Desk just inside on the right
Seven offices in México—headquarters in Guadalajara
Casa de Cambio:
        Cash travelers' checks (need ID)
        Personal checks (need to have an account)
CD's, money market, Mexican mutual funds
Car and medical insurance
About 70% of its clients are foreign customers
Copy machine
Free coffee—sitting area in lobby

Free monthly economic report
Manage house finances for absentee clients
Inquire about a US$ direct deposit account in a Lloyd's account
    with Bank of America in San Diego, CA
Now comfortably airconditioned

Insider's Tip: Should you need to withdraw money from a
bank or an ATM, do it before a weekend or holiday.

Also see *Money Changers (Cambios)*

Bars

The following are a few of the more popular watering
spots in town. Keep in mind that many hotels and restaurants
also offer bar services as well as the dancing/night club places.
While in México try a *tequila con sangrita!* Look for *Hora
Feliz* (happy hour) signs.

1. Casa de Sierra Nevada en el Parque
Restaurant/Bar
El Chorro near Juárez Park
Santa Elena #2
Tel: 152-7155, 152-7154 and 152-7153
Hrs: Daily 1pm-10:30pm
Thursday happy hour (6-8pm) 2x1 drinks, free *botanas*, music
Classy watering spot – relaxing place for a *margarita!*
Music Thurs-Sun 2-4pm and 8-10pm

2. El Campanario
Restaurant/Bar
Canal #34
Tel: 152-0775
Hrs: Daily 1-11pm, closed Thursday
First-class restaurant
Large bar area on left of restaurant
Also a roof-top bar where one can watch the San Miguel sunsets
Friendly waiters and attentive service

3. Tío Lucas
Restaurant/Bar
Mesones #103 (near corner H. Macías)
Tel: 152-4996
Hrs: Daily 12 noon-midnight

Max Altamirano is the friendly bilingual owner
Expanded and renovated bar area
Free appetizers 1-8pm, happy hour 6-8pm (except weekends)
Blues and jazz music nightly from 9pm

4. Harry's New Orleans Café
Restaurant/Bar
Hidalgo #12 (½ block from Jardín)
Tel: 152-2645
Hrs: Daily 12 noon - midnight
        Happy hour: Mon-Fri 5-7pm, Wed 2x1 martinis
Large "New York style" bar in entrance patio
        Nice atmosphere in courtyard
Premium wines and specialty cocktails
Late night bar menu
New name and ownership Dec'03

5. Berlin
Restaurant/Bar
Umarán #19
Tel: 154-9432
Hrs: Mon-Sat 1pm-1am, closed Sunday
        Happy hour: Daily 5-7pm
Credit cards: Master and Visa
Owners: Viajes de San Miguel
Cozy, friendly casual bar plus several small dining areas
Mexican and German menus—popular to eat at the bar
Retractable roof plus two wood fireplaces for the winter
Always good selection of background music
Peter Leventhal artwork on walls for sale
Opened May'04

6. La Vida
Sports Bar/Restaurant (formerly La Lola)
Ancha de San Antonio #31 (west side past Instituto)
Tel: 152-4050
Hrs: Daily 1pm-1am, closed Tuesday
Credit cards: None
Owners: Aniceto and Raúl (from Monterrey, México)
Check out the new horseshoe-shaped bar
Upstairs balcony has small tables plus 2 pool tables
A comfortable neighborhood spot
Daily changing *comida* special (1-7pm)

Daily happy hour 1-9pm
Sports events on TV—bingo Wed 7-9pm
Check out the outdoor grill area
Opened April'97, new ownership Jan'02

7. La Fragua
Bar/Restaurant
Cuna de Allende #3 (just steps away from the Jardín)
Tel: 152-1144
Hrs: Daily 1:30pm-2am, weekends close at 3am, closed Monday
DJ music Wed-Sat (8pm to close) – cover charge during *fiestas*
Old colonial building with retractable roof over courtyard
Nice ambiance with wooden tables and *equipal* chairs
Also a good menu—ask for specials
One of the oldest bars in town
Happy hour (6-8pm) Sunday, Tuesday to Thursday
        Live music (8-10pm) Sunday and Thursday
Reopened with new ownership and major renovation June'99
Also owns **La Coronela Bar,** San Francisco #4, Tel: 152-2746

8. Manolo's Sports Bar
Zacateros #26 (corner of Pila Seca)
(Two entrances, from Casa Payo or from Pila Seca)
Tel: 152-7277
Hrs: Mon-Sat 1-11pm, Sunday 11am-11pm
Credit Cards: Amex, Master and Visa
Five TV's (Direct, Sky and Cable available)
Bottle or draft beer, wine and mixed drinks
        Can order "½ yard" or "yard" beers
Fireplace, dart board and card games
Can order off Casa Payo menu
Opened Sept'03

9. Limerick Pub
Umarán #24 (between H. Macías and Zacateros)
Tel: 154-8642
Web page: www.limerick-pub.com
Hrs: Daily 1pm-1am
Credit cards: Master and Visa
Four owners: All from Argentina
Large open area with bar, fireplace plus two side sitting rooms
Pool table, dart board and two TV's

Irish music plus Irish coffee
Happy hour (2x1 national beers and *margaritas*) Mon-Thurs 4-8pm
Daily executive menu Mon-Fri 1-6pm
Attracts a lively young crowd
Opened Jan'04

Other Bars:
  (1) Petit Bar, Hernández Macías #95, Tel: 152-3229
  (2) L'Invito, Ancha de San Antonio #20 (inside), Tel: 152-7333
  (3) Cantina La Coronela, San Francisco #4, Tel: 152-2746
  (4) Bar Leonardo (Mama Mía's), Umarán #8, Tel: 152-2063
  (5) El Caporal, Mesones s/n, Tel: 152-5937
  (6) La Cucaracha, Zacateros #22, Tel: 152-0196

Insider's Tip: Best place to buy cigars (*puros*): Habanera, Portal Guadalupe #10, Tel: 152-1311, La Europea, Canal #13, Tel: 152-2003, La Divina, front bldg of Plaza Real del Conde, Tel: 154-4190 and La Cuba Vieja, Hidalgo #4, Tel: 152-2125

Bed and Breakfast Places

1. Casa de Liza... Villas en el Parque
Bajada del Chorro #7 (Centro district near *lavaderos* & Juárez Park)
Tel: 152-0352   Fax: 152-6144
E-mail: casaliza@unisono.net.mx
Web page: http://casaliza.com
Owners: Liza and mother Charlotte are always available to meet
        your needs—wonderful experienced bilingual staff
An elegant enclave of luxurious and romantic accommodations situated
        on the paradise-like grounds of an in-town restored colonial estate
Four *casitas* complete with kitchens plus three separate suites
Fountains, fireplaces, antique furnishings, original art and sculpture
Lush grounds on one acre with parrots and orchid-filled greenhouse
Cable TV and telephone in all rooms, laundry service and parking within
Sumptuous gourmet breakfast when and where you like (even in bed)
Hors d'oeuvres around the heated jacuzzi/pool in the late afternoon
Massage, reflexology, manicure/pedicure and hair styling
        available by appointment in the on-site spa or in your suite
No smoking indoors
Well-behaved children welcome
Look for a copy of **The Insider's Guide to San Miguel** in the guestrooms

Four Diamond (one of two in México) rating in AAA México Travel Book
Also available, two *casitas* on nearby Sollano, with all the same amenities

2. Casa de la Cuesta ("house on a hill")
Cuesta de San José #32 (east of Mesones and Núñez)
Tel: 154-4324   Fax: 154-5032
E-mail: info@casadelacuesta.com
Web page: www.casadelacuesta.com
Owned by Heidi and Bill LeVasseur (owners have New England roots)
Both a colonial style B&B and an exquisite art gallery
Six rooms with private baths
      All have outdoor terraces with city views plus sunsets
Decorated with Mexican folkart, textiles, masks and antiques
Breakfast in courtyard or dining room
US$120 per night single or double (+ IVA) - triples available
All guestrooms have a copy of **The Insider's Guide to San Miguel**
Must see separate art gallery full of one-of-a-kind Mexican art and
      artesanía
Opened April'00

3. Casa Schuck
Bajada de la Garita #3 (4 blocks east of Centro)
Tel/Fax: 152-0657   Guest Tel: 152-6618
E-mail: casaschuck@yahoo.com
Web page: www.casaschuck.com
Owners: Tito and Nancy Cordelli (from Westport, CT)
Managers: Susan Cordelli Easter and husband Chuck
A real San Miguel gem!
Exquisite example of Spanish colonial architecture with spacious,
      lush courtyard, gardens and pool
Six luxurious suites each with a private bath
Prices range from US$100-US$150–personal US checks only
Full Mexican or American breakfast
Adults only–smoking outdoors okay
Weddings and special events done on premises – call for pricing
Also: **Casa Cordelli**, Salida a Querétro #117, Tel: 152-0657
      Four *casita* rentals

4. Casa Granada (Pomegranate)
Recreo #58 (3 block walk to Jardín) - Centro District close to
      Plaza de Toros, El Chorro and Juárez Park
Tel/Fax: 152-0577

E-mail: casa_granada@yahoo.com
Web page: www.casagranada.com.mx
Owner: Gerry Gill: artist and salsa dancer–from Cleveland, Ohio
Beautifully restored 300-year-old Spanish colonial home
Three guestrooms, each with full bath and fireplace plus Mexican
    antiques and original paintings by the artist-owner
Owner's art work for sale at **Galería Zacateros 81-B**
US$120 per room plus tax, includes full breakfast
Breakfast in a chapel overlooking a courtyard, fountain, granada
    trees and flowering plants
Also an upstairs, outdoor *sala* and flower filled terrace with
    beautiful mountain and sunset views
Accommodations for in-house massage
Now listed in Frommer's
Opened March'97

5. Casa Calderoni
Callejón del Pueblito #4-A (one block north of Biblioteca)
Tel: 154-6005   or   154-6007
E-mail: ben@casacalderoni.com
Web page: www.casacalderoni.com
Credit cards: Master and Visa
Owners: Ben and Merry Calderoni (bilingual)
    From Houston and lived in Venezuela many years
9 Rooms - each features a different artist
    Includes cable TV, telephone and heaters
Computer available for guests in sitting/reading room
Quiet part of town - unparalleled roof-top terrace views
Very near *artesanías* market
Price range US$85-US$110
No children under 14 years of age and no pets
Owner's artwork and other artwork for sale
First opened June'02

6. Dos Casas
Luxury Bed & Breakfast
Quebrada #101 (corner of Umarán)
Tel: 154-4958
E-mail: doscasas@prodigy.net.mx
Web page: www.livingdoscasas.com
Manager: Jesús Ayala (bilingual)
Beautifully appointed decor

Five suites, including penthouse
    Each room has a gas fireplace
    Rooftop penthouse has a jacuzzi, sauna and two terraces
Lounge has a computer for e-mail
Full breakfast
Secure guest parking available
Opened Jan'04

7. Casa Puesta del Sol ("sunset house")
Fuentes #12 – Atascadero area
Tel: 152-0220   Fax: 152-7232
E-mail: daninmex@unisono.net.mx
Web page: www.casapuestadelsol.com
Credit cards: Master and Visa (personal checks okay too)
Hosts: Daniel and Gabriela Scher from Laguna Beach, CA
Five luxury rooms plus a two-bedroom apartment
Price range US$98-US$165
Also a honeymoon suite with commanding views
Cable TV and telephones in all rooms plus laundry included
In-house computer available for guests
Great colors and artwork throughout
One of the best panoramic views of the city and beyond
Beautifully landscaped grounds with gardens, ponds and a waterfall
Friendly staff of maids, cooks and groundskeepers
Generous breakfast served in gardens or dining room
Includes country club privileges (golf, tennis and swimming)
Opened May'97

8. Villa Scorpio al Puente B&B
Quebrada #93 (next to the Canal bridge)
Tel: 152-7575
E- mail: villascorpio@unforgettable.com
Web page: www.villascorpio.com
Owners: Nick Power (from St Louis) and Penelope Haskew (CT)
Beautiful restored colonial villa
Five rooms, each with a private bath and fireplace
US$100 plus tax per/night, ask about low season rates
Credit Cards: None
Three gardens plus a large rooftop terrace with great views of the
    town and a six person jacuzzi
Large sitting room and library
Full breakfast

In-house spa open daily (by appointment)
    All types of massage and facials
Children are welcome
Opened Jan'00

9. Casa Quetzal Hotel
Hospicio #34
Tel: 152-0501   Tel/Fax: 152-4961
E-mail: info@casaquetzalhotel.com
Web page: www.casaquetzalhotel.com
Credit cards: Master and Visa
Owner: Cynthia Price, artist from Vermont
Six luxury rooms, US$150 - $265
Quiet location, elegant decor
Full breakfast served in your room if you wish (make sure you ask
    for Vermont maple syrup)
Also will arrange private dinners with music
Opened July'00, new ownership Sept'02

10. Villa Mirasol Hotel ("sunflower")
Pila Seca #35 (west part of town)
Tel: 152-6685, 152-8057 and 154-5113 Fax: 152-1564
E-mail: mirasol@unisono.net.mx
Web page: www.infosma.com/villamirasol
Owner: Carmen Avery (bilingual)
Manager: Amparo is pleasant, helpful and bilingual
Ten rooms US$75-$95
Credit cards: Amex, Master and Visa
All rooms have beautiful hand-painted tiled bathrooms and sunny
    private patios plus TV and telephone
Continental breakfast served—coffee, tea and sweets at 5pm
No children between ages 3-12
Ask about in-house suburban airport transportation services

Less Expensive Accommodations:

11. El Jardín de Don Quijote
Calle Orizaba #17-A (also entrance Soledad #7, La Aldea)
Private setting in Col. San Antonio
Tel: 152-3300
E-mail: famgb1@hotmail.com
Hosts: García family (all are bilingual)
Five rooms

Hot water, maid service and cable TV in lounge
Reasonable single and double occupancy rates (call for prices)
Price includes delicious breakfast and lunch (*comida*)
New arrivals get a car tour of the city

12. La Casa de Reyna B&B
Guadiana #45
Col. Guadiana
Tel: 154-7701
E-mail: reynasuarez@yahoo.com
Web page: www.infosma.com
Host: Reyna Suárez (speaks some english)
Five rooms (with private bathrooms)—includes TV
Reasonable prices (includes two home-cooked meals)
Patio

Also: **Casa Diana,** Recreo #48, Tel: 152-0885
E-mail: reservaciones@casadiana.net
On-site Pedro Friedeberg Art Gallery

Biking

1. Bici-Burro
Hospicio #1 (corner of Barranca)
Tel: 152-1526   Fax: 152-3948
Hrs: Mon-Sat 9am - 2pm and 4-7pm, closed Sunday
Owner: Alberto Martínez (bilingual)
Sells and rents mountain bikes
Also accessories plus servicing
Biking and hiking tours
    Half day trips to Atotonilco or Pozos
Family business since 1966
Respect the environment and wildlife!

Also: **Adventuras San Miguel**, Aldama #1-A, Tel: 152-6406
Sol y Luna, Hospicio #10, Tel: 154-8599

---

2. Bicicletas García
Market of Artesanías (adjacent Mercado)
Tel: 152-7937 (*casa*)
Bicycle supplies

Book Stores

1. Libros el Tecolote ("owl")
Jesús #11 (next to Café Parroquia)
Tel/Fax: 152-7395
E-mail: tecolotebooks@yahoo.com
Hrs: Tues-Sat 10am-6pm *(open during siesta)*
　　Sun 10am-2pm, closed Monday
Credit cards: Master and Visa (over US$20)
Owner: Mary Marsh
Large selection of new books about México, fiction and non-
　　fiction, guidebooks and books for learning Spanish
Used books sold, bought and exchanged
　　All subjects, large turnover, some books in Spanish
Also carries greeting cards, postcards and journals
In business since July'94

2. Lagundi
Umarán #17 (corner of H. Macías)
Tel: 152-0830
Hrs: Mon-Sat 10am-2pm and 4-8pm, Sun 11am-3pm
Credit cards: Amex, Master and Visa
Well run by bilingual owners, Fernando and Rocío Ruiz
Large convenient colonial location-since Sept'94
Art books, English-language magazines including monthly satellite
　　TV guides, computer magazines, Mexican videos and CDs
Good selection of art supplies plus framing service
Added small front retail space displaying art work in Jan'03

3. El Colibrí ("hummingbird")
Sollano #30
Tel: 152-0751
Hrs: Mon-Sat 10am-2pm and 4-7pm, closed Sunday
Carmen—bilingual owner (since 1970)
Good selection of English books and magazines (10% discount)
Many English-language paperbacks—also postcards
Spanish-language books, also books on México
Ticket outlet for local performances
Also sell art supplies

4. Tinta y Papel ("ink & paper")
Ancha de San Antonio #6 (also check upstairs)
Tel/Fax: 152-5938

Hrs: Mon-Sat 9:30am-2pm and 4:30-8pm, Sun 10am-2pm
English-language magazines and daily newspapers for sale
Art and stationery supplies
Wrapping paper, boxes and bags
Also cassettes and CDs
Some Spanish books
New ownership Jan'04

Bull Fighting

Plaza de Toros Oriente
Recreo #52—Unusual residential location
Most fights scheduled during winter season and various festivals
     throughout the year
Musical pageantry prior to first bullfight is one of the highlights
Usually 4-6 bull fights on the program
Plaza seats 3,500 people
Seats: *Sombra* (shade) or *Sol* (sun)—different prices
Bring a cushion (or rent one) as cement seats can get uncomfortable
Look for posters advertising the fights around town and in the Jardín
Tickets purchased at entrance of Plaza de Toros
Bring a bota bag full of wine or buy beer or wine in stands

    Bullfighting originated in Spain. It is a pageant of blood and
grace and is as popular as ever in México. First, *picadores*
circling on horses jab the bull in the shoulder muscles with lances.
Next, the same region of the bull's body is targeted by running
fighters called *banderilleros*. Ideally, all three pairs of
banderillas are deposited in the bull. In the third part of the fight,
the *matador* seeks to impress the spectators with various maneuvers
with his red fighting cape (*muleta*) as the bull is bleeding freely.
With the bull exhausted from loss of blood it receives the coup de
grâce into its heart from the *matador*'s sword. It's a good fight if
the *matador* does it right the first time.

    By regulation, posters advertising bull fights must state if you will
be watching *corridas de toros* (full *matadors*) where the bulls are
at least 4½ years and 450 kilos or *novilleros* (aspiring bullfighters)
who fight young bulls between 3½–4 years and 350-400 kilos.

Third Saturday of September
Pamplonada—Popular running of the bulls
The route leaves from the front of the Parroquia, past the Post

Office, San Francisco Church and returning around the Jardín. The route is well barricaded. It is very crowded with young people and can be dangerous. Take care in choosing a safe location to watch. It is also televised locally.

Insider's Tip: In case you are looking for old bull fighting posters, check out Maderería Sánchez, Correo #5. Cost is $15 pesos per poster.

Cafés

1. Bagel Café
Correo #19 (interior)
Tel: 154-6524
Hrs: Mon-Fri 8:30am-3pm, Sat 9am-2pm
Owner: Ron Dumas
Coffee plus fresh fruit and vegetable juices
Bagels and breads baked daily
Try the daily specials plus sandwiches and soups
Call for take-out orders
Also a small art gallery on premises
New ownership Feb'03

2. Café del Jardín
Portal de Allende #2 (west side of Jardín)
Tel: 152-5006
Hrs: Daily 7am-12 midnight—open every day of the year
Small but good location—often crowded
Breakfast, lunch and dinner—small spotless kitchen
Pizzas, pastas, salads, sandwiches and desserts
Expressos, cappuccinos and American coffee - some of the best!
Pedro is an excellent waiter

3. El Cafecito (part of La Buena Vida Bakery)
Hernández Macías #72 (across from Bellas Artes)
Plaza Golondrinas
Tel: 152-2211
Hrs: Mon-Sat 8am-5pm, closed Sunday
Small patio with tables and chairs plus potted flowers
Serve coffee, juice, *licuados* plus fresh baked goods from bakery
Popular spot for shoppers and US Consul and Bellas Artes crowd
Expanded indoor cafeteria
    Just past American Consul entrance

Complete breakfast and light lunch
Try a delicious chicken consommé with brown rice
Daily special (12-5pm) —Mexican *comida*
Attractive sitting area—free daily newspaper to read
Opened Sept'00

4. San Agustín Café

San Francisco #21 (across from San Francisco Church)
Tel: 154-9102
Hrs: Daily 8am-11pm, Sat/Sun 9am-midnight
Credit cards: None
Owner: Margarita Gralia (well known film & TV star from Argentina)
All kinds of coffee plus soft drinks, beer or wine
Three kinds of chocolate served with home-made *churros* (stick sugar donuts)
Breakfast plus light food menu
Try authenic *empanadas* Argentine with *chimichurri* sauce
Also extensive selection of *tapas*
Reasonable prices
Lively ambience and popular with locals
Opened May'02

5. Rincón de Don Tomás

Portal de Guadalupe (*Jardín*)- corner of San Francisco
Tel: 152-3780 and 152-0027
Hrs: Mon - Sat 8:30am-10pm, Sunday 8:30am-9pm
Credit cards: Amex, Master and Visa
Small, busy café facing *El Jardín*–popular with locals and foreigners
      Also a small loft upstairs with three tables
Breakfast, lunch and dinner
Good selection of Mexican specialties
      Beef, chicken and seafood dishes–also soups
Total bar plus cold drinks and all kinds of coffee and desserts
      A good place for a *margarita*
Attentive waiters
It has a new look—light, welcoming, charming
Opened Sept'97

6. Café del Sol

Salida a Celaya #34 (near Telmex office)
Tel: 154-4337
Hrs: Mon-Fri 9am-5pm, Sat 9am-2pm
Owner: Silvia Paz (trilingual)
Small indoor/outdoor café
Good selection of coffees, hot chocolate, muffins and bagels

A variety of egg dishes, hotcakes and quiche
Mexican dishes—everything home-made
One computer (Wi-Fi)—free for customers
Daily newspaper and magazines
Opened Sept'04

7. La Finestra Caffé
Ancha de San Antonio #9
Tel: 152-5784
Hrs: Daily 9am-6pm, closed Tuesday
Owners: Tito Izagirre and Karime Dávila Madrid
Relaxng outdoor courtyard with small chapel (also indoor seating
    in the back)
All kinds of coffee and cold drinks plus beer and wine
Breakfast plus sandwiches, and salads (daily lunch specials)
Gift store in front, Yoga Centre upstairs in back
Also: Canal #21 (interior), Tel: 152-8093

8. El Buen Café
Jesús #23 (corner Cuadrante)
Tel: 152-5807
E-mail: buencafe@yahoo.com
Hrs: Mon-Sat 9am-8pm, closed Sunday
Owned and operated by an American, Kris Rudolph
Breakfast, lunch and dinner–try a fresh-baked dessert
Whole Foods Corner featuring organic natural food products
Homemade deli items to go
Good selection of British and American teas
Magazines to read

9. Las Musas-Café Italian
Bellas Artes patio area
Hernández Macías #75 (near Canal)
Tel: 152-4946
Hrs: Daily 9am-8pm, Sunday 10am-2:30pm
Relaxing atmosphere overlooking patio and garden–should see
Good coffee and light snacks (breakfast and lunch)
Italian owner

10. Cappuccino's
San Francisco #1 (just east of the Jardín)
Tel: 154-8000
E-mail: cappuccinosanmiguel@yahoo.com
Hrs: Daily 9am-10pm

Fresh brewed coffee
Also serves Lavazza Italian blend coffee (#1 in world)
Also sells beans by the package plus a good assortment of teas
Very small with tables in entranceway and courtyard
Rodolfo is the personable bilingual owner-first opened 1992

11. Casa de Café
Hidalgo #18 (near Mesones)
Tel: 154-5312
Hrs: Daily 7:30am-9:30pm
Owner: Marisela Patterson (bilingual)
Roast and grind coffee daily
      Organic beans come from Veracruz
Coffee by the cup or kilo and tea also
Also iced coffee, capuccino or expresso
Four small tables

12. La Ventana ("the window")
Sollano #11
Tel: 154-7728
Hrs: Mon-Sat 8am-8pm, Sunday 8am-3pm
Owners: Josefina and Isaac Toporek
Organic coffee from the high mountains of Chiapas
Roast and grind coffee beans and sell by the kilo
Coffee to drink or to go
      At the window or sit at inside tables
Second location: Plaza Pueblito, Tel: 154-8701
Opened Dec'00

Also: **Café Etc,** Reloj #37, Tel:154-8636
       Petit Four, Mesones #99, Tel: 154-4010
       Café Montenegro, Correo #12-A, Tel: 152-1448

Carpets/Carpet Cleaning

1. La Zandunga (means "full of grace")
Tapetes finos
Hernández Macías #129 (faces Codo)
Tel: 152-4608
Owners Gil and Rebecca Gutiérrez (both are bilingual)
Display room in home of owners (knock or call)

Handmade, 100% wool rugs from Oaxaca
Own productions (design, color and size)
Some 30 rugs in stock, will also special order
Export to USA

2. Eduardo Hernández
Ancha de San Antonio #19
Tel: 152-4227
Hrs: Mon-Sat 10am-2pm and 4-6:30pm, Sun closed
Owner is very pleasant and speaks English
Sells and installs custom wall-to-wall carpeting
Also custom wooden floors, window blinds plus aluminum
        windows and doors
Carpet cleaning
In business since 1988

Other Carpets:
   Oscar Hernández, Codo #12, Tel: 154-4907 (*taller*)
   Lan-Art, Ancha de San Antonio #21 (corner Orizaba)
      Tel: 152-1566 and 152-4591
      Locally made wool carpets (will special order)
      Yucatán sisal (hemp) rugs
   Moroccan Imports, Aldama #30, Tel: 152-8355
   Cos-Az, Recreo #5-B, Tel: 152-6417

Note: The annual 10-day Wool and Brass Fair every November
brings carpet artisans from elsewhere in México.

Carpet Cleaning:

1. Super Limpio
Ancha de San Antonio #47
Tel: 152-3210
Hrs: Mon-Fri 9am-2pm and 4-7pm, Sat 9am-1pm
Owner: María Montserrat Cadena (speaks some English)
Carpets, floors and furniture—in your home or at our shop
Opened May'01

Also: **La Pila**, Jesús #25, Tel: 152-5810

Car/Bike Rental

1. Hola Rent A Car
Hotel Posada de San Franciso (interior)
Plaza Principal #2
Tel/Fax: 152-0198 and 044-415-153-5496 (cell)
E-Mail: holarent@unisono.net.mx
Hrs: Mon-Sat 9am-2:30pm and 4:30-7pm, closed Sunday
Director: José Antonio Quero (bilingual)
New cars plus a suburban—free miles
Daily, weekly or monthly prices (include IVA tax and insurance)
Major credit cards accepted
Can arrange pickup or drop-off at airport
In business since Jan'92

2. Moto Rent
Honda San Miguel
Salida a Celaya, km 1 #97 (near *glorieta*)
Tel: 152-1080 and   152-7100
Hrs: Daily 9am-8pm
Owner/Manager: Lic. Pavel Hernández (bilingual)
Rent motor scooters or ATV's (4-wheelers)
Hourly, daily, weekly or monthly—prices are negotiable
Bring driver's license and credit card
Opened July'03

3. Yamaha
Salida a Celaya, s/n
Tel: 044-415-153-5140 (cell)
Buy-rent-service—motorcycles and scooters
Newest scooters—automatic transmission

Car Maintenance

1. Clínica Automotriz San Miguel
Laureles #5 (from Salida a Celaya turn at Euzkadi Tire)
Col. Allende
Tel: 152-4459   or   154-4612
Hrs: Mon-Fri 8:30am-2pm and 4-6:30pm, Sat 8:30am-2pm
Credit cards: Master and Visa
Director: José Luis Uribe   Service Mgr: Jenaro Gómez (bilingual)

Large, full service repair facility—very clean, organized
American and foreign cars
Mechanical, electrical, suspension, bodywork and painting
Car inspections
Since 1978

2. González Servicio
Mario Talavera (corner of Margarito Ledezma)
Col. Guadalupe
Tel: 152-1202
Hrs: Mon-Fri 9am-6pm, Sat 9am-4pm
Owner: José Juan (Pepe) Castañeda
Tune-up, alignment and brakes
Oil change and tires
Since 1978

3. Peralta Automotriz ("Esso" sign)
Calzada de la Estación #181 (past bus station)
Tel: 152-6589
Hrs: Mon-Fri 9am-7pm, Sat 9am-2pm
Owner: Tec. Juan Carlos Peralta—35 years experience
All types of cars
General mechanical—specializes in fuel injection
Good testing equipment
Car inspections
Same location since 1994

4. Transmisiones Flores
Libramiento a Dolores Hidalgo #15
Col. Independencia
Tel: 154-0174
Hrs: Mon-Fri 9am-7pm, Sat 9am-3pm
Owner: Saul Flores—20 years experience
General repairs—specializes in automatic transmissions
Special training in LA, Calif. for five years
Same location since 1994

5. Pariente
Calzada de la Luz #67-A
Col. Guadalupe
Tel: 044-415-151-2553 (cell)
Hrs: Daily 8:30am-6pm, Sunday 9am-3pm

Owner: Raul Montes
Complete auto detailing
Lubrication and oil change
Wash & clean inside and out—including motor and underneath
Since 1992

6. Godínez Paint Shop
Callejón Valle del Maíz #10 (off Salida a Querétaro)
Tel: 154-6580
Hrs: Mon-Sat 9am-6pm
Owner: David "Pollo" Godínez—20 years experience
All makes of cars
Dupont paint—does good job of matching colors

Also: GM (Webb Motors), Sal. a Qro, Km 1, Tel: 152-2598
      Ford (Ramsa) Sal. a Celaya (next to cable), Tel:152-3439

Cemetery

1. Panteón Municipal
Two blocks south of Hotel Real de Minas (small parallel road
    west of Salida a Celaya). The cemetery is open to the public
    daily from 9am-6pm.
The Twenty Four Hour Association
Application and information contact:
    Bonnie Bisnett
    Secretary
    Tel: 152-3536 alternate Tel: 152-2985(am) 152-6668(pm)

A non-profit service organization, started some 30 years ago, to
help members with burial or cremation. Must be a San Miguel
resident. It is non-secular and open to all nationalities. Pay a very
reasonable one-time fee, depending on the services required.
Includes body removal, funeral needs, plot or crypt, marker and
perpetual care at the 24-hour association section of the above
named San Miguel cemetery. This section is located straight ahead
from the entrance toward the back and on the left by a hedge and
small gate. The association will also notify the US Consul and
next-of-kin. Call for details and current fee schedule.

A date to remember:
November 2nd—All Soul's Day (Day of the Dead)
Graves are decorated on this very important Mexican holiday
The cemetery attracts large and cheerful crowds
You might be surprised to know that the colorful candy fruit,
    skulls and animal figures are made from orchid bulbs
Mark your calendar, a *must* see!

Churches & Religious Organizations

Catholic:

San Miguel de Allende has always been a pious city. Fray
Juan de San Miguel was the first to improvise a chapel in the area.
Later, near the springs known as El Chorro, the church of Santa
Cruz el Chorro was erected. The present day churches reflect the
splendor of bygone years and the great wealth. The ringing of
church bells in San Miguel all have a meaning and are an integral
part of San Miguel life. There are three calls for each mass: 30
minutes before, 15 minutes before and the third announcing the
start of Mass. Also, church bells ring for special *fiestas*, the Ave
María and at times for tributes given to the dead at special Masses
called *rosarios*. Listed below is a partial list of the more than
twenty churches within the city limits.

1. La Parroquia

The most prominent landmark in town. It towers over the Jardín to
    the south and can be seen from a great distance.
It is a parish church and not a cathedral
The structure was built at the end of the 17th century (started 1683)
The facade was constructed in 1880 by a local stone mason and
    builder, Ceferino Gutiérrez, a self-educated Indian. It is said
    that he was inspired by postcard reproductions of European
    churches. The structure was built with pink and tan stone that
    subtly changes color with the changing light.
Inside are murals, a statue of St Michael the Archangel (for whom
    the church is named) and a crypt. Former President Bustamante
    is buried in the basement. Open to the public on the Day of the Dead.
The loudest church bell in San Miguel. The bell is nearly six feet
    in height and 8½ inches thick.
When lit at night, on special occasions, it is a beautiful sight
Sunday Masses: (on the hour) from 6am-1pm and at 6 and 8:15pm

2. Church of San Francisco
Located at Calle San Francisco and Calle Juárez
In front is the Jardín de San Francisco (note a statue of
 Christopher Columbus on the street corner)
It was constructed in 1779 and took 20 years to complete
Donations by wealthy local families and funds from bull fights
 paid for the construction
A fashionable place to be buried as noted by numerous plaques
It has a spacious neoclassical interior
Next to it is the Chapel of the Third Order (*Tercer Orden*)
The simple, austere chapel was built by the Franciscans in 1713
A statue of St. Francis stands in a façade niche
Sunday Masses: 7:15am, 10:30am, 12 noon, 6pm, 7:15pm

3. The Oratorio (of San Felipe Neri)
Located corner of Calle Insurgentes and short street called Pepe Llanos
Large courtyard in front
It was built by local Indians in 1712
Inside are neoclassic Baroque altars and 33 paintings of scenes
 from life of Felipe Neri. The interior is based on a Latin
 cross design.
The Chapel of Loreto was constructed by the Canal family in
 1735 as a replica of Santa Casa (Holy House) which was
 founded in Loreto, Italy. The main entrance can be found inside
 the Oratorio by going down the left aisle, almost to the altar,
 and turning left. Inside gold leaf glitters on the walls. The
 public is always allowed to go in on the Night of Altars (Holy
 Week Thursday) and a few other times each year.

4. La Salud—Church of our Lady of Health
Faces Plaza Allende
The dome is covered with yellow and blue tile.
The church is connected to an old building that was once the
 College of San Francisco de Sales. It was built as a college
 chapel, mostly by money given by a priest.
The tower houses the oldest (1735) bell in town.
Note one of the most beautiful doors in México

5. La Concepción (Las Monjas)
Located at Canal and Hernández Macías
Funds were supplied by a daughter of the Canal family
A royal decree established the convent in 1754 with construction
 starting the next year

Steeple completed in 1842 and the imposing dome in 1891 by
    Ceferino Gutiérrez
Sunday Mass (English)—10am—Father Reynaldo Tapia Martínez
    Right of main church entrance—look for sign

6. San Juan de Dios
San Antonio Abad (near former Tuesday market area)
Tel: 152-0688

7. San Antonio Church
Callejón de San Antonio (south of town)
Col. San Antonio
Parish church one of oldest in the area, some walls date about 1620
Second oldest bell in San Miguel (1762)
Sunday Masses: 7am, 8am, 1pm, 6pm, 8pm

Other Denominations:

1. Anglican
St. Paul's Anglican Church
Calzada del Cardo (across from Hotel Aristos)
Tel: 152-0387
E-mail: rector@stpauls.com.mx
Web page: www.stpauls.com.mx
Sunday 9am Holy Eucharist
Sunday 10:30am Choral Holy Eucharist with sermon and choir
Service first held in December 1965
Center for many community activities
Also offers free psychotherapy referral service
Rector: Rev. Michael Long (since 1997)

2. Unitarian/Universalist
Posada de la Aldea (across from the Instituto)
Ancha de San Antonio s/n (*sin número*)
Meeting Room
Sunday fellowship meeting at 10:30am
UU Fellowship President Robert Hesdorfer Tel: 152-1473
    Vice-president Betse Davies Tel: 154-4353
E-mail: thistle@unisono.net.mx
Web page: www.infosma.com/uusma

3. Jewish Community of San Miguel
Hotel Quinta Loreto (TV room)
Loreto #15
Saturday: 10am traditional Minyan   11am Torah study
Information about other services and holiday celebrations, call the
    Jewish Community at 152-2659
    E-mail: nadel@cybermatsa.com.mx

4. L.D.S. (Mormon)
La Salud #4 (Aldea area)
    Sunday service   9am
    Sunday school   10-11am
    Instruction   11-12 noon

5. Jehovah's Witnesses
Kingdom Hall
Pila Seca #31 (past Quebrada)
Tel: 152-3931
Group of English speaking members and for Spanish speakers

Cinemas

1. Cinemas Gemelos de San Miguel
Plaza Real del Conde (Gigante)
Tel: 152-6408
Twin theaters (each seats 250 people)
Shows daily at 4pm ,6pm and 8pm (best to call for exact starting time)
Opened Sept'94
Floating screen with a decent sound system
Ticket price: about US$3
    (half-price tickets first weekday show and all day Wednesday
    plus Sunday matinee)
Movies change on Friday
Movies are usually in English with Spanish subtitles
Popcorn, drinks and snacks available
Movies announced on FM radio and on outdoor sign in front of
    Gigante Plaza by the highway and in ATENCIóN

2. Cine/Bar
Hotel Villa Jacaranda
Aldama #53

Tel: 152-1015 or 152-0811
Web page: www.villajacaranda.com (see review of movies)
Hrs: Daily at 7:30pm, Sunday matinee at 3:30pm
Movie schedule published in ATENCIóN–changes on Tuesday
Admission about US$6 (includes first domestic cocktail and popcorn)
Wide screen and THX surround sound

3. Cinemateca Santa Ana
Biblioteca Pública
Reloj #50-A (during non-library hours)
Tel: 152-0293
Foreign films, documentaries and films relating to art, music and dance
Original language with English subtitles
Hi-tech state-of-the-art projection and sound equipment
Show times 5:30pm and 7:30pm (depending on the day)–see
        schedule in ATENCIóN or on Biblioteca bulletin board
Seating capacity (85)
Admission approximately US$4
Opened June'00

4. Cineclub Bellas Artes
Bellas Artes Auditorium–second floor
Hernández Macías #75
Tel: 152-0289
Foreign films: English, Spanish or French
Films shown on Monday and Thursday at 5 and 8pm, Sunday at 6pm
Dates/times listed in **ATENCIóN** (calendar page) and at Bellas Artes
Admission: adults about US$2, students US$1
        Buy ticket at the door
Since Sept'98

Clothing Shops

1. Talisman Too
San Francisco #7
Tel: 152-0438
Hrs: Mon-Sat 10am-3pm and 4-7 pm, Sun 10am-2pm and 4-8pm
Credit cards: Amex, Master and Visa
Owner: Esther Ramírez (Swiss)
Ultra chic designs that can be worn from Nantucket to Carmel
This shop is a delight–well accented with fun jewelry and
        exceptional small craft items
Opened Sept'98

2. Goldie
Designs and concierge
Canal #9 (½ block from Jardín)
Tel: 154-7420
E-mail: goldiedesigns@hotmail.com
Hrs: Tue-Sat 11am-6pm (or by appointment)
Credit cards: Amex, Master and Visa
Owner: Diane Goldie from San Francisco
Custom designed elegant clothing
Women's slacks, jackets, blouses and shoes
Creative accessories—own line of jewelry
Enjoy the warm, spacious interior of this *boutique*
Opened Sept'04

3. Girasol Boutique Willa Mina
San Francisco #11 (inside Galería Goded, formerly Kligerman gallery)
Tel: 152-2734   Fax: 152-0951
E-mail: kligerman@prodigy.net.mx
Hrs: Daily 10am-2pm and 4-8pm, Sunday 10am-3pm
Credit cards: Amex, Master and Visa
Owner Willa Mina hand picks her Mexican-made collection of
    fashionable casuals and accessories
Don't miss these colorful Girasol outfits!
Beautifully renovated store with two new fitting rooms
Designer sterling and fashion jewelry-separate showroom in front
First opened in 1989
Discount annex, Guadiana #17-A, Tel: 044-415-151-2718 (cell)

4. DIVA
Hernández Macías #72 (across from Bellas Artes)
Tel: 152-4980   Fax: 154-7260
E-mail: diva@unisono.net.mx
Hrs: Mon-Sat 9am-8pm, Sunday 11am-3pm
Major credit cards welcome
Owner and Creative Director: Christine Anderson
Offers a delightfully original and vibrant line of designer women's
    attire·and accessories for all occasions
Also, jewelry by Robert Lewis, Wanda Lobito, Elena Solow,
    Michael Christofas, Gisela Kriszio and others
Remodeled and renamed Nov'99 (was Mangos Boutique)
Discount (20%) outlet, 2nd floor, Hrs: Mon-Fri 9am-3pm

5. Barbarita Boutique
Zacateros #47 (near Pila Seca)
Tel/Fax: 152-7463
E-mail: info@barbaritaboutique.com
Hrs: Mon-Sat 10am-6pm, Sunday closed
Owner: Barbara Bladen Porter (San Francisco)
Custom designed clothing for women plus accessories
Choose from international collection of fabrics and imported buttons
Reversible clothing—full figure fashions
Also jewelry, art and skin care products
Opened Sept'01, relocated April'02, name changed Jan'04

6. Marcia's Boutique (Black and White shop)
Loreto #20-A
Tel: 154-4493
E-mail: shopgirlmarcia@yahoo.com
Hrs: Tues-Sun 11am-5pm, closed Monday
Credit cards: None
Owner: Marcia Dolce
Ideal traveling clothes in simple natural fabrics—luxurious wraps
Many one of a kind items made by lower income familics
Check out the prison art
Also Alpaca coats and sweaters from Bolivia for men and women
Some men's things
Opened Dec'96, relocated Sept'04

7. Christopher Fallon Design
Fábrica La Aurora
Calzada de la Aurora s/n (north of town)
Tel: 154-5075
Hrs: Mon-Sat 10am-4pm, closed Sunday
Credit cards: Master and Visa
Owners: Christopher and Caroline Fallon
Couture–*prêt à porter* for women
Shirts for men–made in San Miguel
Also home accessories, furniture, antiques, lampshades and more
Good parking
Relocated Sept'03

8. La Colección Judith Roberts
Calle Zacateros #28 (next to Casa Payo)
Tel: 152-3070

Hrs: Daily 10am-2pm and 4-7pm
Credit cards: Amex, Master and Visa
First-class, one-of-a-kind coats, jackets and vests
Accessories plus high-quality folk art

9. El Tocador ("dressing table")
Cuna de Allende #7 (entrance of Posada Carmina)
Tel: 154-8386
Hrs: Daily 10am-8pm, closed Tuesday
Owner: Alejandra Bustamante (bilingual)
Impressive, high quality store
Products from México, Europe and the USA
Everything for women
Clothing, underwear, shoes, hats, handbags, jewelry and lotion
Opened April'01

10. Artesanías "El Inquisidor"
Cuadrante #34 (near H. Macías)
Tel: 152-0433
Hrs: Mon-Sat 10am-2pm and 4-7pm, closed Sunday
Manager: Marina Alvarado González
Small store of locally made women's clothing
Dresses and blouses all 100% cotton
Since 1991

11. Segunda Llamada ("second call")
Codo #3-B
Tel: 044-415-100-4010 (cell)
E-mail: segunda-llamada@cybermatsa.com.mx
Web page: www.segunda-llamada.com
Hrs: Mon-Sat 10am-6pm, closed Sunday
Upscale consignment clothing and accessories for men and women
Excellent quality and good prices
Opened Jan'02, moved Sept'03 (new ownership)

Also: **The Leather Shop,** Umarán #1, Tel: 152-8679
     Casa Canal, Canal #3, Tel: 152-0479
     La Alfonsina, Hidalgo #36, Tel: 152-1429
     Piaf, Correo #6, Tel: 154-5186
     Darla, Recreo (corner of Correo), Tel: 154-5550
     Foto Bazar, Portal de Guadalupe, Tel: 152-2739

Changing your Clothes					
Women's dresses:					
US	6	8	10	12	14	16
México	30	32	34	36	38	40
Men's shirts:					
US	14	14.5	15	15.5	16	16.5
México	36	37	38	39	40	41

Communication Centers

1. Border Crossings
Mesones #57 (Int. of China Palace Rest.)-also entrance on Reloj
Tel: 152-2497   Fax: 152-3672
E-mail: pack@bordercrossingsma.com
Web page: www.bordercrossingsma.com
Hrs: Mon-Fri 9am-6:30pm, Sat 10am-3pm, closed Sunday
Owner: Nelly Lorenzo (bilingual)
Conveniently located message center (1 block from Jardín)
Mailbox rentals–approximately US$18 per month (10% discount
     for annual payment)
     Includes high speed free Internet access for members
     Telephone messages
Mail delivery five times per week (Tues—Sat) from USA
Local and long distance telephone calls
USA mail dropoff ($5 pesos per oz plus postage)
Stateside address:
         % Border Crossings
         413 Interamerica #1, BC-2323
         Laredo TX 78045-8285
Packing & Shipping service (national and international)
     UPS and Estafeta
Permanent collection of folk art and jewelry for sale
Opened July'95, relocated Feb'05

2. La Conexión
Aldama #3 (behind the Parroquia)
Tel/Fax: 152-1599, 152-1687 or 152-6173
E-mail: laconex@prodigy.net.mx
Web page: www.laconex.com
Hrs: Mon-Sat 9am-7pm, Sunday 10am-2pm, closed holidays

Owner: Susan Sargeant
Busy community business center
24-hour message service, bilingual staff
Private mailbox service (US$15 per month minimum)
Mailing address for México and USA (for members)
Daily Express Mail and package service to and from Laredo, TX
Karma mailbox for USA posted mail
Also internet telephone (for members)
Two computer work stations for self-service e-mail (free for customers)
Packing, shipping, forwarding and warehousing
Outlet for Oaxacan wool rugs
Stateside office: (Jan'00)
>   220 N. Zapata Hwy #11
>   Laredo, Texas 78043-4464
>   Tel/Fax: (956) 725-7563
Opened April'91, moved next door March'03
2nd office: Ave. Independencia #74, Tel: 152-4223

3. Solutions
Formerly Mail Boxes, Etc
Recreo #11 (in the back)
Tel: 152-6152   Fax: 152-6153
E-mail: sanmiguelsolutions@yahoo.com
Hrs: Mon-Fri 9am-6pm, Sat 9am-2pm, closed Sunday
Owner: Cristobal Olvera (bilingual)
>   Manager: Mónica Cacho (bilingual)
Mail delivery to and from USA
DHL, UPS and FedEx next day priority mail
Office supplies for sale—also packing and shipping
Stateside address:
>   5411 McPherson Rd #84
>   Laredo, TX 78041-6834
Opened July'96, name changed Jan'04, new owners Dec'04

4. Promotion of Mexican Culture (PMC)
Formerly Travel Institute of San Miguel
Hidalgo #16 (near Mesones)
Tel: 152-1630 or 154-5312   Tel/Fax: 152-0121
E-mail: info@pmexc.com
Web page: www.pmexc.com
Hrs: Mon-Fri 8:30am-2:30pm and 4-7pm, Sat 8:30am-2:30pm
Owner: Marisela Patterson (bilingual)
Helpful bilingual staff

Telephone/Fax/e-mail and copies for a small fee
Mail/message box rentals (US$15 per month)
Van shuttle service to airports
Local tours (historic, arts and crafts)
Also tours to Atotonilco, Guanajuato, Dolores, Pozos, other destinations
Shopping trips to Price Club & Sam's in Qro (need five people)
Spanish lessons (US$12 per hour)
Primera Plus and ETN bus ticket outlet
Relocated Jun'03

5. Pack 'N' Mail

Canal #42 (near Quebrada bridge)
Tel: 152-5461   Fax: 152-0594
E-mail: packmail@cybermatsa.com.mx
Hrs: Mon-Fri 9:30am-6pm, Sat 9:30am-2pm, closed Sunday
Credit cards: Amex, Master and Visa
Owners: Michael and Adriana Vidargas (bilingual)
Courier service to Laredo, TX every Mon, Wed, Fri
Daily worldwide UPS service (documents two day delivery)
Professional packing, shipping, moving and storage
Permanent San Miguel or Texas address mailbox rental (US$20 per
     month) All mailbox rentals have a locked box with its own key
Translations, copies
Community bulletin board
Since 1990, new ownership Jan'00, relocated Dec'01
Stateside office:
            4301 McPherson Road, Suite 105
            Laredo, Texas 78041-5252

Also: **Santa Clara**, Ancha de San Antonio #1, Tel: 152-5141

Message Delivery Services:

1. Mensajería Local

Allende #8 (upstairs) (Col. San Antonio)
Tel: 152-1902
Local delivery service
Complete listing of name, address and person receiving mail
Fee less than local postage rate

2. Perfil Publicitario

San Elias #9-1 (Col. San Antonio)
Tel: 152-2758 (leave message)
Local delivery service
Economical

Community Bulletin Boards

Community members place notices for a wide range of topics, ranging from house/apartment rentals, garage sales, shared rides, sitters and a variety of other personals. Popular locations follow:

1. Helados Holanda (aka **Norman's**)
San Francisco #10
2. Instituto Allende
Ancha de San Antonio #20
(turn left once inside building)
3. Pack 'N' Mail
Canal #42
4. Border Crossings
Mesones #57 (interior)
5. La Conexión
Aldama #3

6. Espino's
Codo #36
7. Academia
Mesones #4
8. Photo Super 30 (Fuji)
Portal Allende (west of Jardín)
9. Chelo's
Canal #26
10. Plaza Colonial
Canal #21 (inside arcade)

Also check the Classifieds in the **ATENCIóN**

Computers/Internet

Internet Service Providers:

1. Unísono Net
Hernández Macías #72-B (upstairs)
Tel: 152-6331 or Tel/Fax: 152-4958
Hrs: Mon-Fri 9am-6pm, closed weekends
Director: Joanie Barcal
Internet service provider (local access)
      E-mail address: unisono@unisono.net.mx
      Web page address: http://unisono.net.mx
Offer a local dial-up or wireless service from home
      Sign up for one month or up to a year
Web mail with world-wide capability
Bilingual technical support staff available for house calls
First opened business in May'96

2. TELMEX
Tel: 01-800-123-2222 (toll free)
Direct Prodigy Internet connection from your home phone (Mar'99)
Cost about US$19 + IVA per month–if you are a long distance
      subscriber with TELMEX–better price if you pay annually
      Charged to telephone bill
      Unlimited hours
      24-hours-per-day techncial assistance

Also high-speed **Prodigy Infinitum** Internet (Mar'02)
   3 speeds:
      256 kbps   approx. US$ 50 + IVA per month
      512 kbps   approx. US$ 90 + IVA per month
   2,048 kbps   approx. US$400 + IVA per month
   No dial-up—always on-line—direct to server
   Installation approx. US$300
   Call 01-800-123-3456   Ext. 4 (English)

3. CYBERM@TSA
Tele Cable
Salida a Celaya, km 1 (just past Ford agency)
Tel: 152-1942 and 152-3442   Fax: 152-1145
Hrs: Mon-Fri 8:30am-2pm and 4:30-5:30pm, Sat 9am-2pm
High speed cable internet (no need for telephone line)
Cost depends on speed deisred:
    64 kbps   approx. US$22 per/mo
   128 kbps   approx. US$37 per/mo
   256 kbps   approx. US$45 per/mo
Cable modem and installation extra (as is basic cable service)
Connected 24 hours a day
Service started June'01

Cybercafés:

1. Café Etc.
Reloj #37 (across the street from Biblioteca side entrance)
Tel/Fax: 154-8636
Hrs: Mon-Sat 9am to 7pm, Sunday sometimes open in afternoon
Owners: Juan and Rocío Ortíz (bilingual)
Six work stations-fast DSL line (Prodigy Infinitum)
   Scanner and printers available
Fifteen *pesos* per/hour or prepaid card
Computers and accessories for sale
Espresso bar- a variety of hot and cold drinks
   Quality and price better than Starbucks
Eat inside or in small courtyard (7 tables)
Delicious inexpensive sandwiches and soups
   Ask about tasty home-made daily specials
Mexican coffee beans sold by the pound
Best CD collection (2000 +) of jazz music in town
Opened Apr'02, relocated Mar'04—a fun place to go!

2. Estación Internet
Correo #12-A (next to La Morada Hotel) at Sollano
Tel: 152-7312
Hrs: Daily 9am-9pm
E-mail address: email@estacioninternet.com
Web page address: www.estacioninternet.com
Owner: Adolfo Cervantes (bilingual)
Four fully networked multimedia stations
Computers can be rented (ask for hourly rates) for word
    processing and graphic arts, also a printer is available
High-speed cable Internet connection (broadband)
        Flat-screen technology—printer and scanner available
Oldest cybercafé in San Miguel
Also a café and **Sierra Madre** outlet
Opened Nov'96 and relocated March'02

3. Punto G
Hidalgo #23
Tel/Fax: 152-4493   044-415-153-6160 (cell)
E-mail: laskersma@hotmail.com
Hrs: Daily 10am-10pm
Owner: Hugo Alonso (bilingual)
Workstations: Eight—high-speed cable Internet connection
Reasonable rates, cheaper with purchase of five-hour card
Printer and scanner available
Light food, soft drinks and cable TV—nice sitting area
Also location of San Miguel Chess Club
Opened Mar'01, relocated Mar'02, name changed Feb'04

4. Net@ San Miguel Cybercafé
Aldama #60 (near Parque Juárez)
Tel: 152-5672
Hrs: 10:30am-10pm, closed Sunday
Owner: Christian Ramírez (bilingual)
Six work stations
Fast internet connection (cable)
Only $10 *pesos* per/hour
Also international telephone service
    Lowest prices in town
    USA: $2.50 *pesos* per/minute
    Canada: $1.50 *pesos* per/minute
Opened Oct'03

5. Araiz@.com
Canal #120
Tel: 154-5934
E-mail: araizacom@prodigy.net.mx
Hrs: Mon-Sat 10:30am-8pm, closed Sunday
Owner: Francisco Mtz. Araiza (bilingual)
Seven work stations
Sell computers, supplies and make repairs
Also give classes and consultations
Opened Sept'99

6. Internet Fácil
Plaza Real del Conde (Gigante) - near front entrance
Tel: 154-6950 (also the computer line)
Hrs: Mon-Sat 9:30am-8:30pm, closed Sunday
Owner: Luís Ricardo Ferro Baeza
Cyberm@tsa—high-speed cable Internet
Eight private work stations (cubicles)
     Attractive layout with small lounge area
Minimun charge—$16 *pesos* per/hour
     Discount cards available
Printer and scanner available
Good parking
Opened Feb'00

7. Cybernet
Mesones #10 (next to a *cantina*)
Tel: 152-3573
E-mail: cybernet@sanmiguelense.com
Web page: www.cybernct.sanmiguelense.com
Hrs: Mon-Sat 10:30am-9pm, Sunday 10am-3pm
Seven work stations—high-speed connecton
Two printers (one color) and one scanner
Reasonable prices—$15 *pesos* per hour
Opened March'00, moved Feb'04

The Computer Center:

Biblioteca (upstairs from Café Santa Ana)
Formerly the Mickler Computer Center
Insurgentes #25
Tel: 152-1210
Hrs: Mon-Fri 10am-2pm and 4-7pm, Sat 10am-2pm

Separate lab and class area
Fast DSL internet connection—free for library members
Computer classes in English for fee-scheduled on request
Free computer skills classes for Mexican youths
Reopened Dec'01

Additional E-Mail Locations:
1. La Conexión, Aldama #3, Tel: 152-1599, send/receive (fee)
2. PMC, Hidalgo #16, Tel: 152-1630, send/receive (fee)
3. Border Crossings, Correo #19, Tel: 152-2497, send/receive (fee)
4. Santa Clara, A.de San Antonio#1,Tel:152-5141, send/receive(fee)

The OFFICIAL **Insider's Guide to San Miguel** web page:
http://insidersma.tripod.com

Web page design:
Diseño.i
Francisco Marquez #17-A (Col. Independencia)
Tel/Fax:154-0245
E-mail: mail@diseno-i.com
Web page: www.diseno-i.com
Hrs: Mon-Fri 9am-2pm and 4-7pm, Sat 9am-2pm
Owners: Claudia and Francisco Vázquez (bilingual)
Web page design, domain hosting and construction services
Also sell computers, related equipment and supplies
Fast growing local client list
Several awards for web design
Started April'00, relocated July'04

Computer Stores:
1. Equipos y Sistemas
Indio Triste #7—Los Frailes
Tel: 044-415-153-7222 (cell)
E-mail: delera@unisono.net.mx
Hrs: Daily 9am-5pm, closed Sunday
Owner: Ing. Eduardo Lera Salinas (bilingual)
Assemble, upgrade and sell computers (with local warranty)
Software and accessories for sale
Also repair computers, will do house calls
In business since 1988, relocated Jan'04

2. Sistemas Integrales en Computación (SIC)

Núñez #15-B (no name/number outside)-left from Mesones
Tel: 152-6064   Tel/Fax: 152-4859
E-mail: gposic@prodigy.net.mx
Hrs: Mon-Fri 9am-2pm and 4-7pm, Sat 9:30am-2pm
Manager: Alejandro Zavala (bilingual)
Sell computers, software and supplies—reasonable prices
Repair PC's— will make house calls

> Also: **Electroserc**, San Francisco #51-B, Tel: 152-4698
> **La Esencia,** Canal #59-A, Tel: 154-8003

> Insider's Tip: Looking for a printer cartridge, check out Centro Papelero de San Miguel, located at Ancha de San Antonio #55, Tel: 152-1937 or Insurgentes #134-A, Tel: 154-8780. They stock a good selection of various brands. They also deliver.

Computer Classes:

The Computer Center
Biblioteca (upstairs from Café Santa Ana)
Separate classroom area
Classes in English at all levels by computer professionals
Free afternoon computer classes for Mexican youths
Class schedules in ATENCIóN and on Biblioteca bulletin board

Computer Club Meeting:
San Miguel Computer Club (PCs)
Biblioteca Municipal—Pepe Llanos #14
Every Tuesday at 10am
Newcomers and beginners welcome

Computer Consultation:

1. Edwin Sours
Tel: 152-6782
E-mail: smaedwin@yahoo.com

2. Juan Francisco Martínez Araiza (bilingual)
Canal #120
Tel: 154-5934   044-415-153-3230 (cell)
E-mail: paco5_mtz@yahoo.com

> Also you might try **Larry Gassler** (Tel: 154-4736) or E-mail: larsma@cybermatsa.com.mx, for installation, upgrades and service.

Cooking Classes/Catering

1. Patsy DuBois
Rancho Las Hadas Madrinas (road to Dolores Hidalgo)
Tel: 185-2151   044-415-153-5303 (cell)
E-mail: mexcooking@prodigy.net.mx
Mexican country cooking classes
Simply the best chocolate chip cookies anywhere!
Party facilities available on site
Also runs a busy catering business

2. Sazón
Correo #22 (just around the corner from Pegaso)
Tel: 154-7671
E-mail: srateresa@aol.com
Web page: www.sazonsanmiguel.com
Hrs: Mon-Sat 10am-6pm, Sunday 11am-3pm
Owner: Teresa Jones from Minneapolis and Tucson
A busy and exciting new cooking school
State-of-the-art kitchens and equipment
Pickup a newsletter with listing of classes and events
Will create a private cooking party for your special ocassion
Experienced local chefs and guest chefs from around the world
Opened Jul'02, moved Nov'03

3. Chef María
Calle de la Luz #12 (Col. San Antonio)
Tel: 152-4376
E-mail: cocimari@hotmail.com
Hrs: Daily 10am-1pm
María Laura Ricaud (bilingual)
Cooking classes (in English) for 1-8 people
Also individual classes for the same price
Old family recipes—featured in Texas Monthly (Nov'01)

4. Reyna's Cooking Class
Cri-Cri #25 (Col. Guadalupe)
Tel: 152-4193
E-mail: reyna53@prodigy.net.mx
Mexican cuisine workshops—needs minimum of five people
        Creative, fun and taught in English
Cook and then eat full *comida* (drinks included)
Keep printed recipes of Mexican regional dishes

5. The Night Kitchen
Michele Vallon–from New York City
Tel:152-3099
Catering, take-out and artcakes
International, New York and ethnic food
The artcakes are one-of-a-kind and creatively personalized and decorated
Palatable prices
Total 30 years experience in NYC and San Miguel

6. Flavors of the Sun
Victoria Challancin
Tel: 152-5912 and 152-1852   Fax: 152-6153
E-mail: flavorsofthesun@yahoo.com
Web page: www.infosma.com/flavors
Classes cover "Sun Belt" cooking from México through Italy, the
        Mediterranean, Middle East and Far East
Private or group classes
Member of IACP (International Association of Culinary Professionals)
Published own cookbook, *Flavors of San Miguel de Allende* (Apr'98)

7. Indonesian Catering
Col. San Antonio
Tel: 152-3074
Sra. Murgiati (Mur) Dipoyoso
Authentic Indonesian food
        Gado gado (salad), *nasi goreng* (fried rice), chicken curry,
        spring rolls (*lumpia*) and much more
Catering for 6-30 people—minimum two-day notice
Home delivery (dishes are warm)
Menu with prices upon request

8. Servicio de Banquetes
Juan de Dios Peza #37 (Col. Guadalupe)
Tel: 152-6507 (office), 152-2166 (home)
Guadalupe Ramírez ("Bola")
Will cater any special event
Food and serving
Also tables, chairs, dishes, glasses, etc. for rent

Insider's Tip: Holly's comfort food. Will deliver or in-home cooking. Fresh daily specials, classic entrees, desserts and *hors d'oeuvres*. Call Holly at: 152-1274.

Other Caterers:
   ChaCha González, Los Frailes, Tel: 152-1837
   Armando Camacho Guzmán, Centro, Tel:154-5250
   El Pegaso, Corregidora #6, Tel: 152-1351
   El Buen Café, Jesús #23, Tel: 152-5807

Copy Places

1. Copias Artículos de Ingeniería
Zacateros #27
Tel: 152-1209
Hrs: Mon-Fri 9am-3:30pm and 4-8pm, Sat 9am-2:30pm, closed Sun
Engineering and architectural copies
Good reproduction equipment
Five copy machines
Also bindings and lamination

2. Video Geminis
Zacateros #43
Tel: 152-2056
Hrs:Mon-Sat 9am-2pm and 4:30-8pm, closed Sunday
Owner: Agustín Valadez—family business since 1936
Photos (studio, passport, etc.), videos and cassettes copies
4 copy machines (including large blueprint one)
Enlargement/reduction, lamination and binding
Color copying also
Fax service

3. Copi Jusa
Insurgentes #92 (west of Hidalgo)
Tel: 152-6054
Hrs: Mon-Sat 9am-2pm and 4-8pm, Sun 10am-2pm
3 copy machines including one for blueprints
Bindings, paper supplies and lamination

Also: **Mexisano**, Hidalgo #1-B, Tel/Fax: 152-7072
      Galarza, Insurgentes #40 (across from Loreto), Tel: 152-3180
   Imprenta Lasser, Zacateros #85, Tel: 152-3737
         Does color copying
There are also copy machines in numerous stationery stores.

Country Club

Malanquín Golf and Country Club
Road to Celaya (3 kms south of town, just north of Los Frailes)
Tel: 152-0516 or 154-8210   Tel/Fax: 152-6721
E-mail: malanquin@prodigy.net.mx
Web page: www.malanquin.com
Hrs: Tues-Sun 7am-9pm, closed Monday
General Manager: María Cristina Lambarri (bilingual)
Opened July 4, 1970
Golf—9-hole course
4 Clay tennis courts, swimming pool and driving range
Hole in One Restaurant/Bar for daily breakfast and lunch
     No membership required

Share Membership (transferable): about US$8,000
     Plus monthly dues (single or family)
Non-Voting Membership: about US$4,250
     Plus monthly dues (single or family)
Guest:
     Golf (special price after 2pm)—lessons available
     Tennis and swimming
     Pay daily, weekly or monthly
     Also rent golf clubs and carts
Inquire about a summer camp program for children (mid-July to
     mid-August)
Full-time members have reciprocal privileges at some 18 clubs in
     México, including the Country Club of Querétaro, the Country
     Club of Juriquilla (Qro) and the Country Club of Celaya.
Membership—approximately 400 members

Dancing/Night Clubs

1. La Cava de la Princesa
Restaurant/Bar—one of the oldest in town
Recreo #3 (near corner of Calle Correo)
Tel: 152-1403
Hrs: Daily 6pm-3am, closed Monday
Credit cards: None
Owner: María Eugenia Riba (since Nov'01)
Popular night spot for the over 40 crowd
Live music daily from 10pm until closing
     Small cover charge on weekends

Small intimate dance floor
Food service with limited menu—reasonable prices
     Karaoke (daily 6-10pm)—5,000 songs in Spanish and English
Also a pool table near the bar

2. Mama Mía's
Umarán #8 (near Jardín)
Tel: 152-2063
Hrs: Regular hours 9pm-2am—(closed when no customers)
Live salsa and rock music—starts around 10pm
Sometimes a small cover charge
Small, but interesting layout—some balconies
Mama Mía Restaurant and **Bar Leonardo** at same location

3. Pancho and Lefty's
Mesones #99
Tel: 152-1958
Hrs: Thurs-Sunday 10pm-3am
Three bars in one
     Main bar-rock and roll music
     Ivy bar (upstairs)-DJ music
     Patio bar-country music
Reopened Sept'02

4. El Ring
Disco/Bar
Hidalgo #27 (near Insurgentes)
Tel: 152-1998
Hrs: Wednesday-Saturday 8pm-3am
Large, interesting decor—formerly a cockfighting hall
Ground floor plus two tiers—should see!
Draws a young, lively, late crowd (live music)
Sometimes a cover charge
     Club 27
     Hidalgo #27
     Thursdays 6:30pm-midnight
     All kinds of music for an older crowd
     Entrance fee: $50 *pesos* (incl 2 drinks)

5. El Grito
Umarán #15
Tel: 152-0048
Hrs: Friday and Saturday 10pm-3am

Drinks only–no food
Upscale Mexican atmosphere
Named for Father Hidalgo's independence speech
　　Note a painting of Hidalgo behind the bar
Capacity–400 people (mostly age 25 and under)
DJ music–be prepared for a cover charge
A pool table can be found in front room
Roof- top patio open during favorable weather
Opened August'98

Delis

1. La Cava
Zacateros #40 (corner of Tenerías)
Tel: 152-1549
Hrs: Mon-Fri 10am-3pm and 5:30-8:30pm, Sat 10am-4pm
　　Closed Sunday
Imported foods (good selection of cheeses)
See owners in advance for Thanksgiving and Christmas turkeys
Since March'95

2. Harry's Market
Gourmet and seafood
Hidalgo #10 (½ block from Jardín)
Tel: 152-3838
E-mail: specialdelivery@harrys-gourmet.com
Hrs: Mon-Sat 10am-6pm, Sunday 10am-2pm
Manager: Karla Rosales (bilingual)
Fresh fish and shellfish (from the world's largest outdoor market
　　in México City)—delivered daily
Imported certified USDA Angus beef
Imported cheeses and specialty food items
Fine wines by the bottle
Same owner as Harry's restaurant (next door)
Opened Nov'01

3. Mexisano
Hidalgo #1-B (next to American Express)
Tel/Fax: 152-7072
Hrs: Mon-Fri 9am-5pm, Sat 10am-2pm
Owners: Miguel and Cristina (bilingual)
Healthy, nutritous deli food

Sandwiches, baguettes, salads and muffins
Soy products, yogurt, cheese, nuts and dried fruit
Home-made breads, brown rice, organic pastas and vegetables
Cold water fish
Cold drinks including water
Also party plates and gift baskets
Will deliver home or office
Copy machine and stationery supplies
Reopened Sept'04

4. Bee Natural
Jesús at corner of Terraplén
Tel/Fax: 154-8629
E-mail: tiendasma@yahoo.com
Hrs: Tues-Sat 10am-5pm
Owner: Jorge Catalán (bilingual)
Organic store
Bread, rolls and cookies
Grains including brown rice
Yogurt, tofu, honey, cheese and teas
Food for special diets
Opened July'04

Also: **El Atrio La Capilla**, Cuna de Allende #10 (Gd/F), Tel: 152-0698

Dentists

1. Dra. Laura Elías Urdapilleta
San Jorge #12 (corner San Elías) – Col. San Antonio
Tel: 152-4330 (office) 152-4262 (*casa*)
Hrs: Mon-Fri 9am-8pm
Sensitive bilingual professional
Certified by the Mexican Dental Association (ADM)
General dentistry: cleaning, crowns and root canals
Reasonable fees
Since 1985 practicing in México City and San Miguel

2. Dr. Jorge Vargas
Libramiento Qro-Dolores #10 (south of town)
Tel: 152-1081 and 152-1986
Office Hrs: Mon-Fri 9am-2pm and 4-7:30pm, Sat am
Certified by the Mexican Dental Association (ADM)

Complete dentistry
Consultation by appointment only
Many local patients
Bilingual
Son Dr. Jorge Vargas, San Francisco #35 (Int), Tel: 152-4966

3. Dra. Cecilia Berrospe
General Dentistry
Hospital de la Fé San Miguel (upstairs in medical building)
Libramiento Highway to Dolores Hidalgo
Tel: 154-6474
Trained in México City and practiced in LA, CA two years
Certified by the Mexican Dental Association (ADM)+(ADA)
Appointments only
Speaks English

4. Dra. María Guadalupe Tejeda Gómez
General dentistry plus orthodontics
Barranca #3 (near Correo)
Tel: 152-2065
Hrs: Mon-Fri 9am-1:30pm and 4-8pm, Sat 9am-1pm
Trained at UNAM in México City
Practicing in San Miguel since 1983
Bilingual

**Check 1996 San Miguel Medical Directory of
Professionals & Services for further listings**

Out-of-Town:
Dr. Alfonso Vera Soto
S.L. Potosí #29 Sur (near old bus station)
Querétaro
Tel: 01(442) 212-1704 and 01(442) 212-9551
State-of-art equipment
Excellent work
Bilingual

Doctors

Specific hospitals and doctors are not recommended in this text, as individuals should make their selection based on their own needs and research. Care should be taken. Costs plus insurance coverage, if applicable, need to be discussed during the initial visit. Getting sick in México is not exactly the same as getting sick in the United States or Canada.

1. Medical Center
Hospital de la Fé San Miguel
Libramiento Hwy. #43 (to Dolores Hidalgo)
Tel: 152-2233, 152-2320 and 152-2329
Some 29 specialists including:
> Dr. Arturo Barrera (Internist)—bilingual
> Dr. Salvador Quiróz (Internist)—bilingual
> Dr. Jorge Alvarez (Cardiologist)—bilingual
> Dra. Lillian Hernández (ENT)—bilingual

**Check 1996 San Miguel Medical Directory of
Professionals & Services for further listings**

---

2. Dra. Ma. Silvia Azcárate
General Practitioner
Codo #9-A (flat iron building-upstairs)
Tel: 152-1944   044-415-149-0232 (cell)
> Emergency Tel: 120-3895 (*casa*)
Office hours: Mon-Fri 11am-1:30pm and 5-7pm
Trained at UNAM in México City
Trilingual: speaks English, Spanish and French
More than twenty years experience
San Miguel practice since 1993
Makes house calls seven days a week

3. Dr. Jorge A. Martínez (bilingual)
General practitioner
Tel: 044-415-153-8832 (cell)
E-mail: margonjo@hotmail.com
Will make house calls

4. Dra. Juliana L. Taylor (bilingual)
General practitioner
Casa/office: Minerva #36
Col. Olimpo (overlooks bus station)
Tel: 152-3718   or   044-415-149-6572 (cell)
Make an appointment
Will make house calls

5. Dra. Blanca E. Farías de Villarreal
Dermatologist—Trilingual
Umarán #20-B (upstairs) - just west of H. Macías

Tel: 152-2321
Hrs: Mon-Fri 9am-2pm. Sat 10:30am-2pm
    Make appointment first
Trained in México City-Practiced in San Miguel since 1989

6. Dr. Fidel G. Dobarganes
Hospital de la Fé San Miguel
Libramiento Hwy. to Dolores Hidalgo
Tel: 152-2233, 152-2320 and 152-2329
Orthopedist (from Querétaro)—bilingual
Consultation: about US$30
Hrs: Wednesday only in SMA–11am-2pm and 4 -6pm

Chiropractors:

1. Mary Lawson, DC
Chiropractic physician
San Elias #3-A (Col. San Antonio)–near bus stop
Home/Office
Tel: 152-2917
Gentle, low force chiropractic, acupuncture, muscle rehab
Nutritional consultant
Applied kinesiology
Accredited in USA and México
Treatment time: 30 min/US$50

2. Dr. Gabriel Monterrubio (bilingual)
María Greever #14 (Col. Guadalupe)
Tel: 152-1603
E-mail: agui28@prodigy.net.mx
Trained in USA (Palmer College)
Consultations: Mon, Tues, Thurs, Fri 9am-2pm and 4-7pm

Physical Therapists:

Rosa María L. Rabern
Esperanza #3 (Col. San Antonio)
Tel: 152-4733
Studied at ABC Hospital/México City
Worked 9 years for Centro de Crecimiento
Mostly referrals by local doctors
Clinic at home (also hospital and house visits)
Since 1981
Bilingual

> Also: **Manuel Castillón Hansen** (bilingual)
> Tel: 044-415-117-8225 (cell)
> Makes house/hospital calls

Neuro-Muscular Therapist:

Sergio A. Ortega
Certified neuro-muscular therapist (USA—bilingual)
The Reflex Center
Aparicio #48-A (east of Mesones and Núñez)
Tel: 154-6903(make an appointment first)
E-mail: ortega@unisono.net.mx
Web page: www.portalsanmiguel.com/ortega
Studied in México, Europe and USA
    Graduated from San Francisco School of Massage
He combines elements of neuro-muscular therapy, acupressure,
    deep tissue work, reflexology, polarity and myofascial
    trigger point release
Has a staff working for him
Also a unisex beauty salon
    Hairstyling, coloring and facials plus manicure, pedicure,
        and nail treatment for both men and women
Since 1973, relocated to San Miguel Aug'99

Reflexologist:
Linda Sorin
Trained and certified in reflexology in USA
Pípila #11 (Col. San Antontio)
Tel: 154-4069
E-mail: lindasorin@yahoo.com
Firm, but gentle acupressure on feet (and hands)
For relaxation and wellbeing as well as chronic and acute health problems
Treatments in home office or your home
Has been in health care for almost 40 years

Also check **Health Salons** for additional listings

Caretakers:

1. Oscar Peña
Trained EMT (bilingual)
San Miguel Medical Services
Tel: 154-6810   044-415-101-4814 (cell)

E-mail: emsm@unisono.net.mx
Skilled home nursing care
Part-day or 24-hour service
Also equipment rentals (walkers, wheelchairs, etc)
Since 1999

2. Premium Home Healthcare Providers
Owner: Robin Fell (bilingual)
Worked many years in medical equipment business in Latin America
Tel: 152-5555
E-mail: robinfell@cybermatsa.com.mx
Web page: www.premiumhomehealthcareproviders.com.mx
Service provides full and part-time nurses, nannies and companions
All staff trained and certified
Schedule in-home consultation at no obligation
Started Dec'04

Drugstores

1. Botica Agundis (aka "Chelo's")
Canal #26 (corner of H. Macías)
Tel: 152-1198
Hrs: Daily 10:30am-11pm (open 365 days of the year)
Owner: Chelo (bilingual)–over 50 years' experience
Drugs (also shots), cosmetics, perfumes and dental products
Extensive supply of medical products
Favorite spot of the foreign community—good place for advice
Sell popular generic drugs in large quantities
Ask about a senior discount

2. Botica de Santa Teresita
Reloj #28 (corner Mesones)
Tel: 152-0147
Hrs: Daily 9am-2:30pm and 4-8:30pm, Thur 9am-2:30pm, Sun 9am-4pm
Interesting old-fashioned pharmacy - first opened 1846
Pharmacist Manuel Martínez is bilingual
Good prices

3. Farmacia Guadalajara
Ancha de San Antonio #13
Tel: 154-9047   Fax: 154-9048
Hrs: Daily—open 24 hours!
Credit cards: Amex, Master and Visa

Large store offering, medicines, personal care products,
household, and food items
Soft drinks, snack foods, ice, candy, deli items, bread, cereals,
    eggs and bottled water
Film processing plus batteries
278 branches in México
Opened June'03

4. Farmacia Guanajuato
Insurgentes #74 (across from the Biblioteca)
Tel: 152-6090
Hrs: Daily—open 24 hours a day!
Owner: Sra. M. Obdulia Rangel
Prescription medicine 30% discount
Free delivery
Since 1993

5. Farmacia Humac
Hospital de la Fé
Libramiento Hwy #43
Tel: 152-2233, 152-2320 and 152-2329
Hrs: Daily 8am-8pm (will open for emergencies)

6. Farmacia Homeopática
Mesones #67
Tel: 152-0230
Hrs: Mon-Sat 9am-2pm and 4-8:30pm, Sun 11:30am-2:30pm
Husband/wife owners:
    Dr. Antonio García González/Sra. Carmen Précoma Berra
Working in San Miguel since 1982

Also: **Gigante Pharmacy**, Plaza Real del Conde, Tel: 152-4047
  Farmapronto, Insurgentes #78, Tel: 154-8330 and
                Ancha de San Antonio #39, Tel: 154-4998

Electrical Shops

1. El Jonuco Eléctrico
Juárez #23
Tel: 152-4982
Hrs: Daily 9am-8pm, Thur and Sun 9am-3pm
Owners: María Gloria and Martín Tellez (bilingual)

2. Ferre-Plomería
Quebrada #3 (no number on bldg)-near Insurgentes
Tel: 152-0605
Hrs: Mon-Fri 8:30am-6:30pm, Sat 8:30am-3pm, Sun 10am-2pm
Owner: Javier Zúñiga (very friendly)
Small electrical and plumbing store
Will make home repairs
Some hardware items plus keys made
Adjoining store sells tiles and bathroom fixtures
Since 1994
2nd store: Calzada de la Luz #104, Tel: 152-2288

3. Electrosistemas Hepco
Núñez #15 (near upper Mesones)
Tel: 152-4616
Hrs: Mon-Fri 9am-2pm and 4-7pm, Sat 9am-2pm
Install, service and sell electrical material

The electrical system in México is 110 volts, 60 cycles, as in the USA and Canada. Older hotels and homes may have electrical outlets for flat two-prong plugs. You may need an adapter for using any modern electrical apparatus that has an enlarged end on one prong or that has three prongs to insert.

Government Offices

1. Presidencia Municipal (center of city government)
Carretera a Dr. Mora, km 1, on road to Querétaro past Gigante
Move expected to be completed in March'05
Tel: 152-0001
Web page: www.sanmiguelallende.gob.mx
Hrs: Mon-Fri 8:30am-4pm, closed weekends and holidays
Municipal Treasury (office for payment of all city fines, 9am-1:30pm)
Office of Foreign Affairs
    Lic. Christopher Finkelstein (bilingual)
    Tel: 152-0001
    E-mail: relacionesinternacionales@sanmiguelallende.gob.mx
Also: Presidencia Municipal office
    Plaza Principal #8 (north side of Jardín), 2nd/floor
    Municipal Hall opened in 1736, but later destroyed and then was rebuilt. It was remodeled after the May 1911 fire.

Meetings held in Mayor's office and Council Hall (Sala de
   Cabildos) where there are life-sized statues of General
   Allende and Father Hidalgo and a large wall plaque honoring
   the illustrious citizens of the town.

Insider's Tip: Should you need a document certified I would
recommend that you go to the Presidencia Municipal office.
The cost is very reasonable

2. Municipal Tourist Office
Plaza Principal #6 (left of Presidencia entrance)
Hrs: Mon-Fri 8:30am-7pm, Sat/Sun 10am-5pm
Web page: www.sanmigueldeallende.gob.mx
Director: Myrna Veronica Salinas (bilingual)
Also an information kiosk (north side of Jardín)
Relocated April'02

3. Tránsito Municipal
Carretera Dr. Mora, km 1
Salida a Querétaro #134 (*glorieta* past Gigante)
Tel: 154-8420
Hrs: Mon-Fri 9am-4pm (office hours)
Known as "The stop lights of San Miguel"
Handle local traffic, including illegal parking
Policemen will remove license plate if you are parked illegally
Wear light gray uniforms

4. Police Station (Policía)
Carretera a Dr. Mora km 1
Salida a Querétaro #134 (*glorieta* past Gigante)
Tel: 152-0022
All police matters except traffic
Motorcycle squad patrols the town (as of May'98)
A small municipal jail is located in the back
Place to report missing items. Also see **radio station** listing
Wear dark blue uniforms
Small sub-station, Plaza Principal #10

Should you find yourself a victim of a crime, you must make a
report to: **Agencia del Ministerio Público** (DA's Office), not the
local police. The office is located at: Alfonso Esparza Oteo #17,
Col. Guadalupe (north of town), Tel: 154-9450, 154-9451 &
154-9452. It is open 24 hours.

Emergency Hot Line: Tel: 152-0911

Few dispatchers speak English. Be prepared to give:
Name, Address and Telephone Number

A Spanish word or two would be helpful in describing the problem:

Very noisy—*muy ruidoso*	Sick—*enfermo*
Quarrel—*pleito or riña*	Dead—*muerto*
Hurt—*lesionado*	Drunk—*borracho*
Shot—*balazo*	Unconscious—*desmayado*
Robbed—*robado*	Car stolen—*robo de coche*
Stabbed—*puñalada*	Ambulance—*ambulancia*

Direct contact with the Red Cross (Cruz Roja), Fire Department
(Bomberos), Police Station, Traffic Police (Tránsito) and
Highway Police (Policía Federal de Caminos)

5. Oficina Federal de Hacienda Oficinas del Gobierno del Estado
State government offices
San Francisco #23
Ground floor: State Treasury
First floor: Civil registrations (births, deaths), property registrations

6. Delegación de Tránsito y Transporte del Estado
Correo #26
Tel: 152-0164
Ground floor: Office of District Attorney
First floor: Tránsito administration offices, vehicle registration
and driving licenses
Hrs: Mon-Fri 9am-1:30pm, closed weekends and public holidays

7. Policía Judicial
Plain clothes detectives
Headquarters at state prison (CERESO) located on the road to Querétaro
Tel: 152-2018

8. Municipal Court
Plaza Caracol (near PEMEX station)
Tel: 152-1315

Civil Court
Plaza Caracol
Tel: 152-2998

9. Secretaría de Hacienda y Crédito Público (SHCP)
Counter at the Post Office
Process income tax forms
Headquarters located in Celaya
Juan Bautista Morales #200
Tel: 01(461) 618-5122

Hrs: Mon-Fri 8am-3pm and 5-8pm
Local office at Mesones #71 (ground floor in the back)
Tel: 152-0037 Hrs: Mon-Fri 8am-3pm

10. State Government Tourist Office
Plaza Principal s/n (south side of Jardín and next to Parroquia)
Tel/Fax: 152-6565
E-mail: cotursanmiguel@hotmail.com
Hrs: Mon-Sat 10am-5pm, Sun 10am-2pm (flexible hours)
Source of information for San Miguel and the state
Some English brochures
Adminstrative office: San Francisco #1 (upstairs)
Manager: Lic. Jesús Ledezma (June'01)
Office assistant: Sra. María Elena (bilingual)

11. Delegación Regional de Servicios Migratorios
Calzada de la Estación, s/n
Glass Factory building - near train station
(take Central-Estación bus on Canal at Las Monjas)
Tel: 152-2542 Tel/Fax: 152-6939
Hrs: Mon-Fri 9am-1pm, closed weekends and holidays
Regional Director: Lic. Salvador Oyanguren Espinosa (Apr'01)
Second in command: Lic. Samuel Jurado Guzmán (bilingual)
General reorganization March 1994, new location Aug'02
Extension of a Tourist Visa up to 180 days
Issuance or extension of FM-3 (*Visitante*) permit
Can ship household effects duty free during first six months
If obtained outside México, one must open an account and
register San Miguel address within one month after arrival
Accept applications for FM-2 (*Inmigrante*) document
Each case acted on individually
Most cases, must be resident of México five years
Restricted time per year outside México

**The author encourages you to take your concerns and questions
to this office. You will find the bilingual staff provides a service
which is helpful, prompt, efficient and courteous.**

For English speaking advice and/or help in typing and translations
for FM2 and FM3 documents, see Paula at the
American Consular Agency.

For a modest fee, **Patty García** (bilingual)
Tel/Fax: 152-0049 or 044-415-149-3122 (cell)
E-mail: patgar5@yahoo.com

Will do all the leg work on your behalf when you need to renew
your immigration papers. (She will also act as a trouble-shooter
should you have any other problems). Honest, dependable and
highly recommended!

Also a copy place called **Escritorio Público** is nearby new
Immigration offices and is open the same hours.

12. Post Office
Calle Correo #16 (one block east from Jardín)
Tel: 152-0089
Mon-Fri 9am-5pm, Sat 9am-1pm, closed Sun and holidays
Listed in separate chapter named Post office

13. COFOCE
Guanajuato World Trade Commission
Plaza San Juan
San Francisco #35 (Interior)
Tel: 152-6500   Fax: 154-9500
Hrs: Mon-Fri 9am-5pm, closed weekends
Director: Lic. Alma Lilia de la Rosa (bilingual)
Promotes regional products for export
        Helps facilitate exports between manufacturer and customer
Opened April'02

14. PROFECO
Federal Office of Consumer Protection
Local office closed Feb'03
Contact Celaya office—Tel: 01(461) 609-0461

Grocery Stores

1. Bonanza
Mesones #43-A (next to Apolo XI restaurant—same owner)
Tel: 152-1260
Hrs: Mon-Sat 8am-8pm, Sunday 8am-5pm
Good selection of general grocery items
Deli—local and imported cheeses and cold cuts
Natural health foods—nuts and grains
Friendly owner—willing to special order items if not in stock
Store expansion—doubled the size (June'01)

2. Espino's
Codo #36
Tel: 152-1009
Hrs: Mon-Sat 8:30am-8pm, Sunday 9am-2pm

Large self-help store with a good selection of grocery items
Also a good selection of liquor and wine
Newspapers for sale
Excellent fresh vegetables (green beans, celery, spinach,
  cauliflower) are sold at the front entranceway daily by an
  outside vendor

3. Super San Francisco II (commonly known as Martin's)
Salida a Celaya s/n (next to PEMEX)—Parking in front
Tel: 152-3833
Hrs: Daily 8:30am-10:30pm
Fresh produce, canned goods, cold drinks and yogurt
Sells wholesale to restaurants

4. El Tomate
Codo #36-B (next to Espino's)–relocated September '97
Tel: None
Hrs: Mon-Sat 9:30am-3:30pm, closed Sunday
Erika Jankay is the German owner (trilingual)
Very efficient and helpful staff
High quality food items
Fresh vegetables and fruits, organically grown lettuce and sprouts
Imported items: horseradish, pretzels, plus frozen vegetables,
  frozen blueberries and blackberries
Large variety of spices

5. Kike's Super Mercado
Stirling Dickinson #28 (street alongside Real de Minas Hotel)
Tel: 154-8170
Hrs: Mon-Thurs and Sun 8am-9pm, Fri/Sat 9am-10pm
Credit cards: Master and Visa
Manager: Juan Antonio Esponda (bilingual)
Medium-size grocery store—good selection
Plenty of parking
Will deliver
Opened Nov'01

6.Carey's Especialidades Internacionales
Ancha de San Antonio #75 (across from the Aristo's entrance)
Tel: 152-2038
Hrs: Mon-Sat 10am-7pm, closed Sunday
Owner: Raquel Carey (bilingual), Manager: Eduardo (brother)
High quality imported foods (canned goods, frozen things and hard
  to find items) from the USA

Community bulletin board
Since 1992, relocated Jan'01

7. Susazón
Plaza Real del Conde (Gigante)
Tel: 152-5820
Hrs: Mon-Sat 9am-8pm, Sun 10am-3pm
Speciality store
Extensive line of frozen meats
Frozen prepared meals plus desserts
Good selection of spices and sauces
Opened Dec'02

8. Menutre
Codo #9
Tel: 044-415-149-9195 (cell)
Hrs: Mon-Fri 10am-7pm, Sat 10am-4pm
Frozen foods
      100% natural fruit and vegetables—also some Mexican foods
Opened Oct'04

9. La Mezzaluna
Umarán #23 (near Zacateros)
Tel: 154-9788
Hrs: Mon-Sat 10am-6pm
Owner: Paolo Mancini
Wide variety of fresh pastas and ravioli
Also *salsas*—organic ingredients
Take-out
Opened July'04

10. Abarrotes y Semillas (groceries and seeds)
Puente de Umarán #23 (side street by Mercado)—also known as
      Plazuela de Fresno
Tel: 152-3268
Hrs: Daily 8am-8pm, Thur and Sun 8am-3pm
Owner: Elvira Gómez and family
Bulk supplies: rice, beans, corn for popping (*palomitas de maíz*)

Also check out *Supermarket/Markets* chapter

Candy Stores:

1. Sensual
Chocolatiers
Mesones #57 (interior)—China Palace courtyard
Tel: 154-6947 (*casa*)
Web page: www.sensualchocolatiers.com
Hrs: Daily 11am-8pm, Sun 11am-6pm
Owner: Michael McKenna
Made fresh daily in San Miguel
Attractive glass and silver colored tin boxes for sale
Opened July'04

2. La Carreta
Dulces Típicos Mexicanos
Ancha de San Antonio #3 (next to Santa Clara)
Tel: 152-3883
Hrs: Mon-Sat 10am-2:30pm and 4-8:30pm, Sun 10am-2:30pm
Owners: Jesús and Clemen Ayala Chavez
All products made in México-some special candy made locally
Opened Jan'01

3. Dulcería Loreto
Insurgentes #14 (corner of Pepe Llanos)
Tel: 152-3160
Hrs: Daily 9am-8pm, Sun 9am-2pm
All kinds of local candies and cookies
Owner: David García

Petit Four, Mesones #99, Tel:154-4010—For chocolates
El Atrio de la Capilla, Cuna de Allende #10, Tel: 154-4944

Gyms-Aerobics-Meditation-Yoga

1. Ramiro's Club (formerly called Lobo Gym or Wolf Gym)
Potrero #8 (Col. San Antonio)
Take street next to Hotel Real de Minas and turn right at first
    intersection and go to nearby large stone building on right
Tel: 152-2707 (*casa*)
Hrs: Mon-Fri 6:30am-10pm, Sat 6:30am-2pm
Owner: Ramiro Ramírez (bilingual)

Daily, weekly, monthly or yearly rates
Personal trainer available for extra fee
Also racquetball court
Opened in 1977
San Miguel Medical Clinic (Upstairs)
> Dr. Cesar Gil Hoyos—general practice
> Mon-Sat 4-8pm

2. San Miguel Health and Fitness Center
Formerly Body Limit
Plaza Pueblito
Stirling Dickinson #27 (Col. San Antonio)
Tel: 154-8395
Hrs: Daily 6:30am-10pm, Sat 8am-3pm and Sun 9am-1pm
Owner: Ross Macdonald—Director and Certified Personal Trainer
Large exercise studio
> State-of-the-art CYBER equipment (treadmills, Stairmaster and
> crosstrainer)
Weights, aerobics and stationary bikes
Men's and women's showers, sauna and lockers
Cold drinks available—also good selection of vitamins for sale
Ask about monthly or yearly membership
Plenty of parking
Opened Feb'02, new ownership Apr'03

3. San Miguel Sport Center
Salida a Celaya (100 yards past *glorieta*)—on bus route
Tel: 152-2796
Hrs: Mon-Fri 6am-9pm, Sat 6am-7pm, closed Sunday
Owner: Armando Barraza (bilingual)
Large, spacious fitness center
All new, top of the line equipment
> Lifefitness and Hammer Strength
Free and machine weights, cardio equipment
Spinning classes and indoor rock climbing
Aikido classes and aerobics
Certified personal trainers
Beauty and massage spa
Lockers, showers and steam rooms—also snack bar
Daily, weekly, monthly or yearly plans
Good parking
Opened July'02

4. Santo Domingo Sports Club (Club Deportivo)
Santo Domingo #55 (up the hill from Correo)
Tel: 154-7545
E-mail: spinningsma@hotmail.com
Hrs: Mon-Fri 7am-8pm, Sat 7am-2pm, closed Sunday
Manager/Trainer: Antonio Martínez (bilingual)
Daily, weekly or monthly membership
Weight room with treadmill, weight equpment and stationary bikes
25-meter semi-Olympic covered heated (83°F) pool
    Swim team plus classes for adults and kids
    Also aquaerobic classes
Lockers, showers and steam rooms
Also a spinning room for classes
Large outdoor grass area—good parking
Opened July'00

5. Axis Gym
San Francisco #40
Tel: 154-5874
Hrs: Mon-Fri 7am-9pm, Sat 8am-2pm, closed Sunday
Weights, machines and stationary bikes
Bathrooms available
Opened Feb'96, relocated Oct'02

Fitness Consultant:
Liz Montes (bilingual)
Tel: 152-4115
E-mail: lizmontes@prodigy.net.mx
Certified personal trainer
Training and fitness programs—muscle rehabilitation
Nutritional counseling
Make appointment

---

6. En Forma Aerobics Studio
Mesones #14 (inside second courtyard)
Tel: 152-0002
Hrs: Class Schedule (Mon-Fri)
    7am, 8am, 7pm and 8:15pm
    9:30am low-impact class for seniors
Owned and operated by Linda Cooper
Separate weight room—personal training also available
Studio started 1981

7. Joan Nagle
Aquatic Specialist
Col. San Antonio
Tel: 152-4821 (call for information between 8-9am—Oct-April)
E-mail: aquajoan@yahoo.com
Hrs: Mon, Wed and Fri at 10am
Current certification by AEA and US Water Fitness Association
Water aerobics with WOGA
Master swimming

8. Studio Pilates
Grillo #18 (Col. Guadiana)
Tel: 152-4169 (make appointment)
Jeanette Gordon-Certified instructor
Complete repertoire-all levels
Stott Pilates
Post rehabilitation
Private or semi-private sesions
Teaching in UK and San Miguel since 1998

Also: **Sue Lawrence,** Guadiana #25, 044-415-149-0176 (cell)
Certified instruction beginner through advanced
On equipment and mat - Private duets and classes

---

9. Curves
Ancha de San Antonio #15 (Aldea Hotel)
Tel: 152-8400
E-mail: noblemh@cybermatsa.com.mx
Hrs: Mon-Fri 8am-2pm and 4-7pm, Sat 9am-12 noon
Owner: Melissa Noble
Women only
Scripted 30 minute workout to music
Modest one-time membership fee (good at any other location)
Fastest growing franchise—over 90 in México
Opened Oct'03
Also **Bambu Day Spa**
Inside La Aldea Hotel
Tel: 044-415-103-0240 (cell)
Hrs: Mon-Fri 9am-4pm, Sat 10am-3pm
Massage, facials, nails, etc.

Meditation Center/Yoga:

1. Meditation Center of San Miguel
Callejón Blanco #4 (just off Quebrada)
Tel: 152-0536, 152-7016 (*casa*) and 152-0461 (*casa*)
E-mail: dogiefrank@unisono.net.mx
Hrs of meditation: Mon-Fri 8-9:30am, Sat 10-10:40am
One may enter and leave quietly at anytime during the above hours
All forms of silent, still meditation welcome
Video presentations offered on selected Thursdays
        See ATENCIóN for dates and times

2. Yoga with Norman
Successful Living Yoga
Meditation Center
Callejón Blanco #4
Tel: 152-5912 and 152-1852
E-mail: slyoga@yahoo.com
Web page: www.yoganorman.com
Hrs: Mon-Fri 10-11:15am
Specializing in healing, stress management and health improvement
Gentle guidance in and for:
        Weight control   Breathing   Healing
        Flexibility   Meditation
25 years' experience
All levels welcome
Therapy, private counselling and classes by appointment

3. Moola Bandha Yoga School
Ancha de San Antonio #9 (in back and upstairs of La Finestra Café)
Tel: 154-6137
E-mail: gauthierfabienne@hotmail.com
Web page: www.moolabandha.com
Classes: Mon-Fri 10am (just show up), Tues & Thurs 4pm (beginners)
Owner: Fabienne Gauthier
        Teaching Ashtanga Yoga in San Miguel since 2001
        Attended national yoga conference in México City
Centrally located, light-filled, hardwood floor studio
Ask about week long yoga retreats in San Miguel and other parts of México
Relocated Oct'04

4. Yoga at Bellas Artes (cooperative)
Mascha Beyo *sala* —ground floor
Calle Hernández Macías #75
Classes every Monday, Wednesday and Friday
Hatha Yoga, intermediate and advanced level 8-9:30am
Gentle yoga for newcomers & people with limitations 9:30-11am
Classes emphasize strength, stamina, flexibility and peace of mind

5. LifePath Retreats
Recreo #11 (upstairs above Solutions)
Tel: 154-8465   From the USA: 1(888) 667-3873
E-mail: info@lifepathretreats.com
Web page: www.lifepathretreats.com
Co-founders: Joseph Dispenza and Dr. Beverly Nelson
A six-day program in personal growth, retreats held each month
Ongoing weekly classes Enneagram, Dreamwork, traditional
    group therapy and massage therapy
Trained, certified massage therapist Mike Herbert
Opened 2000

Hair Salons

1. Salon & Spa de Robert
Zacateros #83-A (next to Galería Dos Culturas)
Tel: 154-8188
Hrs: Mon-Fri 9am-6pm, Sat 9am-4pm
Proprietor/Hair stylist: Robert Albury (moved from Houston, TX)
    Over 40 years experience—licensed in six states
Very impressive, large salon with stone columns and walls-below street level
Full service salon and day spa for men and women
All hair services, manicures, pedicures, facials, acrylic nails,
    reflexology and massage
Retail hair products for sale
Walk-ins welcome—street parking
Opened Nov'03

2. The Cutting Garden
Codo #4 (near Tenerías)
Tel: 154-9130
Hrs: Mon 10am-2pm, Tues-Sat 10am-6pm, closed Sunday
Owner: Christine Conway (born in London)

By appointment
Hair cutting and tinting—also waxing, manicures and pedicures
Men and children as well
Owned a salon in México City for 20 years
Opened Dec'99, relocated Nov'02

3. Marín Estética
Núñez #14 (east on Mesones and then left on Núñez)
Tel: 152-4771
Hrs: Mon-Sat 10am-2pm and 4-8pm, closed Sunday
Hair stylist: José Marín (bilingual)
By appointment only
Also manicures and pedicures
Good selection of magazines to read
Very popular with the foreign community

4 Sala de Belleza Evangee
Jesús #6
Tel: 152-1099
Hrs: Mon-Sat 10am-2pm and 4-7pm, closed Sunday
Owner: Teresa (understands some English)
Appointments helpful
Also manicures and pedicures

5. Sala de Belleza Carmela
Canal #9 (inside courtyard behind La Antigua)
Tel: 152-1346
Hrs: Mon-Sat 9:30am-2pm and 4-7pm, closed Sunday
Hair styling, cut or trim, permanent and hair coloring
Also manicures and pedicures–acrylic nails available
First opened in 1960

Also: **Esteto Clínica,** Codo #16, Tel: 152-2935
Zarco Salon, Zamora Ríos #10-B, Tel: 154-6851
Unisex Beauty Salon, Aparicio #48-B, Tel: 154-6903

Barbershops:

1. El Pípila Peluquería
Sollano #3 (near Correo and behind church)
Tel: None
Hrs: Mon-Sat 10am-2pm and 6-9pm, closed Sun (flexible hrs)
Small, old fashioned barbershop—2 chairs, 1 barber
Proprietor: Jorge (speaks only Spanish)

Over 30 years' experience
Trim in Spanish: *"corte solamente un poco"*
Inexpensive

2. Estética Unisex Bandála
Hernández Macías #62 (across from Sautto Hotel)
Tel: None
Hrs: Daily 9am-8pm, Sunday 9am-2pm
TV for viewing from barber chair
Also manicures and pedicures plus other services

Hardware Stores

1. Don Pedro Ferretería
Ancha de San Antonio #123 (no outdoor sign)-near Oxxo store
Tel: 152-1714
Hrs: Mon-Fri 8am-5pm, Sat 8am-2pm, closed Sunday
Manager: Alberto González (speaks some English)
Good selection of hardware items, also has building materials
Worth a visit to meet likeable English speaking owner Don Pedro
Other stores: Calzada de la Aurora #20 and Carr. a Queretaro #61

2. Tlapalería y Ferretería Don Pedro
Colegio #33-A (branch store near old Mercado)
Tel: 152-2214
Hrs: Mon-Fri 9am-2pm and 4-7pm, Sat 9am-2:30pm
    Sunday 10am-2pm
Clerk José speaks some English
Keys also made

3. Ferretería Cedelco
Insurgentes #8 (in front of Oratorio)
Tel: 152-3233
Hrs: Mon-Sat 8:30am-8pm, Sun 8:30am-2pm
Owner: Van Rijn Stewart (bilingual) and very helpful
Good selection of hardware items—keys made
In business since 1991
Second store at Plaza Allende #4 (faces Civic plaza)
    Sells tile and bathroom fixtures
Third store at Calzada de la Estación #147
    Tel: 154-8181
    Hrs: Mon-Sat 8:30am-5:30pm

4. Cementos Apasco
Ancha de San Antonio #3 (corner of Orizaba)
Tel: 152-1796
Hrs: Mon-Fri 8am-2pm and 4-7:30pm, Sat 8am-2pm
    Closed Sunday
Leonardo speaks some English
Duplicate keys made

5. Hierro Comercial
Salida a Celaya, km 1
Tel: 152-1956
Hrs: Mon-Fri 8am-7pm, Sat 8am-2pm, closed Sunday
Five outlets in state of Guanajuato
Manager: Humberto speaks English
Building materials—duplicate keys made

6. Lara
Ferretería y Cerrajería
Hidalgo #100
Tel: 152-2686
Hrs: Mon-Fri 9am-2pm and 4-8pm, Sat 9am-7pm, closed Sun
Duplicate keys made—will make house calls

7. El Volcán
Ferretería y Tlapalería
Canal #43-A (just west of Hotel Posada de Las Monjas)
Tel: 152-1482 or 152-0946
Hrs: Mon-Sat 9am-3pm and 5-8pm, Sunday 9am-2pm
Owner: Ricardo Olvera Garavito (speaks some English)
Family business since 1910
Large variety of hardware supplies plus building materials and
    materials for *papier mâché*

Locksmiths:

1. Cerrajería Ceballos
Terraplén #13 (no sign—between #11 and #13)
Tel: 154-7181 and 152-6292 (after hours)
Hrs: Mon-Fri 10am-7pm, Sat 10am-2pm, closed Sunday
Owner: Hugo Gil
Duplicate house or car keys—will make house calls
Opened Sept'00

2. Key Stand
Old Mercado (covered market), booth near meat section

Most local hardware stores also make keys (see above)

> Also: **Ferretería Torres**, Umarán #90-B, Tel: 152-0296

Hat Shops

1. La Colombina 30/30
Formerly known as El Sombrero
San Francisco #30 (moved from San Francisco #14–Dec'98)
Tel: 152-0504
Hrs: Daily 10am-2pm and 4:30-8pm
    Closed Thursday and Sunday afternoon
Owner: Margarita (bilingual)
Family business—more than 85 years!
Hats all made in México
Also leather products: belts, vests and purses
Brother has a leather workshop in back of store

2. Hat Shop (no name)
Outside old Mercado (north side) Shop #96 and #97
Tel: None
Hrs: Daily 9am-5:30pm
All *sombreros* made in México
Lowest price in town

> Also: **The Leather Shop,** Umarán #1, Tel:152-8679

Health Salons

1. Health and Beauty Center
Casa de Sierra Nevada
Hospicio #46 (interior)—next to reception entrance
Tel: 152-3427 and 152-1302   Fax: 152-8503
E-mail: smaspa@yahoo.com.mx
Web page: www.smaspa.com
Hrs: Mon-Sat 9:30am-7pm, Sunday 10am-4pm
Treatments are supervised and given by Antonette Lim (trilingual)
Offers: Body exfoliation, body wraps of algae and rose petal
    extracts, facials, massages, reflexology and aromatherapy waxing
Women and men welcome—appointment only

Ten percent gross sales help support S.O.M.E. (So Others May Eat)
Also wedding floral arrangements and spa treatments
Operated since 1984, relocated Oct'01

2. Mónica Juárez
Col. San Antonio
Tel: 152-6305
All types of body massage
Men or women
Make appointment (will also come to your home)
Many satisfied customers
Reasonable prices

3. Jasmine
Jesús #25-A (upstairs) - near corner of Cuadrante
Tel: 152-7973 and 154-4578 (*casa*) or 044-415-149-6849 (cell)
E-mail: mckinney@unisono.net.mx
Hrs: Mon-Sat 10am-6pm, Sunday by appointment
Owners: Susan and Juan Carlos Ortega (bilingual)
Massages, facials, body treatments, manicure and pedicure
        Deep tissue massage a specialty
Also sells Virgin of Guadalupe things (tin *nichos*, etc)

4. Patricia
Facial and body treatments
Ladrillera #1 (near Pila Seca)
Tel: 154-8104
Hrs: Mon-Fri 10am-2pm and 4-7pm, Sat 10am-2pm
Massages, manicure, pedicure, facials, reflexology, waxing and
        body wraps
Some at-home services
Opened April'04

5.María de Valle
Armonía Corporal
Jacarandas #15 (Fracc. La Lejona)—south of town
Tel/Fax: 152-4582   044-415-153-3755 (cell)
All types of massage for men or women
At her place or your home
Uses "Just" oils from Switzerland
Over ten years of experience
María is bilingual

6. Esteto Clínica
Codo #16
Tel: 152-2935
Hrs: Mon-Fri 10am-7pm, Sat 10am-1pm, closed Sunday
Owner: María Ofelia–certified massage and skin technician
Body massage, facial, manicure and pedicure
Reasonable prices

Also: **Salon & Spa de Robert,** Zacateros #83-A, Tel; 154-8188
Rhea's Massage, Canal #135-A, Tel: 152-8971
Body harmony—colon hydrotherapy

Check "Therapists" under **Doctors** heading. Also, check
ATENCIóN classifieds for additional massage listings.

Holidays

Mexican and San Miguel:
This is an important part of the San Miguel scene as many are here to enjoy not only the siestas, but the fiestas as well! The following is a partial listing of some of the better known holidays.

January (enero)
1   New Year's Day
6   Three Kings' Day (children receive gifts)
17   St. Anthony's Day (blessing of animals in front of several churches)
21   Birthday of General Ignacio Allende (parades and fireworks)
24   Pilgrims depart for San Juan de los Lagos in the state of Jalisco

February (febrero)
2   *Candelaria* Day—Plant and seed sale at Parque Juárez
     Start of the planting season (spring)
5   Constitution Day
Moveable: Ash Wednesday (start of Lent)—40 days before Easter
24   Flag Day

March (marzo)
Moveable: First Friday in March—Feast of our Lord of the
     Conquest. *Los Concheros* pay homage in music and dance to
     their patron and one of their most important and colorful
     religious celebrations. The Indian dancers are worshippers

not performers. It starts mid-morning in front of the Parroquia
and lasts all day. Not to be missed!
21   Birthday of Benito Juárez
Moveable: Two Sundays before Easter—image of *El Señor de
   la Columna* is carried all night from Atotonilco to the Church
   of San Juan de Dios (San Miguel) arriving at dawn
Moveable: Friday before Holy Week—*Viernes de Dolores*—
   Day of the Altars in the homes
Moveable: Sunday before Easter (Palm Sunday)—the beginning
   of Holy Week—the high point of the Catholic year
*Moveable:*Thursday of Holy Week—Day of the Altars in churches
Moveable: Friday of Holy Week—holy images are carried from
   the Oratorio to La Parroquia in the late afternoon and ends in
   the early evening with a candlelit procession
Moveable: Sunday of Holy Week—Easter—*papier mâché*
   "*Judas*" figures are exploded in front of the Presidencia
   (Jardín) around mid-day

**Insider's Tip: Buy Pat Collins' excellent book called Holy Week in
San Miguel (1994) at a local book store for about US$10.**

May (mayo)
1   Labor Day—honored with parade of workers & school children
3   Holy Cross (Santa Cruz)—day of the masons and builders
5   *Cinco de Mayo*—anniversary of the Battle of Puebla
*Moveable:*Ascension Day, a religious fiesta (40 days after Easter)
Moveable: Late May, early June—Corpus Christi Day
   Elaborate religious procession–commences in early evening
   from one of the principal churches–beautiful to watch as are
   the home altars around the town center

June (junio)
Moveable: Los Locos–first Sunday after June 13 starting
   around 11am–clowns dance to music and floats proceed
through the main streets of town–fun to watch–starts at
   Instituto Allende
26   Anniversary of General Ignacio Allende's death

July (julio)
Moveable: Usually 3rd Sunday of July—*Fiesta* at Atotonilco
16   *Fiesta de la Virgen del Carmen*
30   Anniversary of Father Hidalgo's death

September (septiembre)
13 Death of Child Heroes celebrated
15-16 Independence Day (celebrated with fireworks, dances and
      speeches)—The *Grito* is read at 11pm the evening of the
      15th from the balcony of Allende Museo at the Jardín
29 St. Michael's Day (celebrated on the nearest weekend) in
      honor of the city's founder. The greatest religious celebration
      in the city. Parades, dances, music, bullfights and fireworks.
      Also, the *Sanmiguelada* (started in 1973), the running of the
      bulls around the Jardín on Saturday.

October (octubre)
 8 *Fiesta de San Francisco*
12 Columbus Day (*El Día de la Raza*)

November (noviembre)
 1 All Saint's Day
 2 All Soul's Day—Day of the Dead when graves are
      decorated with food, candles and flowers. A very important
      religious and Indian festival in México. The only day that the
      crypts in the Parroquia, San Francisco Church and Las
      Monjas are open to the public.
20 Anniversary of the 1910 Revolution–largest non-religious
      parade of the year (all school children participate)

December (diciembre)
12 Feast of México's Patron Saint, the *Virgen de Guadalupe*
16-24 *Posadas* (traditional processions visiting local homes)
25 Christmas Day
31 Traditional midnight dinners and church services

> Tip: Often one hears a series of loud firecrackers in
> the early morning. This is to announce a holiday, a local *fiesta*,
> a birth or a death and in most probability is not a revolution.
> Why the wee hours of the morning? To get your attention!

The following are legal holidays for which employees are paid:

Jan 1	New Year's Day	Sep 16	Independence Day
Feb 5	Constitution Day	Nov 20	Revolution Day
Mar 21	Benito Juárez B'day	Dec 25	Christmas Day
May 1	Labor Day		

Horseback Riding

1. Coyote Canyon Adventures
Rodrigo and Cristiana Landeros (bilingual guides)
Tel: 154-4193 (*casa*)   044-415-153-5005 (cell)
E-mail: info@coyotecanyonadventures.com
Web page: www.coyotecanyonadventures.com
Located Rancho Xotolar (Mexican cattle ranch)-10 miles from SMA
Offer horseback riding, hiking, mountain biking and camping
Half day, full day or overnight
Group or individual–all ages welcome
Ranch style meals prepared at a campfire
Ask about swimming, cattle herding, cow milking or cheese making
Summer adventure camp for kids
Reasonable prices

2. Horseback Riding
Andrés or Jesús Romo
Tel: 152-2057
Also equestrian classes plus moonlight riding (just outside town)
US$15 per hour
Make appointment first–ride any day

3. Horse Tours
Rancho "El Batán" de la Huerta
Comonfort
Tel: 044-415-103-2944 (cell)
E-mail: ranchodepancho@hotmail.com
Web page: www.ranchodepancho.com
Joshua Adams is from Alaska
Great riding country
    Pancho Villa's last camp
    See second largest tree in Mexico
$150 *pesos*/hour (2 hr minimum), $600 *pesos* per half day
    $800 *pesos* full day and $1000 *pesos* overnight
Can arrange transportation and food
Rides for all skill levels

Additional riding info: Canales Equestrian Center
Calle Pedro Paramo #37 (thru Los Frailes)-Col. Mirador
Tel: 152-3386 (stables)   Tel/Fax:152-3282
E-mail: ecanales@unisono.net.mx

Also: **Rancho La Loma,** Road to Dolores, Tel: 152-2121
Adventuras San Miguel, Aldama #1, Tel: 152-6406
Horse Boarding, Rd to hot springs, Kit Carson, Tel: 044-415-100-4313 (cell)

Hospitals

1. Hospital de la Fé San Miguel
Libramiento #43(Highway to Dolores Hidalgo behind bus station)
Replaced **Unión Médica Hospital** in April 1995
Tel: 152-2233, 152-2320 and 152-2329 (for appointments and
    non-emergency calls)
Tel: 152-2545 (medical emergency only–24 hours)
E-mail: hospitaldelafe@yahoo.com
Administrator: Francisco de Asis Luna (bilingual)
Medical Director: Dr. Hugo Rosas Hernández
Six doctors in partnership, 22 staff physicians
Adjacent Medical Building contains Administration Office plus
    private doctor and dental offices
Full-service community medical facility with modern equipment
17 beds (2 suites, 7 private rooms plus male & female wards and a pediatric ward)
Visiting hours: 11am-8pm
Provides general in-patient and out-patient medical care
Emergency services
Accepted as a Bluecard worldwide hospital by the World Access
    Blue Cross Blue Shield International hospital network for outpatient
    and inpatient care (www.bluecares.com/worldwidehospitals.htm)
Computer hookup with Mayo Clinic for consultations
Medical Directory (1996) available at Hospital
Ask about becoming a Tree of Life contributor
Offers a hospitalization insurance plan (November'98)
Also on-site clinical lab and pharmacy—good parking available

2. Hospital Civil (General)
Reloj #56 (north of Insurgentes)
Tel: 152-0045 or 152-6015
Director: Dr. Jorge Vidargas
Open 24 hours per day (Emergency Room doctor and staff)

3. Instituto Mexicano del Seguro Social (IMSS)
Social Security Hospital/Clinic
Calzada de la Aurora s/n km2 (north of Centro)
Tel: 152-0699 or 152-0278
Hrs: open 24 hours

Director: Dr. Héctor García Villanueva (family practice)
    IMSS office
    Gregorio Guelati s/n (street behind clinic)
    Tel: 152-2186
    Hrs: Mon-Fri 8:30am-2pm
    Open enrollment year-round (Mexican and non-Mexican)
    Pay annual fee (US$88-$235 depending on age)
    Complete application and take fee to:
            Departamento de Afiliación
            Sopeña #1 (next to Teatro Juárez)
            Guanajuato
            Tel: (473) 732-9509
            Mon-Fri 8:30am-2pm
    Basic medical exam/tests
    Take photos (2), copy of immigration papers, birth certificate
    One month waiting period after payment
    Universal coverage in México
        Free doctor visits, medicines and hospitalization

Red Cross Ambulance (*Cruz Roja Mexicana*)
Carretera Celaya km 1
Tel: 152-1616, 152-4225, 152-4121
24-hour service
Service to community since May 1980

Medical Equipment:

1.**Durable Medical**
Salida a Querétaro #157 (west side of street)
Tel: 152-6405
Hrs: Mon-Fri 10am-2pm and 4:30-8pm, Sat 10:30am-4pm, closed Sun
Owner: Rosana Sánchez
Medical rehabilitation equipment for sale or rent
Wheelchairs, crutches, walkers, orthopedic shoes, etc.
Delivery service available
Relocated July'03

2. Ortopedia Ortíz
Zacateros #41
Tel: 152-6004
Hrs: Mon-Sat 10am-2pm and 4-7pm, closed Sunday
Owners: Family of doctors in Guadalajara
Manager: Patricia Ortíz Márquez

All kinds of medical rehabilitation equipment
  Wheel chairs, crutches, orthopedic shoes and more
Opened Sept'03

3. Community Loan Closet
St. Paul's Church outreach program
Church office Tel: 152-0387
One can call to inquire about _free_ use of wheel chairs, walkers,
  crutches, canes, etc.
Two-month limit

Out-Of-Town:

1. Hospital Angeles de Querétaro
Formerly Hospital Internacional Querétaro (HIQ) – Aug '98
Bernardino del Razo #21, Querétaro
Col. Ensueño (San Miguel side of the city – 50 minutes away)
Tel: 01(442) 216-9717   Fax: 01(442) 216-2751
Director: CP Fernando Ladrón de Guevara
Emergency room
60 beds
Half-day checkups (7:30am-1pm) – make appointment
Since changeover many new doctors and new state-of-the-art
      diagnostic equipment

2. Centro Médico del Potosí
Antonio Aguilar #155
San Luis Potosí, SLP, México 78200
Tel: 01(444) 813-3797 or 01(444) 811-6363 Fax: 01 (444) 813-1377
E-mail: cmptyc@prodigy.net.mx
Research hospital
150 medical specialists
Tel: 01(800) 480-6300 (toll-free) Patient Service Department
      Mon-Fri 9am-7pm (except 2-4pm), Sat 9am-2pm
Rated by the Gov't in the top 2% of all hospitals in México
Offers a hospitalization plan
Call Mark Melhado in San Miguel at 152-6483 for information
3 hours from SMA

3. Hospital de Nuestra Señora de la Salud
Madreperia #435
San Luis Potosí, SLP, México 78090
Tel: 01(444) 824-5224

Level 3 hospital services (highest in México)
65 medical specialists
State-of-the-art equipment and technology
Offers a hospitalization plan (call for details)
3 hours from SMA

4. ABC Hospital (American British Cowdray Hospital)
Calle Sur #136 (corner Av. Observatorio-near West Bus Station)
Col. Las Américas, México, DF 01120
Tel: 01(55) 5230-8000
University Hospital—first opened 1886, merged in 1941
Closed staff of Board certified specialists
Patients: 92% Mexican, 8% Foreigners
4 hours from SMA

5. Hospital Angeles del Pedregal
Camino a Santa Teresa #1055
Col. Heroes de Padierna
México, DF
Tel: 01(55) 5652-2011 or 01(55) 5652-0422

6. Querétaro (1 hour from SMA) and Celaya (1 hour from SMA)
have a Social Security Hospital and some good private hospitals

Hotels

There are accommodations of a wide variety available for
visitors in San Miguel. Keep in mind that rooms may be difficult to
find around certain *fiestas*, such as Independence Day and the Patron
Saint festival (mid to late September), Christmas week, *Semana
Santa* (Easter week) as well as the months of January and February
when the "snow birds" are here to escape the winter up north. Make
reservations as far in advance as possible. Hotels are grouped by a
combination of price, quality and services offered.

Expensive:

1. Casa de Sierra Nevada Quinta Real
Reception/Concierge–Hospicio #46 (Nov'99)
Tel: 152-7040   Fax: 152-1436
Toll-free numbers: (01) 800-500-4000 (national)
E-mail: reservaciones-csn@quintareal.com
Web page: www.quinta-real.com

Suites: 33 (in seven separate nearby locations)
Credit cards: Amex, Master and Visa
Management Company: Quinta Real Hotel (Oct'01)
General Manager: Mónica Díaz Serralde (bilingual) (Jan'05)
Restaurant: excellent food (Mexican and international)
New state-of-the-art kitchen–Nov'99
Breakfast 8-11am, Lunch 1-4pm, Dinner 8-11pm
Indoor and outdoor dining in attractive courtyard
Former residence of the Archbishop of Guanajuato (1580)
Member of Summit Hotels and Resorts
Inconspicuous when viewed from the street
Favorite of the "Rich and Famous"
Tastefully decorated in antique colonial furnishings
Also a health spa and pool
Ask about horseback riding

Casa de Sierra Nevada Quinta Real en el Parque
Santa Elena #2 (El Chorro near Juárez Park)
Tel: 152-7155, 152-7154 and 152-7153   Fax: 152-7152
Five suites plus a first class bar and dining room
Opened March'97

2. Antigua Villa Santa Mónica
Baeza #22 (East side of Juárez Park)
Tel: 152-0427 and 152-0451   Fax: 152-0518
E-mail: vsmonica@prodigy.net.mx
Web page: www.antiguavillasantamonica.com
Rooms: 14 suites
Credit cards: Amex, Master and Visa
Restaurant: Nice outdoor courtyard setting
     Hrs: Daily breakfast 8am-12 noon
        Lunch/dinner 1:30-10pm
Manager: Pedro Pérez (bilingual)
Restored 18th century Spanish *hacienda*, originally built by a
     wealthy silver baron over 200 years ago. José Mojica, a film
     and opera star in the 1930s owned and lived in it a few years.
San Miguel's Betty Kempe (from Fort Worth, Texas) owned the
     hotel from Dec'69- Oct'85
Beautiful well-groomed grounds with outdoor heated swimming pool
No room guests under age 12
Weekends are usually busy

3. La Puertecita Boutique'Otel
Santo Domingo #75 (Atascadero residential area)
Tel: 152-5011, 152-2275 and 152-2250   Fax: 152-5505
    Toll-free number within México: 01 (800) 711-1860
E-mail: lapuertecita@lapuertecita.com
Web page: www.lapuertecita.com
Rooms: 33 (10 suites), some have fireplaces and patios
1 villa (across the street)
Ask about special package rates (including room, meals and bicycles)
Credit cards: Amex, Master, Visa
Restaurant Hrs:
    Breakfast daily 8-11:30am
    Lunch 1-4pm
    Dinner 7-9pm
Indoor and outdoor dining (terrace faces landscaped gardens)
Texas-style barbecue (Thursday 1:30-4pm and 6-8pm)
Fresh seafood (Friday lunch and dinner)
Mexican lunch buffet (Sunday 1:30-4 pm) – live entertainment
East of Centro, halfway up the hill (parking available)
Owner: Claudia Escalante Kay-John Kay died Aug'02
Manager: Sr. Donato Ortega (bilingual)
A *boutique* hotel, said to be more residential than commercial
    Only one in all of México
Large outdoor garden, two swimming pools and a jacuzzi
Non-smoking hotel
Van service to the Jardín
Body massage and facials available (extra cost)
Check out health club (US$70 per month for non-guests)
AAA Four Diamond Award

4. Villa Rivera Hotel
Cuadrante #3 (behind La Parroquia)
Tel/Fax: 152-2289, 152-0742, 152-2601 and 154-4787
    Toll Free: 01(800) 024-4787 (national)
E-mail: hotel@villarivera.com
Web page: www.villarivera.com
Rooms: 12 (all have names related to the city)
Credit cards: Master and Visa
Restaurant/Bar
    Hrs: Daily 8am-11pm
    Happy Hour: Thurs and Sat 7-10pm—live music
    Inside or outside—very nice ambiance

Director: Jesús M. Calvo García
    Also owns Pueblo Viejo Restaurant
All rooms have telephone, cable TV and small refrigerator
    Some have small patio
Includes continental breakfast
Attractive lawn area with heated swimming pool
Residential area, western views include the Parroquia
Formerly Hotel Villa del Sol–completely renovated Mar'99
Parking for hotel guests

5. Vista Real Hotel
Callejón de Arias #4 (follow the signs up the hill)
Tel: 152-3984   Fax: 152-3996
E-mail: info@vistarealhotel.com
Web page: www.vistarealhotel.com
Suites: 21 (master and junior suites plus standard rooms)
    All rooms have cable TV, telephone and security box
    Colonial decor—soft colors
Credit cards: Amex, Master and Visa
Gorgeous property with unbelievable panoramic city views
Restaurant La Vista (main dining room or private)
    Breakfast 9am-12 noon, lunch/dinner 1-10pm, closed Monday
    Chef Fernando Padilla (bilingual)—CIA'95 graduate
Large spacious grounds with beautiful gardens
Heated swimming pool
Bar La Paloma Azul
    Happy Hour (Tues and Wed 5-8pm)
    Good place to watch the sunset
Large conference room—seats 70 people
Transportation service available from La Morada Hotel every 30
    minutes between 9am and 10pm
Also good parking
Opened Jan'00, new name and management Sept'03

6. Hotel Casa Linda
A luxury spa hotel
Mesones #101 (across from Teatro Angela Peralta)
Tel: 154-4007
E-mail: reservations@hotelcasalinda.com
Web page: www.hotelcasalinda.com
Rooms: 8 (two are 2-room suites & one is a 3-room suite)
    All have bathtub, fridge, coffee-maker, microwave, VCR and stereo

Credit cards: Amex, Master and Visa
Owner: Linda McLaughlin—from Texas
Built around beautiful courtyard, water fountains and gardens
Cyber weight room (open to guests only)
Day spa (open to public by appointment)
Plus lap pool, jacuzzi and steam room
Extensive video and CD collection
Continental breakfast
Private parties and weddings
Sign up for yoga and tai chi classes
Opened May'02

7. Hotel Hacienda de las Flores
Hospicio #16 (near Chiquitos)
Tel: 152-1808 and 152-1859 Fax: 152-8383
E-mail:hotelhaciendadelasflores@cybermatsa.com.mx
Web page: www.haciendadelasflores.com
Rooms: 16
Credit cards: Master and Visa
Owner: Alicia Franyutti de Cornish (trilingual)
High season (Dec 20-Holy week and July-Sept)—prices higher
Restaurant: upstairs on first floor
    Hrs: Daily breakfast 8am-12 noon
    Luncheon and parties by appointment
Colonial style hotel in residential area-property over 460 years old
Beautiful landscaped gardens, large trees and swimming pool
Cable TV, telephone, electric blanket, heater, refrigerator, microwave
    oven and iron in each room
Suites with living/dining/kitchenettes fully furnished
Long-term rentals available
New bar located in the garden with cable TV
Sheltered roof-top area with jacuzzi
Also a conference room (up to 150 people)
AAA Three Diamond Award plus several European quality awards

8. Hotel Casa Rosada
Cuna de Allende #12 (behind the Parroquia)
Tel: 152-0382 and 154-5410 Fax: 152-8123
E-mail: hotelcasarosada@hotmail.com
Web page: www.casarosadahotel.com
Rooms: 16
Credit cards: Amex, Master and Visa

Large ground floor lobby-originally part of 300 year old Parroquia
All rooms include cable TV and telephone- eclectic decor
    Also safe boxes and cable modems for computers
Small indoor-outdoor eating area—very attractive
Restaurant serves breakfast and light lunch (soup, salad and sandwiches)
Hrs: Daily 8am-3pm
Second level has large manicured garden and lawn
Separate bar area—Hrs: Daily 3-11pm
Valet parking
Opened Sept'02

9. Hotel Villa Jacaranda

Aldama #53 (south of Centro and near Parque Juárez)
Tel: 152-1015 and 152-0811   Fax: 152-0883
    Toll-free number from USA: 1-800-310-9688
E-mail: reservations@villajacaranda.com
Web page: www.villajacaranda.com
Rooms: 16 (doubles and suites)
Free guest phone at desk
Credit cards: Amex, Master and Visa
Restaurant/Bar: Dirona dining award
    Hrs: Daily 7:30am-10:30pm
    Inside and outside dining
    Comfortable, quiet and relaxing setting
English-speaking owners: Don and Gloria Fenton
Gazebo, roof-top jacuzzi, satellite TV and protected parking
Cine/Bar (upstairs): movies nightly at 7:30pm
Bar/lounge (with Wurlitzer jukebox) near front entrance
Small pets are allowed with overnight guests

10. Rancho el Atascadero

Prolongación Santo Domingo
Tel: 152-0206 and 152-0337   Fax: 152-1541
    Toll-free numbers: 1 (888) 881-6635 (from USA)
    01 (800) 466-0000 (in México)
E-mail: atascadero@redmex.com.mx
Web page: www.hotelatascadero.com
Rooms: 47 plus 4 suites (all have fireplaces)
Credit cards: Amex, Master and Visa
Restaurant/Bar
    Hrs: Daily 7:30am-10:30pm
Converted 18th-century *hacienda*, beautiful colonial ranch style hotel
Extensive grounds include parking

2 kms east of Centro on top of the hill
Tennis courts, swimming pool, sauna and fronton court
Some of the staff speak English
Hotel shuttle bus to town every hour between 8am-3pm

11. Hotel Real de Minas
Calle Ancha de San Antonio s/n (south of town)
Tel: 152-2626, 152-2997 and 152-2838   Fax: 152-1727
    Toll-free number within México: 01 (800) 466-5800
E-mail: realdeminas1@prodigy.net.mx
Web page: http://unisono.net.mx/realm
Rooms: 215 (air conditioned)
Credit cards: Amex, Master and Visa
Restaurant/Bar
    Hrs: Daily 7:30am-10pm
Very large lobby—shops in arcade
Landscaped grounds—swimming pool, tennis courts (2)
One of a chain of six hotels in México
Conference rooms for special events or meetings

Also: **El Santuario Hotel**, Terraplén #42, Tel: 152-0335

Moderate:

1. Posada Carmina
Cuna de Allende #7-A
Tel: 152-0458 and 152-8888   Fax: 152-1036
E-mail: hotel@posadacarmina.com
Web page: www.posadacarmina.com
Rooms: 24
Double and single rates—reasonable price, good value
Credit cards: Master and Visa
Restaurant: Hrs: Daily 7:30am-11pm, closed Sunday night
    Happy Hour: Mon-Fri 5-8pm—all drinks 2x1
Managers: Francisco and Rodrigo García (Carmina's grandsons)
Courtyard and inside restaurant (rebuilt stable)—a favorite of
    local residents, especially for the mid-day *comida*
Great location, only a few steps from the Jardín and La Parroquia
Spanish atmosphere
Building dates back to 1784
    1964 Carmina and husband arrrived in San Miguel-managed
        Hotel Taboada on Cuna de Allende
    1967 rented present building (for 18 years)

1985 bought the building and five years later purchased
adjacent property behind hotel and fronting Jesús street
Additional twelve rooms (opened Apr'02)
Limited inside car parking for guests (from Jesús street)
Also: **Carmina Suites,** Salida a Querétaro #100 (Mirador)-14 suites
Hotel El Caracol, Jacaranda #2 (La Lejona), 154-6561

2. Hotel Posada de San Francisco
Plaza Principal #2
Tel: 152-7213 (through 16)   Tel/Fax: 152-0072
E-mail: hposadasanfranciso@prodigy.net.mx
Web page: www.naftaconnect.com/hsanfrancisco
Rooms: 46
Manager: José Luis Devesa (bilingual)
Jr. suites are more expensive
Credit cards: Amex, Master and Visa
4-story hotel that overlooks the Jardín–best location in town
Built in 1938 by the Zavala family
Convenient meeting place—clean bathrooms and public telephone
Courtyard has bar and food service
Satellite TV and telephone in rooms
Also a coffee shop (**Café San Francisco**), money exchange, travel
agency and insurance company on ground floor

3. La Mansión del Bosque
Aldama #65 (next to Parque Juárez)
Tel: 152-0277   Fax: none
E-mail: manruth@unisono.net.mx
Web page: www.infosma.com/mansion
Rooms: 23 (no two are alike)
Room price includes breakfast and evening meal
Credit cards: None
Well managed by proprietor Ruth Hyba
Dining Room: Hrs: Daily 8-10am breakfast
Dinner 7:30pm (one sitting)—except Sunday when main
meal is served at 2pm
Carefully planned meals and an opportunity to meet other guests
An intimate charming guest house with small, sunny patio area
Library lounge with fireplace
Small pets are allowed with overnight guests
Ask to see Ruth's cookbook, **Gourmet My Way** (Feb'03)
Since 1968

4. Pensión Casa Carmen
Correo #31 (near post office)
Tel/Fax: 152-0844
E-mail: ccarmen@unisono.net.mx
Rooms: 12
Price includes breakfast and lunch
Ask for special monthly rates
Credit cards: None
Owners: Horace and Natalie Mooring (bilingual)
Dining Room: Hrs: Breakfast 8-10am, Lunch 1-2:30pm
Nice convenient location—only minutes from the Jardín
Small, sunny, plant-filled patio
Rooms are gas heated with private baths
Usually full with repeat guests during the winter season
First opened in 1958

5. Hotel Quinta Loreto
Calle de Loreto #15 (north of Biblioteca)
Tel: 152-0042   Fax: 152-3616
E-mail: hqloreto@cybermatsa.com.mx
Rooms: 40 plus 6 apartments
Rooms with cable TV slightly higher (also one or two meals optional)
Credit cards: Amex, Master and Visa
General Manager: Georgina Sautto de Martínez (bilingual)
Restaurant: Breakfast 8 -11am, Lunch 2-5pm
    Reputation for quality food—very popular dining spot
    Cozy place in the winter with a fireplace, summertime
       outdoor tables on verandah
50's type motel with cars parked inside compound
May be hard to find as it is tucked away—several blocks north of
    the Jardín—near the old Mercado and Plaza Lanaton
    (market of *artesanías*)
Simple but pleasant rooms (hotel located in a large garden setting)
Many of the same *norteamericanos* return every winter
Small pets allowed with overnight guests

6. Hotel Posada de la Aldea
Calle Ancha de San Antonio #15 (across from the Instituto)
Tel/Fax: 152-1022, 152-1026, 152-1296 and 152-1664
E-mail: laaldea@prodigy.net.mx
Web page: www.naftaconnect.com/hotellaaldea
Rooms: 66
Student room discount with Instituto registration and payment

Credit cards: Master and Visa
Restaurant Hrs: Daily 8am-5:30pm (breakfast and lunch only)
Extensive grounds in front of hotel with rest areas, gardens and a fountain
Colonial style, very nice rooms
Satellite TV and telephone in all rooms
Swimming pool and tennis courts (2)—small fee for non-guests
Parking inside grounds—ask at the desk for tunnel directions and key
Hotel opened August'79

7. Hotel Aristos
Calle del Cardo #2 (across from St. Paul's church)
Tel: 152-3510, 152-0149 and 152-0392   Fax: 152-1631
        Toll-free tel: 01 (800) 901-0200 (within México)
E-mail: reservaristol@hotmail.com
Rooms: 58 standard, 4 suites plus apartments
Credit cards: Amex, Master, Visa
Restaurant Hrs: Daily 7:30am-10:30pm
        Sunday buffet (includes tennis and swimming) 12 noon-5pm
Manager: Gerardo González (bilingual)
Bar has large screen TV
Cable TV and telephone in all rooms (English channels extra)
Extensive grounds behind the Instituto (nice view of La Parroquia)
Very quiet and away from the downtown noise
Swimming pool (heated), tennis courts (2)—hard surface
Chain of six hotels in México
Check-out 1pm

8. La Morada Hotel
Formerly Rincón del Cielo Hotel
Correo #10 (at Sollano)
Tel: 154-4496 and 152-1647   Fax: 152-0017
        01-800-221-7432 (toll-free within México)
        1-877-587-6748 (toll-free from USA)
E-mail: info@lamoradahotel.com
Web page: www.lamoradahotel.com
Rooms: 15 (three deluxe plus 12 suites)
Credit cards: Amex, Master and Visa
Large rooms, most have *bóveda* ceilings, wet bar, fireplace and
        jacuzzi–also cable TV, telephone and small refrigerator
Cybercafé on ground floor (serves snacks and drinks)
You'll like the location and room size– "a real sleeper"
New management Jan'02

9. Posada La Ermita

Salida a Querétaro #64 (east of Centro)
Tel/Fax: 152-0777 and 152-0788 E-mail: laermita64@hotmail.com
Rooms: 24 junior suites
Credit cards: Amex, Master and Visa
Part condo time-share (RCI) and part hotel
Once the home of Cantínflas, México's top actor/comedian
A series of separate buildings built on a hillside
Suites have cable TV, telephone and fireplace
Heated pool, inside parking, interesting lobby mural
Short hike down hill to Centro–stop to see small, charming church next door
Built in 1970

10. Mansión Virreyes (formerly Central Hotel)

Canal #19 (½ block from Jardín)
Tel: 152-0851 and 152-3355   Fax: 152-3865
E-mail: mansionvirreyes@prodigy.net.mx
Rooms: 25
General Manager: Rubén Pérez Fryman (bilingual)
Price includes breakfast
Credit cards: Amex, Master and Visa
Restaurant: (outside/inside courtyard) Hrs: Daily 8am -9pm
Bar has large cable TV, live music Fri/Sat *comida* only
Cable TV and telephone in upgraded rooms

11. Hotel Arcada

Calzada de la Estación #185 (near bus staton)
Tel: 152-8940 and 152-8950   Fax: 152-8960
Rooms: 52
Manager: Lic. Carlos Beltrán (bilingual)
Credit cards: Amex, Master and Visa
Each room has a telephone, cable TV and fan
Restaurant
    Hrs: Daily 7am-10pm
    Three meals–Mexican and some international
Large covered patio–lots of sunlight
Bar area, meeting room and covered guest parking
Opened Apr'98

Economical:

1. Hotel Posada de las Monjas

Canal #37 (several blocks west of Jardín)
Tel: 152-0171   Fax: 152-6227

E-mail: bigboy@prodigy.net.mx
Web page: www.posadalasmonjas.com
Rooms: 64 (a wide variety in size and lighting)
Credit cards: Master and Visa
José López (father and son) work the front desk—both are bilingual
Check for economical rooms at time of check-in (no reservations)
Restaurant: 2nd floor   Hrs: 8-11am, 2-4pm and 8-10pm
Small bar open on weekends (Thur-Sat) 3-11pm
Large lobby with fireplace, TV and guest telephone
Interesting old-style building, several levels
Near bus station, inside parking

2. Hotel Parador de San Sebastian
Mesones #7 (across the street from Academia)
Tel: 152-7084
Rooms: 12 (all with private bathrooms)
Credit cards: None
New office and reception area
Restaurant: None
Old-style building with open courtyard
Plus 14 small apartments in back

3. Hotel Sautto
Hernández Macías #59 (down the street from Bellas Artes)
Tel: 152-0051 and 152-0052   Fax: None
Rooms: 20
Credit cards: None
Bella Italia Restaurant:
> Hrs: Daily 1:30-11pm
> Inside and outdoor courtyard
> Very good food—sometimes live music in the evenings

Colonial *hacienda* belonging to one of San Miguel's early families
Large open courtyard with fruit trees and flowers
Rooms have a worn look, but are comfortable
Quieter rooms are away from the restaurant area
Small pets allowed with overnight guests
Enclosed parking lot in back

4. Hotel Posada Los Insurgentes
Hernández Macías #92
Tel/Fax: 152-0283
E-mail: hotellosinsurgentes@unisono.net.mx

Web page: www.travelbymexico.com
Manager: Sonia Caballero (bilingual)
Rooms: 20 (each with a bathroom)
Clean and very comfortable beds—some rooms have cable TV
Small courtyard area—cold drinks for sale
Inexpensive rates

5. Casa de Huéspedes
Mesones #27 (directly across from Calle Juárez)
Tel: 152-1378
Rooms: 7 plus two roof-top apartments (nice view)
Credit cards: None
Restaurant: None
Busy part of town
Rooms located upstairs on first floor
Many potted plants on first floor open-air corridor
Manager: Sra. Saleta le Desma

6. Huéspedes Feliz
Calle del Codo #30 (south of Centro)
Tel: 152-0854
Rooms: 7 (all have a small kitchen and bathroom)
Prices are very reasonable
Credit cards: None
Restaurant: None
Convenient location between Centro and the Instituto
Micaela is the friendly, bilingual owner
Small lounge area with books and telephone
Usually full with long-term guests during the winter season

7. Hotel La Casa de Café
Hidalgo #18 (near Mesones and one block from Jardín)
Tel: 154-5312   and   152-1630   Fax: 152-0121
E-mail: correo@pmexc.com
Web page: www.pmexc.com
Credit cards: None
Rooms: 10 with private bath, cable TV (extra) and very clean
Inexpensive (ask about long-term rates)

8. Hotel D'Allende
Hidalgo #22 (near Mesones)
Tel: 154-7920   Tel/Fax: 152-7929
E-mail: hotel_d_allende@yahoo.com.mx

Rooms: 14 (on two floors)
Includes private bath and cable TV
Inexpensive double and single rates
Near school and disco
Opened April'01

9. Casa Olvera (Guest House)
Hospicio #39 (next to Casa de Sierra Nevada)
Tel: 152-1057
Central residential neighborhood
Eight individual rooms with private bathroom and telephone extension
Full use of family living room with TV, dining room and kitchen
      plus rooftop terrace
Daily or monthly–very reasonable rates

10. Hostal Alcatraz
Reloj #54 (2½ blocks from Jardín)
Tel: 152-8543
E-mail: alcatrazhostal@yahoo.com
Web page: www.mexlinks.com/hostel.htm
Owner/Manager: Rosalinda (bilingual)
Male/female dorms with bunk beds
      Sleeps up to 18 people
      Approximately US$9 per/bed per/night
Member of Hostelling International
Open kitchen, patio and TV room
Opened July'99

11. Hotel Vista Hermosa Taboada
Cuna de Allende #11 (½ block from Jardín)
Tel: 152-0437   Fax: 152-2636
Rooms: 18 (telephone and some rooms have a small balcony)
Double/single rates are the same
Apartments (4) (more expensive)—ask about weekly/monthly rates
Credit cards: Master and Visa
Old-style building, 3 floors (nice view from roof-top)
Small courtyard lobby

12. La Siesta
RV Park/Hotel (29 rooms)
Salida a Celaya #82
Tel: 152-0207   Tel/Fax: 152-37-22

E-mail: lasiesta@unisono.net.mx
Owners: Raúl and Cecilia Araiza (bilingual)
Opened Oct 1960

Look under **Bed and Breakfast** and **Apartments** for
    additional places to stay.

When looking for a place to stay, the following Spanish
    words and expressions may prove helpful:

I need a room	*Yo necesito una habitación.*
How many people?	*¿Cuantas personas?*
one person	*una persona*
two people	*dos personas*
Can I see a room?	*¿Puedo ver una habitación?*
with bathroom	*con baño*
room	*habitación (cuarto)*

single	*sencillo*	key	*llave*
double	*doble*	pillow	*almohada*
bed	*cama*	blanket	*cobija (manta)*
double bed	*matrimonial*	towel	*toalla*
twin beds	*individual*	soap	*jabón*

Ice Cream/Yogurt Shops

1. Dolphy
Formerly called Bing
Plaza Principal #24 (corner of Reloj)—north side of Jardín
Tel: 152-2744
Hrs: Daily 10am-10pm
Cones, ice cream bars, cold drinks and coffee
Chain in México—opened Nov'94—renamed June'01

2. Helados Holanda (aka Norman's)
San Francisco #10
Tel: 152-0567
Hrs: Daily 11am-9pm
Owner: Guadalupe Kruk (bilingual)—Norman died Aug'01
National franchise
Cones, popsicles, sundaes, milkshakes and bulk ice cream
Also sells fresh popcorn and cold drinks
Large community bulletin board

Copy machine
Relocated April'01

3. Santa Clara
Ancha de San Antonio #1 (near Aldea arches)
Tel/Fax: 152-5141
E-mail: staclara@mpsnet.com.mx
Hrs: Daily 10am-9pm
Franchise — Cal is the Canadian owner
Ice cream, yogurt, cottage cheese and coffee (+ coffee beans)
    Best to get American-type sour cream on Mondays
Mail boxes available, telephone, fax and e-mail service
Staff well trained and friendly

4. Nutri Yogurt
Salida a Celaya s/n (alongside Pemex gas station)
Tel: None
Hrs: Daily 8am-9pm, Sun 9am-3pm
Organic yogurt (plain or with fruit)
    No sugar, preservatives or artificial coloring
Made daily in San Miguel
Also sells honey, granola and coffee
Opened Dec'03

Labs (Clinical)

Perform blood and urine tests plus throat cultures

1. LABSAM
Mesones #51 (near Reloj)
Tel: 152-2222
Hrs: Mon-Sat 8am-8pm, Sunday 8am-3pm
Computerized
Owner: Carlos Rosales (bilingual)

2. San Francisco Clínico Laboratorio
San Francisco #51-A (up the hill on the south side)
Tel: 152-4612
Hrs: Mon-Sat 7:45am-7:30pm, Sun 8am-2:30pm

Also: **Hospital de la Fé**, Libramiento #43, Tel: 152-2233
    Bios-Lab, Hidalgo #22 (interior), Tel: 154-7322

Laundromats

1. Lavamágico
Pila Seca #5
Tel: 152-0899
Hrs: Mon-Sat 8am-8pm, closed Sunday
English spoken by Guadalupe
Reasonable price (approx US$3) for 4 kg load

2. Express Laundry
Canal #127
Tel: 152-7086
Hrs: Mon-Fri 9am-7pm, Sat 9am-5pm, closed Sunday
Owner: Carlos (bilingual)
Prompt service
Free pickup and delivery
Reasonable prices
Opened Dec'97

3. Lavandería El Reloj
Reloj #34-A (near Genesis)
Tel: 152-3843
Hrs: Mon-Fri 8am-8pm, Sat 8am-5pm, closed Sunday
Rafael Ramírez López—very personable owner
Completely renovated with new equipment

4. Lavandería Franco
Zacateros #54-B (flat-iron building)
Tel: 154-4495
E-mail: lavafranco@yahoo.com.mx
Hrs: Mon-Fri 9am-7pm, Sat 9am-5pm, Sunday closed
Owner: Francisco Antonio Oliveros (bilingual)
4 kg load cost approx. US $4—four hour service
Free pickup and delivery
2nd location: Ancha de San Antonio #15-A, Tel: 152-4362
    Dry cleaning—two day service

5. Lavandería Automática de San Miguel
Potranca #18 (Col. Guadiana)
Tel: 152-2082
Hrs: Mon-Sat 8am-8pm, closed Sunday
First laundromat to open in San Miguel (1984)

6. Lavandería Ana
Umarán #45 (near Quebrada)
Tel: 044-410-153-0105 (cell)
Hrs: Mon-Sat 8am-8pm, closed Sunday
Same day service
Paid by the weight

Dry Cleaning
La Pila
Jesús #25 (near corner of Cuadrante)
Tel: 152-5810
Hrs: Mon-Fri 9am-7pm, Sat 9am-2pm, closed Sunday
Owner: Juan Barragán (bilingual)
Electronic dry cleaning and laundry (state-of-the-art equipment)
Also clean rugs and curtains—will pickup and deliver
In addition, wash, polish and wax floors

Public Laundry
El Chorro
Near Benito Juárez Park and the waterworks (south end of Recreo)
Women scrub clothes in outdoor tubs
Morning time best for viewing

Lawyers

There are some 30 lawyers (*abogados*) in San Miguel, of which 13 are notary publics. Real estate transactions with notarized deeds, will preparation and legal business involving the government require a notary lawyer. They are more highly qualified than ordinary lawyers. Today they should have a Masters in Notary Law and are appointed by the state government when a vacancy occurs. A few who have worked with the foreign community with good results are the following.

1. Lic. Salvador Soto Guerrero
Abogado y Notario Público No. 5
Hospicio #40
Tel: 152-0301   Fax: 152-6587
Hrs: Mon-Fri 10am-2pm and 5:30-7:30pm
Real estate contracts, wills and some litigation
PhD and Law professor at Guanajuato University

Member of the Instituto Mexicano de Derecho Procesal and
      Instituto Ibero-Americano de Derecho Procesal
Practicing law 25+ years
Bilingual

2. Lic. Engelbert Meyenberg
Abogado **Mexico Advisor**
Correo #24
Tel: 152-6932   or   152-0586   Fax: 152-5723
E-mail: engelbert.meyenberg@mexadv.com
Web page; www. mexadv.com
Hrs: Mon-Fri 10am-7pm, closed weekends
Bilingual
Educated at UNAM in México City
Specializes in real estate and corporate law
Mexico Advisor office opened Sept'02 (est. in México City'98)

3. Lic. María de la Luz Martínez de Carbajo
Abogado y Notario Público No. 8
Hidalgo #6 (across the street from Amex travel office)
Tel: 152-4901   Fax: 152-0801
Hrs: Mon-Fri 9:30am-2:30pm and 5-7pm, Sat 9:30am-1pm
Speaks a little English

4. Lic. Roberto Zavala V. (father)
Abogado y Notario Público No. 6
Juárez #5 (across from Jardín de San Francisco)
Tel: 152-3813 and 152-0587   Fax: 152-2592
Hrs: Mon-Fri 10:30am-2pm and 4:30-7pm
Father and son are both lawyers in same office
Some English spoken

5. Lic. Jorge García García
Abogado y Notario Público No. 9
Hidalgo #35 (corner of Insurgentes)
Tel: 152-0249   Fax: 152-2088
E-mail: notaria9@puma.cybermatsa.com.mx
Hrs: Mon-Fri 11am-3pm and 6:30-9pm
Speaks some English
Since 1969

Library

1. Biblioteca Pública
Insurgentes #25   (APDO #119)
Tel: 152-0293   Tel/Fax: 152-7048
E-mail: sandra@bibliotecasma.com
Web page: www.bibliotecasma.com
Hrs: Mon-Fri 10am-7pm, Sat 10am-2pm
        Sunday and public holidays closed
One of the largest bilingual (English/Spanish) collections in México
        Some 45,000 books (over half are English titles)
Large outdoor courtyard
Friendly and helpful bilingual reception staff
Library card:
        Temporary membership ($100 *peso* refundable deposit) +$20 *pesos*
        Yearly membership $50 *pesos* (3/03)
4 Hardcover/4 Paperback books for 2 weeks
4 Tapes for 1 week
Started Nov 23, 1954, and supported by the foreign community
        50th anniversary (Nov'04)
1958 moved to present location (17th century structure) with the
        help of the state government

Summer 1996 first phase of new construction to open back
        courtyard, **Quetzal Room** and **Café Santa Ana**
Quetzal Room—muralist David Leonardo painted an impressive
        four-wall *Quetzalcoatl* and *Aztec* mural portraying everyday
        activities of the ancient peoples of México (Mar'03)
Summer/Fall'98 opened new reception area, office and store
Teatro Santa Ana (with the Player's Workshop) opened Jan'99
        Cinemateca opened June'00

Also:
Office of ATENCIóN (weekly English newspaper)—located upstairs
The Computer Center (located upstairs from Café Santa Ana)
Teatro Santa Ana and **Cinemateca**–enter Reloj #50-A after 7pm
Children's library
Music room (cassettes and sheet music)–over 2,000 tapes
English-language book section
Sala Quetzal (Latin American studies)–adjacent Café Santa Ana

Recommended Reading List:
1. *Distant Neighbors: A Portrait of the Mexicans* by Alan Riding
2. *Many Méxicos* by Lesly Byrd Simpson
3. *Frida—A Biography of Frida Kahlo* by Hayden Herrera
4. *Mornings in México* by D.H. Lawrence
5. *Life in México* by Fanny Calderón de la Barca
6. *Another México* by Graham Greene
7. *Como Agua Para Chocolate* (*Like Water for Chocolate*)
    by Laura Esquivel
8. *On Mexican Time* by Tony Cohan

This is only a partial list as many more selections, including
    art books, are available. Stop in and see for yourself.

Periodical section of used newspapers and magazines
Center for various community service projects
Copy machine (used for library material only)
Pay telephone for local calls
La Tienda Gift Shop (just inside entrance to the left)
Café Santa Ana–snacks, light food and drinks (in back and right
    of main courtyard)

Activities:
1. *Conversaciones con Amigos*
    Practice your Spanish and English—Tues and Thurs 5-6:30pm
2. *Bodega de Sorpresas*
    Rummage sale—Thursday 10am-1:30pm
3. *House & Garden Tour*
    Sunday 11am-2pm—US$15 or *peso* equivalent
4. Public lectures (see ATENCIóN or bulletin board at
    the library for announcements)

2. Biblioteca Municipal
Pepe Llanos #14
Tel: 152-7855
E-mail: saber@unisono.net.mx
Hrs: Mon-Fri 8am-8pm, Sat 9am-2pm
Reading room, computers for research and all kinds of classes

In México City:
Benjamin Franklin Library (USIS)
Londres #16
Tel: 01 (55) 5080-2000 ext. 3482 (through the US Embassy)
Hrs: Tues, Wed and Thur 10am-3pm, Mon and Fri 3-7:30pm
Founded in 1942—first American library overseas

Liquor Stores

1. La Europea
Canal #13
Tel: 152-2003
Hrs: Daily 10am-8pm
Chain of 13 stores in México
Central location—entire store airconditioned
Spirits plus imported wines, water and ice
A good selection of canned snacks and condiments
Large humidor displays Mexican and Cuban cigars
Best prices around

2. Vinos y Licores Don Quijote
Salida a Celaya s/n (south of town)
Tel: 152-3748
Hrs: Daily 9am-9pm
Corona beer distributor
Good selection of whiskey, wine, beer, soft drinks and snacks

3. La Divina
Casa de los Vitrales ("Stained Glass House")
Plaza Real del Conde (large building adjacent to parking lot)
Road to Querétaro (2 km southeast from Centro)
Tel: 154-4190
Hrs: Daily 10am-8pm, closed Thursday
Credit cards: Master and Visa
Manager: Roberto Zamora (bilingual)
29 stores in México
Self-service warehouse
> Ground Floor
>> Liquor, wine, beer and soft drinks–good prices
>> Canned deli items from Conservas San Miguel
>> Sausage from La Barcelonesa
>> Gift baskets
>> Cigars (national and Cuban), pipes and tobacco
> 2nd Floor
>> *Tequila* museum
>> 150 kinds of *tequila* (purchase by bottle, ½ case or case)
>> Mexican handcrafts plus *equipal* furniture
>> Large mural depicting history of *tequila* in México (1873)
>> 32 stained-glass windows
Opened Nov'98

4. Macro Corpovino
Zacateros #83 (near Aldea)
Tel: 152-2219
Hrs: Mon-Sat 10am-9pm, Sunday 10am-2pm
National chain, some 20 stores in México
Manager: Miguel Angel Garcia
Good sized store with large selection—self serve
Liquor, wine, beer and soft drinks
Free delivery
Opened July'96

5. Vinos y Licores
Pepe Llanos #4
Tel: 152-0836
Hrs: Daily 8am-9pm
Owner: Mario Pérez (bilingual)
Small store (liquor, wine and beer)

Also a good selection at:
Espino's, Codo #36, Tel: 152-1009
Gigante at Plaza Real del Conde, Tel: 152-4047

Meat and Poultry Stores

Meat:

1. Carnicería "Cervantes"
Jardín de Zaragoza #26 (across from Oratorio Church on Insurgentes)
Tel: 152-0108
Hrs: Daily 8am-5pm
Owner: Miguel Angel Cervantes Rosas
Busy butcher shop
Place to get a good cut of meat
Family business—more than 25 years

2. Carnicería La Paloma
Colegio #25 (near civic plaza and Mercado)
Tel: 152-1484
Hrs: Daily 8am-4pm
Fresh beef and pork
Family business since 1946—run by Antonio Sánchez Méndez

3. Carnicería San Miguel
San Pedro #10 (corner of Indio Triste)
    Near Mercado de San Juan de Dios
Sign painted on building above entrance
Tel: 152-3010
Hrs: Daily 7am-5pm
Juanita is the owner
Started business 1988

4. Barbecue Bob's Kitchen
Salida a Celaya #6 (just before Pemex)
Tel: None
Hrs: Mon-Sat 10am-4pm, closed Sunday
American style cuts of meats
Home-made sausage
Organically grown vegetables and herbs
Also sells BBQ sauces, sauerkraut, honey, dill pickles and pickled
    beets, squash and peppers
Kitchen decorations of dried vegetables and herb plants
Opened June'03

Poultry:

1. Pollo y Huevo
Codo #1 (corner of H. Macías)
Tel: 152-3631
Hrs: Mon-Sat 7:30am-3:30pm and 6:30-10pm
    Sunday 6:30am-10pm
Fresh, clean local chicken (9am-12 noon)—no chicken delivery on Wed
Can order by telephone
Owners: Patrícia and Antonio (both speak English)

2. Pollería Zaragoza
Insurgentes #15
Tel: None
Hrs: Daily 7:30am-4:30pm, Wed and Sun 7:30am-2pm
Miguel speaks English
Fresh local chicken (about US$2 per kilo)
Chicken ranch closed on Wednesday
Also sell fruits and vegetables (fresh on Mon, Thur and Sat)

Medical Insurance

1. Centro Médico del Potosí Hospitalization Plan
San Luis Potosí (3 hrs from San Miguel by car)
144 full-time doctors, 56 specialties
Continually updates diagnostic equipment
Acceptance dates (Nov-Feb) — coverage begins Jan 1st
No age limit, pre-existing condition exclusion or physical exam
Deductible US$110 (first night hospitalization), no co-insurance
Annual premium: reviewed annually
Sum insured: $125,000 *pesos* and $15,000 *pesos* if accident on
     public transportation
Free outpatient consultations and lab work for members
San Miguel contact: Mark Melhado (Tel: 152-6483)
Since 1984 plan available to San Miguel residents
Call for details of plan

2. BUPA International (British United Provident Assoc.)
London, England
Latin America rep – Raúl de Alba (Querétaro) – bilingual
     In San Miguel every Saturday 11am-2pm
     Ancha de San Antonio #81, Apt #14
Tel: 01-442-253-3242 (Qro) or 044-552-151-8483 (cell)
E-mail: bupalba@prodigy.net.mx
Worldwide hospitalization medical coverage
No deductible, no co-insurance and no age restrictions
Enroll first day of any month
Select one of three levels of limited coverage
     (excludes pre-existing conditions)
Premium payment: quarterly (+5%) or annually
     Check or Master/Visa card
Optional air ambulance plan—also sells travel insurance
Call for details – offered since Nov'98

3. Grupo Nacional Provincial (GNP)
Casa Canal (interior)
Canal #3
Tel: 152-1086 or 044-415-100-5420 (cell)
E-mail: riverariocar@hotmail.com
Hrs: Mon-Fri 10am-2pm (or call and make an appointment)
Carmen Rivera Río Rocha (bilingual)—San Miguel resident
Represents GNP—largest insurance company in México

Major medical insurance (domestic and worldwide)
Also, life, homeowners and car insurance

Also: **Patton Ins Group**, Hidalgo #8, 2nd/F, Tel: 154-7658

A number of other medical plans are known to be available to expatriates who need worldwide coverage. They are International Medical Group (IMG) in Indianapolis, IN, International Health Insurance from Copenhagen, Denmark, Blue Cross/Blue Shield of Delaware and SRI of Arizona.

Med Air Services Assoc (MASA)	**Sky Med Int'l**
Tel: 152-7363 (RE/MAX)	001-866-805-9624 (toll free)
Web Page: www.masamexico.com	www.skymed.com

Insider's Tip: Go to www.medtogo.com to learn about a México health and safety travel guide in English. It is a directory of the best hospitals and English speaking physicians in some 40 destinations in México.

Money Changers (Cambios)

1. INTERCAM
Formerly called Deal Consultores
Correo #15 (also at Juárez #27 and San Francisco #4)
Tel: 154-6676, 154-6707 and 154-6660
Hrs: Mon-Fri 9am-6pm, Sat 9am-2pm, closed Sunday
Authorized to do money exchange by Treasury Department of México
Cash, travelers' checks, money orders and wire transfers
Bring ID/passport
Personal checks (with previous application only)
Posted exchange rate
Very efficient and no paperwork
62 branches in México
Since 1988

2. Dicambios
Foreign currency exchange
Correo #13
Tel: 152-3657
Hrs: Mon-Fri 9am-4pm, Sat and Sun 10am-2pm

US dollars, travelers' checks and personal checks (residents only)
Bring ID (passport or FM3)
New ownership Nov'99
Second location: Juárez #1 (at San Francisco), Tel: 154-8020

3. Monex
Mesones #80 (next door to Teatro Angela Peralta)
Tel: 154-9996 thru 98   Info: 01-800-426-6629 (toll free)
Web page: www.monex.com.mx
Hrs: Mon-Fri 9am-3pm
Foreign exchange (cash, travelers' checks or personal checks)
     Bring ID (passport or FM3)
Also electronic transfers
Offers investment funds
Efficiently run small office—opened May'02
43 branches in México—since 1985—largest exchange in México

4. DESERVE
Posada San Francisco Hotel
Plaza Principal #2, (second left inside hotel entrance)
Tel: 152-5050
E-mail: deserve@prodigy.net.mx
Hrs: Mon-Fri 10am-6pm, Sat 10am-3pm, Sunday closed
Cash (buy/sell dollars), travelers' checks
Personal checks if a resident
Rarely have to wait

Also: Lloyd, San Francisco #33
        BANAMEX, BANORTE, BANCA SERFIN, HSBC
        (all located on Calle de San Francisco)
        BBVA-BANCOMER on Juárez

Insider's Tip: You can have US funds transfered from the USA to San Miguel via an American Express(Hidalgo #1-A) moneygram or Western Union "dinero express" for pick up at the Elektra store (Zacateros #36). The transfer is sent electronically and pickup in San Miguel is in pesos less a commission. You will need a reference number and ID.

CURRENT EXCHANGE RATE: (Feb 2005)
        One (1) US Dollar = 11.20 *Pesos*
        Floating rate since Dec. 20, 1994
        Jan 1, 1996 "new *pesos*" became just "*pesos*"

Museums

1. Allende Museo
Cuna de Allende #1 (cradle of Allende)
Corner of Umarán (faces La Parroquia and the Jardín)
Tel: 152-2499
Hrs: Tues-Sun 10am-4pm, closed Monday
Home and birthplace of Don Ignacio Allende (hero and martyr
    of Mexican independence)
Beautiful colonial building and courtyard
Built in the 18th century around 1760
Neoclassic design with baroque decorations
The Latin inscription above the entrance says, "He who was born
    here is known everywhere."
Note a statue of General Allende on the outside corner of the house
    facing the Jardín
Now houses a museum and gallery (also a second floor)
Pre-Columbian archaeological pieces, also weapons and
    objects from the Mexican independence movement
Some art openings as announced in the ATENCIóN
Admission: approx US$3 – free on Sunday

2. History of San Miguel Museum
Former location of Presidencia Municipal which opened in 1736,
    was later destroyed and then rebuilt. It was remodeled after
    May 1911 fire.
Plaza Principal #8 (north side of Jardín)
Opening mid-2005

> **Also: Museo de Arte Popular**, Rancho Jaguar, Atotonilco
>   Jennifer Hass, Tel: 152-0804 (make an appointment)

Music

Music Store:

Tienda Allegro
Umarán #1 (interior)—across the street from Mama Mía's
Tel/Fax: 152-4245
Hrs: Mon-Sat 10am-2pm and 4-7pm, closed Sunday
Owner: Mercedes Millan (bilingual)
Large selection of guitars, wind instruments and accessories
Also music books and private lessons
Guitar teachers available for lessons
Relocated Dec'02

Lessons:
Javier Estrada
c/o Border Crossings, Mesones #57 (interior)
Tel: 152-2497 (leave message)
Guitar lessons (mornings Monday-Friday)
Bilingual
35 years' teaching experience

Insider's Tip: Music for all occasions: Mariachi Los Camperos
Leonardo Tovar, Col San Antonio, Tel: 152-2865 or 044-415-153-3986

Newspapers

ATENCIóN San Miguel
Weekly English newspaper (comes out on Friday)
Published by the Biblioteca Pública
Founded in 1975 by Connie Moore and Eve Greene
Located upstairs from Café Santa Ana (March'98)
Cost: $8 *pesos* per copy
Sold at Biblioteca, plus some 20 retail outlets (i.e.; Lagundi,
        Espino, La Conexión, El Pegaso, Jardín newsstand, etc)

Note the center pullout "What's Going On" regional supplement
with a listing of activities, a calendar and ongoing events.

ATENCIóN office hours: Mon-Fri 10am-4pm
Tel/Fax: 152-3770 and 152-7049
E-mail: atencionedit@bibliotecasma.com
Subscription about US$70 per year (in México)
        US$180 per year (USA and Canada)-reflects new Mex postal rate
Send a copy to a friend for about US$2

ATENCIóN publication deadlines (same week of publication)
Display ads—Friday at 12 noon for next publication
Classified ads—Monday at 2pm (rates: 1-30 words approx US$5)
Ads ordered at office or sent by e-mail (must be paid in full)
        Email to: atencionads@bibliotecasma.com
Articles and Letters to the Editor—Tuesday at 10am at office or
        send via e-mail: atencionedit@bibliotecasma.com
        for publication in the same week

Insider's Tip: Ordering one copy or a subscription to the local ATENCIóN newspaper, prior to moving or visiting here, might not be a bad idea.

Look for the **Herald** (Int'l English edition of the Miami Herald) at the Jardín, Mesones #69 and Espino's on Ancha de San Antonio (2/03). It comes out daily and costs $7 *pesos.*

Nurseries/Flower Shops

1. Viveros Paraíso (paradise nursery)
Calle Cinco de Mayo at 16 de Septiembre
Col. Allende
Tel: 152-4635
Hrs: Daily 10am-7pm
Proprietor: Benito Paredón Alvarez
In business since 1984 (from Dolores Hidalgo)
Good selection of plants, fruit trees, rolls of grass, soil and clay pots
Also located at: **Libramiento a Querétaro** #4 (near Dr Vargas' office) and **Paseo del Parque** (behind Espino)

2. Floriade
(Mr. MacGregor's Garden)
Libramiento s/n (near Hospital de la Fé)
Tel: 154-4881 or 044-415-151-2029 (cell)
E-mail: floriade@cybermatsa.com.mx
Hrs: Mon-Fri 9am-6pm, Sat 9am-1pm, closed Sunday
Owner: Ing. Germán MacGregor (bilingual)
Complete garden center
    Trees, bushes, plants, grass and pots
Also garden design, maintenance, landscaping and irrigation systems
Opened March'98, moved Dec'03

Also: **Vivero Primavera**, Salida a Celaya (before Ford agency) and Salida a Celaya (between Pemex and Telmex)

Recommend the following books:
    About the Garden by Fen Lasell Taylor, Jun'97– about US$9
    Some Common & Interesting Plants of San Miguel de Allende by John and Anne Parker, Mar'99 (bilingual with color photos) – about US$15
    Both are for sale at the Biblioteca

Also check:
> **Terra,** Cuadrante #6, for garden supplies and seeds,
> plus landscape and gardening services by
> appointment with Alfonso Alarcón (Tel: 152-7754)
> **Cantadora,** Calzada de la Aurora, s/n, Tel: 154-8302
> Cantera stone
> **Tuesday Market** has limited plants and pots
> **La Yucca,** Hidalgo #17, Tel: 152-4738, artificial flowers
> **Las Colonias** at the Botanic Garden offers landscaping
> and plants in exchange for a donation
> **Portal de Allende** (west of Jardín)-dried flowers

Insider's Tip: Fresh roses are sold at various sidewalk locations in *el Centro*. Look for Rosa Tellez's family down the street from Pegaso Restaurant, in front of Espino's and the corner of H. Macías and Mesones (Teatro water fountain). Also sold on Aldama near corner of Cuadrante and across the street from Bellas Artes (H. Macías #72).

Also: **Mercado** (near Civic Plaza)—several fresh flower stands

Insider's Tip: Lupita Juárez, at the Mercado (Tel: 152-1635 or FAX: 152-8995) can make flower arrangement deliveries in San Miguel. Also, through FloraMex, national and international deliveries can be made.

Optical Stores

1. Optica San Miguel
Juárez #7 (interior)
Tel/Fax: 152-3151 and 154-4546
E-mail: optsanmi@yahoo.com
Hrs:Mon-Fri 10am-2pm and 4-8pm, Sat 10am-2pm, closed Sun
Most credit cards accepted
Owners: Alberto Carrera López and wife Beatriz (bilingual)
Bausch and Lomb authorized center
Eye examinations—Dra. Julieta Nebradt, an ophthalmologist from
       Irapuato, sees patients every Tuesday by appointment
Prescription glasses to order—hard and soft lenses
Repair service
Relocated April'00

Also: **Optica Jess & Karen,** Plaza Real del Conde, Tel: 152-6151

Photo Shops

1. Photo Super 30 (Fuji)
Portal Allende #6 (west of Jardín) -all green decor
Tel: 152-2696
Hrs: Mon-Sat 9am-9pm, Sunday 10am-6pm
Print processing time (1 hour), including APS prints
    Slides (1 week) and enlargements
Also sell film, cameras, albums and video tape
Busy location

2. La Fotografía
Aldama #13
Tel: 152-1431
E-mail: kip_gadc@hotmail.com
Hrs: Mon-Fri 10am-7pm, Sat 10am-4pm, closed Sunday
Owner: Hilario García—professional photographer
One day service—attention to detail
Film, supplies and equipment for sale
Postcard images of San Miguel also for sale
Since 1996

3. Foto Americana
Kodak Products
Mesones #68 (near Hidalgo)
Tel: 152-6573
Hrs: Mon-Sat 9:30am-9pm, Sunday 9:30am-3pm
Processing takes 1½ hours
Sell Kodak film, cameras and Polaroid photos

4. Foto Fácil
Elektra Appliance Store
Zacateros #36 (just inside store to the left)
Tel: 152-6930
Hrs: Daily 9am-9pm except Tues and Fri closed from 3-5pm
Print processing—1 hour service
Cameras for sale
Best prices around

5. Fotografía Iris Profesional
Calle San Rafael #19 (west side of San Juan de Dios Mercado)

Tel: 044-415-153-8417 (cell)
Hrs: Mon-Sat 9am-7pm, Sunday 9am-2pm
Studio photos, also passport photos
Most are ready within 24 hours
Also: **San Carlos,** Mesones #5, Tel: 044-415-153-3575 (cell)

6. Radio Shack
Plaza Real del Conde (Gigante)
Tel: 152-4140
Hrs: Daily 10:30am-8:30pm
Large selection of digital cameras
Also mobile phones, TV's and sound systems
Good selection of electronic accessories
Opened Sept'04

Also: **Foto Estudio San Miguel,** H. Macías #41-B, Tel: 152-8083
Processes colored slides
Mini-Lab Processing (formerly The Perfect Image)
Callejón de San Antonio #29, Tel: None
Hrs: Mon-Sat 9am-2pm and 4-8pm

Post Office

San Miguel de Allende C.P. 37700
Servicio Postal Mexicano
Calle Correo #16 (one block east of Jardín)
Tel: 152-0089
Hrs: Mon-Fri 8am-4pm, Sat 8am-12 noon
        Closed Sunday and public holidays
Postmaster: Armando Ríos Gallardo (May'02)

Postal rates:	*México*	*USA/Canada*	*Europe*
Letter *(carta)*	6.00	8.50	10.50
Postcard *(tarjeta postal)*	6.00	8.50	10.50
Postage prices above are in *pesos* (5/02)			

Post Office doesn't always stock exact denomination of stamps
        needed so in some instances be prepared to pay a little more
Glue on counter is to be used on Mexican stamps

Large stamps may be placed on back of envelope
General Delivery mail (*Lista de Correos*)—daily list of names on counter
Public pay telephone located on the east wall for local calls
Post box rentals (APDO—*Apartado*)—approx US$10 annually
    (rent from first of the year)

Proper local address:

                Name
                APDO # _____ (or street address)
                San Miguel de Allende, GTO
                37700 MEXICO

MEX POST (Express mail)
Calle Correo (next to Post Office)
Tel: 152-6421
Hrs: Mon-Fri 8am-4pm, Sat 8am-12 noon
México and International—3 days (México), 5 days (USA)
Parcel: ½ kilo approx US$15 (about US$4 each additional kilo)
    Max 20 kilos (USA)—México starts at approx US$4
Insurance not available
Carta:(México)about US$3.50 1-2 days, USA same as parcel rate

US Mail drop-off places:
1. **La Conexión,** Aldama #3, Tel: 152-1599
    Express Mail, daily, with/without US stamp, fee
    Karma mail, free service with US stamps (mail drop in front door)
2. **Pack 'N' Mail,** Canal #42, Tel: 152-5461
    Regular letters, Mon, Wed, Fri with/without US stamp, fee
3. **Solutions** (formerly MBE), Recreo #11, Tel: 152-6152
    1-oz letters, Mon, Wed and Fri, with/without US stamp, fee
4. **Border Crossings,** Mesones #57 (interior), Tel;: 152-2497
    Regular letters, daily, with/without US stamp, fee

Radio/TV Repair

1. Radio Servicio Vega
Mesones #70
Tel: 152-0719
Hrs: Mon-Sat 10am-2:30pm and 4:30-9pm, closed Sunday
Proprietor: David Vega and son David (bilingual)

Repair TV's, radios, stereos, VCR's
Good service, honest, fair appraisals

2. Electroserc
San Francisco #51-B (up the hill near Murillo street)
Tel/Fax: 152-4698
Hrs: Mon-Fri 9am-2pm and 4-7pm, Sat 9am-2pm, Sun closed
Owner: Ing. Geova Ramiro Rodríguez (some English)
All kinds of electronic repairs and cleaning
    Computers, printers, TV's, stereos, VCR's, fax machines,
        cell phones, cameras, etc.
Good service and fair prices

3. Radio TV San Rafael
Canal #91 (near San Pedro)
Tel: 152-3270
Hrs: Daily 9am-9:30pm, Sunday 9am-2pm
Owner: Pedro Ledesma (bilingual)
Repair TV's (color and black & white), also VCR's
Fair prices with estimate first
Since 1981 (previously worked in LA, Calif.)

Real Estate Offices

Like most places in the world: "location, location, location"
is the key ingredient for real estate. San Miguel is no exception. If
you are looking to invest, you quickly learn that prices today are
already quite high. You no doubt know that San Miguel is a very
popular tourist destination and "*gringo*" retirement community.
Here we live in a dollar economy and as a result most real estate
transactions are in US dollars.

If you are shopping for property you will need to identify
which neighborhood would be best suited for you. Some of the
more popular areas are: Los Frailes, Country Club, Guadiana, Los
Balcones, El Atascadero and El Centro. The price per square
meter of land varies widely among the different areas. Prices are
considerably lower in the various *colonias* that surround the town.
To build, the average price quoted today is approximately
US$400-$600 per square meter (US$40-$60 per sq ft). Home
prices range from US$80,000 for condos and small homes to over
one million dollars for a special colonial home.

If you are serious about buying here (and foreigners can now own property outright instead of going through a bank trust) you will need a reputable realtor and *notario público* (government appointed lawyer) who can draw up real estate contracts. If you do not use an English-speaking lawyer you will need to bring along a translator. It is interesting to know in México that both buyer and seller often use the same lawyer, although this may not be advisable. Title insurance is now available in México through Stewart Title and First American. They also offer US escrow accounts. You can contact Andrea Soto at **México Advisor**, Tel: 152-0586, for more information.

Real estate transactions begin after a purchase offer has been accepted by the seller and a promissory contract is signed by both parties. The usual 10% deposit is paid at this time, usually in the form of a cashier check. The balance will be paid when the *escritura pública* (official deed) is signed, at which time you become the legal owner. Generally in México mortgages are not available so sales are in cash. Occasionally, selected US companies offer Mexican mortgages. All closing documents are drawn up by the *notario público.* The *notario* will certify at the public property registry that the property is free of debt, liens and mortgage and receives a non-lien certificate along with a tax statement from the Treasury Office in order to insure the proper transfer. In México it is common practice for the buyer to pay the transfer tax (2% of the appraised value) and all the closing expenses and the seller pays the capital gains tax and the realtor's commission (2-6%).

The above is intended to be an overview and one should consult a lawyer should you have specifc questions. Good luck!

1. Allende Properties
Cuna de Allende #15 (½ block from Jardín)
Tel/Fax: 154-5000
E-mail: info@allendesma.com
Web page: www.AllendeSMA.com
Hrs: Mon-Fri 10am-7pm, Sat 10am-2pm, closed Sunday
Owner: Richard Dupuis (from Toronto)
Manager: Joanie Barcal
Beautiful new office in downtown location
Real estate sales and services
Complete on-line catalog of San Miguel properties
Separate closing offices (upstairs)

Manager: Ben Calderoni
Ass't Manager: Laura Hernández (also FM3 services)
Bilingual staff

2. RE/MAX Colonial
Portal de Guadalupe (east side of Jardín)—at Correo
Tel: 152-7363, 152-7365 and 152-7364   Fax: 152-7952
E-mail: mail@realestate-sma.com
Web page: www.realestate-sma.com
Hrs: Mon-Fri 10am-6pm and Sat 10am-2pm
Manager: Lane Simmons (active in the community)
Each office independently owned and operated
      60,000 real estate agents, 3,800 offices in 35 countries
      Lead industry in sales
Exclusive buyer representation
Recommend buying in-house, **Foreign Buyers Guide To Real Estate Transactions in San Miguel**
Recommended by International Living
New management since April'98, relocated July'04

3. Select Real Estate
Correo #24 (near Recreo)
Tel: 152-2322 or 154-9242
E-mail: sales@selectrealestate.com.mx
Web page: www.selectrealestate.com.mx
Hrs: Mon-Fri 10am-7 pm, Sat 10am-2pm
    Other times by appointment
Partners: Richard McClarty and Christian Sarvey
Virtual tour technology
Lowest commission rates in San Miguel (2%)
Opened: Jan'04

4. Colonial Real Estate
Cuna de Allende #19-A (centro)
Tel: 154-4971   Tel/Fax: 154-4972
E-mail: info@colonialre.com
Web page: www.san-miguel-real-estate.com
Hrs: Mon-Fri 9:30am-2pm and 4-7pm, Sat 9:30am-2pm, closed Sun
Broker/Owner: Alma Cecilia Ramírez (bilingual)
Sales only—offer wide range of properties
Many satisfied customers
Since 1995

5. San Miguel Properties
Formerly Casas de San Miguel
Hidalgo #4 (½ block from Jardín)
Tel: 154-9402 and 152-5096   Tel/Fax: 152-2096
E-mail: sales@sanmiguel-properties.com
Web page: www.sanmiguel-properties.com
Hrs: Mon-Sat 10am-6pm, Sunday by appointment
Owner: Steve Prichard/San Antonio, TX
Sales of homes, ranches and commercial properties
Nice looking in-town office
Also sell homeowner, car and medical insurance
New location Sept'03, name changed Jan'04

6. Abraham Cadena
Ancha de San Antonio #47
Tel: 152-1638   Fax: 152-2313
E-mail: ach@unisono.net.mx
Web page: http://www.unisono.net.mx/ach
Hrs: Mon-Fri 9am-2pm and 4-6:30pm, Sat 9am-12:30pm,closed Sun
25 years in business
Bilingual staff - Lucha is the long time, efficient office manager
Sales, long and short term rentals plus property management
Also sells Sanborn's car and homeowners insurance

7. Bueno Real Estate
Salida a Celaya #52 (between PEMEX and Corona building)
Tel: 152-1636   Tel/Fax: 152-1842
E-mail: c21bueno@prodigy.net.mx
Hrs: Daily 9am-2 pm and 3:30-6:30pm, Sat 9am-2pm, closed Sunday
Owner: Armando Bueno (American)
Real estate sales and rentals (houses, apartments, condos, ranches)
Office opened Feb'91, relocated Dec'01, changed name Nov'03

8. ABC Realty
A.B.C. of San Miguel (architecture, real estate and construction)
Canal #55
Tel: 152-3500 and 152-5000   Fax: 152-5825
E-mail: moreno@abcrealty.com
Web page: www.abcrealty.com
Hrs: Mon-Fri 9am-7pm, Sat 9am-3pm, Sunday by appointment
Owner: Architect Salvador Moreno (bilingual)
     More than 20 years experience in San Miguel

Large listing of available properties
Stop in to see one of a kind brass and copper relief of San Miguel
Second office: Cuna de Allende #11, Tel: 152-6000

9. Real Estate San Miguel
Broker/Owner: Michael Mervin Herrera
Cuadrante s/n (corner of Aldama) and Hospicio #50
Tel: 152-2284 and 152-6510   Tel/Fax: 152-7377
E-mail: info@sanmiguel-mx.com
Web page: www.sanmiguel-mx.com
Hrs: Mon-Fri 9am-2pm and 4-6:30pm, Sat 9am-2pm, closed Sunday
All types of listings (only sales)
Convenient location behind La Parroquia
Bilingual realtors

10. La Margarita
Formally Zavala-Garay Real Estate
Sollano #27 (corner of Cuadrante)
Tel: 152-5389   Tel/Fax: 152-2893
E-mail: lamargarita@cybermatsa.com.mx
Web page: www.sanmiguelhouses.com
Hrs: Mon-Fri 10am-2pm and 4:30-7pm, Sat 10am-2pm, closed Sun
Owner: Peggy Taylor (bilingual American) long-term resident
Specializing in sales only: uptown—downtown—out of town
Elegant, colonial or rustic listings
Conveniently located *centro* office
Reorganization April'02

11. Century 21 Parroquia
Aldama #10-B
Tel: 154-6050 and 154-6565   Fax: 152-0908
E-mail: century21parroquia@prodigy.net.mx
Web page: http://www.century21mexico.com
Hrs: Mon-Fri 10am-2pm and 4-7pm, Sat 10am-2pm
Directora: Lydia Gómez Herrera (bilingual)
Largest real estate company in the world
125 franchises operating in México
Sales and rentals
Opened Nov'03

12. Dotty Vidargas
Casas Coloniales
Canal #36 (corner of Zacateros)

Tel: 152-0286 and 154-5731   Fax: 152-2347
E-mail: vidargas@unisono.net.mx
Web page: www.dottyvidargas.com
Hrs: Mon-Sat 9:30am-2pm and 4-7:30pm, closed Sunday
Buying? Selling? Furnishing?
Homes and lots in town or in the country
First real estate agent in San Miguel – since 1960
Also an interior design store

> **Insider's Tip: Caution should be used regarding the amount of deposit paid for accommodations (hotel, B&B, houses and apartments) that you have not personally inspected. Deposit refunds could prove difficult to collect.**

Home Rental Companies:

1. Casas Elegantes
Vacation rentals
Tel: 152-7351
In USA: 1-(214) 413-2131 (answered in San Miguel)
E-mail: casaselegantes@aol.com
Web page: www.casaselegantes.com
Owner: Bob Latta (from Ft. Smith, AR)—attention to detail
High-end premium rentals
Personalized agency with trained professional staff
Offers unique home grocery stocking service
Since 2001

2. San Miguel House Rentals
Tel: 154-6848   or   044-415-103-0541 (cell)
    In USA: (512) 351-4304 (answered in San Miguel)
E-mail: anniel@san-miguel-house-rentals.com
Web page: www.san-miguel-house-rentals.com
Owners: Annie Reutinger and Jay Clark (from San Francisco)
Associate: Dar Burleson
Some 60 mid-priced to luxury in-town vacation residences
Since 1996, new ownership Sept'03

3. Premier House Rentals
Formerly Casas de San Miguel
Tenerías #36 (home)
Tel: 154-9460
E-mail: katharine@premiersanmiguel.com
Web page: www.premiersanmiguel.com

Owner: Katharine Hibberts
Good selection of rentals
New ownership and name Mar'04
San Miguel Management Company
Formerly Casas de San Miguel
Hernández Macías #111
Tel: 152-4416 and 152-0187   Fax: 152-3471
E-mail: peggy@sanmiguel-mgmt.com
Owners: Graciela Loyola and Peggy Blocker
Residential/commercial property management and construction
Also sell all kinds of insurance

4. HERHER
Construction, Maintenace and Property Management—Rentals
Owners: Judith Arnold Hernández and David Hernández
Tel/Fax: 152-3337
E-mail: sanmiguelrentals@yahoo.com
Web Page: www.sanmiguelrentals.com

5. Vacation Homes San Miguel
Joanne and Jennifer Rockett
Sollano (Centro)–Apdo #1053
Tel/Fax: 152-2110   1-(512) 853-9416 (from USA or Canada)
E-mail: smarent@yahoo.com
Web page: www.vacation-homes-san-miguel.com
Lived in San Miguel since 1986

6. Los Ensueños de San Miguel
Tel: 044-415-149-6434 (cell)
E-mail: nishiguchi@prodigy.net.mx
Web page: www.ensuenos.com
Local manager: Yoko Nishiguchi (trilingual)
Rentals and property management—some less expensive properties

Insider's Tip: It is a local custom to tip the private home help
(housekeeper and cook). You should discuss this with your
host or rental agent. General wages are low in México and service
jobs pay very little. A general guideline of $100 *pesos* per/guest
per/week is acceptable.

NEW SAN MIGUEL PHOTOBOOK:

VISIONS OF SAN MIGUEL THE HEARTLAND OF MEXICO

Cobblestones in color, Fiestas, La Parroquia and more.......
132 Pages
160 Colorful images
Taken by 30 talented photographers
9 1/2" x 8 1/2" tabletop book
Printed in Hong Kong

Cost of each book:	US$ 26.95	Faster Delivery
S&H (USA):	+ 3.00	
Total per/book	US$ 29.95	**Order on Internet**
(Canada add add'l US$3)		smabooks@yahoo.com

Send this form with your check to:

A. S. Dean
BC-2323
413 Interamerica #1
Laredo TX 78045 - 8285

IG 0305

SHIP TO:

DATE: _____   AMOUNT: US$_____

PLEASE SEND_____ COPIES TO:

NAME: _____

ADDRESS: _____

_____

TEL/EMAIL: _____

• PLEASE ALLOW 2 WEEKS FOR DELIVERY •

¡MUCHAS GRACIAS!

Rentals (Appliances, etc.)

1. Sol y Luna
Hospicio #10
Tel: 154-8599   044-415-103-4112 (cell)
Hrs: Mon-Fri 9am-7pm, Sat 10am-5pm, Sun 12 noon-5pm
E-mail: reynaldo_vazquez_tours@yahoo.com.mx
Rent TV's, VCR's, DVD players and cell phones
Also heaters, fans and small refrigerators
Plus bicycles, scooters, 4 wheelers, kayaks and camping equipment
Rent by the day, week or month
Deliver and pickup for additional $50 *pesos*
Also offer babysitters, cooks and maids
Translation services available

2. Servicio de Banquetes
Juan de Dios Peza #37 (Col. Guadalupe)
Tel: 152-6507
Guadalupe Ramírez (caterer)
Will rent tables, chairs, dishes, glasses, etc.

3. Casa Bonita
Plaza Real del Conde (near Café La Plaza)
Tel: 152-8955
Hrs: Mon-Fri 10am-2pm and 4-7pm, Sat 10am-2pm, closed Sun
Owner: Claudia Contreras (bilingual)—ten years experience in Qro
Rent tablecloths, china, glassware, chairs, umbrellas, etc.
Also will organize your social event
Opened Mar'98

Restaurants

The restaurants listed in this guide are extremely careful about food handling and preparation. Go ahead, join the locals, and enjoy salads and fruits
Eating out is one of the great pleasures for residents and travelers alike. San Miguel has the best quality and variety of restaurants of any city of its size in México. One can choose from a wide selection of Mexican and international cuisine, prices and ambiance. It is the author's experience that restaurants in San Miguel catering to the North American and tourist population take special care with ice, drinking water and in the preparation of fruits, vegetables and lettuce; however, it is always advisable to be cautious in this regard and not hesitate to ask questions. Try some local

dishes, such as *mole, tacos al pastor, chiles rellenos, carnitas* and chicken *enchiladas*. Following are more than fifty of the best eateries in town. ***Buen Provecho*** (Enjoy!)

Jump to the end of this section for a list of some of ***The Insider***'s favorite treats.

Insider's Tip: Buy an annual VIP club card for a 20% discount at more than 40 local restaurants. For info; Tel: 152-7363 or E-mail: vipsma@cybermatsa.com.mx

Let's Go Out For Breakfast!

1. Café de la Parroquia
Jesús #11
Tel: 152-3161
Hrs: Tue-Sat 7:30am-4pm, Sun 7:30am-2pm, closed Monday
Credit cards: None
Inside or outdoors—very pleasant atmosphere
Breakfast—Fresh brewed coffee, fresh fruits, energy drinks and
        omelettes, special pancakes or *pan francés* (French toast)
        Some vegetarian dishes on the menu
Great lunch place also—*comida* specials change daily
Some of the best tasting food in town
French-run, Françoise speaks Spanish, English and French
On the Day of the Dead and at Christmas the owner's creative
        displays–Christmas branch–are unique and a must see
Opened 1989
La Brasseríe (same location)
        Tues-Sat 5-10pm, closed Sunday & Monday
        Serving light dinners

2. Amigos
Jesús #5 (near Umarán)
Tel: 154-7730
Hrs: Daily 8:30am-10pm
Credit Cards: None
Owners: Raymond and María (bilingual)
Small, attractive *café* with larger seating area upstairs
Breakfast, lunch and dinner
Baguette sandwiches, soups and salads
Coffees, juices and smoothies—plus beer and wine
Home-made fresh pasteries
Take-out available
Re-opened July'04

3. Genesis Tienda Naturista
Reloj #34-B
Tel: 152-2016
Hrs: Mon-Sat 9am-8pm, Sunday 10am-2pm
Owner: Cecilia Loera Mata (bilingual)
Small sit-down bar—very clean!
Fresh squeezed fruit, vegetable juices and *licuados*
Granola cereal with yogurt and nuts, dried fruits and honey
Fresh baked muffins and bagels
Also sell health products and vitamins
Since 1983

Check out the **Café** listings in this book as most of them also
serve a complete breakfast. Other recommended breakfast
places listed in **Restaurant** chapter: **Posada Carmina,
El Pegaso, Villa Santa Monica** and **Pueblo Viejo**

Comida: (Lunch)
Comida corrida is a set 3-4 course meal and a popular way
to order the mid-day meal

4. Posada Carmina Restaurant
Ground floor courtyard of Posada Carmina Hotel
Cuna de Allende #7-A (very close to Jardín)
Tel: 152-0458 and 152-8888
Hrs: Daily 7:30am-11pm, closed Sunday night
Breakfast 7:30am-12 noon
Special lunch menu 12:30pm until finished
Dinner 7-11pm, closed Sunday night
Happy Hour: Mon-Fri 5-8pm All drinks incl. beer 2x1 (with snacks)
Credit cards: Evening meal only
Efficiently run by Carmina's grandsons
(Doña Carmina died July'00)
Courtyard (three orange trees) and inside dining room (once a stable)
A favorite of local residents, especially for the the mid-day *comida*
Consistently good food at reasonable prices—a balanced meal
Comida corrida (4 courses)—changes daily and menu posted at
entrance—look for weekly menu in the ATENCIóN
Also highly recommend the trout (*trucha*) off the menu
Don't forget this place for breakfast as the 4-minute soft-boiled
egg is done to perfection
Also cappuccino and expresso coffee
Special events and weddings
Experienced waiters

La Felguera Fusión Restaurant
(Named after Carmina's home-town in Spain)
Posada Carmina Hotel
All new dinner menu
Hrs: Mon-Sat 7-11pm, closed Sunday night
Live music
Opened Sept'04

5. El Pegaso
Corregidora #6 (side street across from Post Office)
Tel: 152-1351
Hrs: Mon-Sat 8:30am-10pm, closed Sunday
E-mail: robin@unisono.net.mx
Credit cards: Master and Visa
Owners: Robin and Beto Díaz
Excellent chef and experienced waiters (the best in town!)
Serving breakfast, lunch and dinner
Very tasty international daily specials
Ask Fernando to make you a chicken caesar salad from scratch at your table
Not to be missed, fresh raspberry pie!
Often warm cheerful fire in cool months
Popular with the foreign community–since 1982
Ticket sales outlet
Good collection of contemporary Mexican folk art for sale
Customers note a new no animal policy and non-smoking room to
    the left. A first in San Miguel!

6. Food Factory La Aurora
Fábrica La Aurora (inside to the left)
Calzada de la Aurora s/n (north of town, just past bridge on right)
Tel: 152-3982
Hrs: Mon-Sat 11am-6pm, closed Sunday
Credit card: None
Owner/Chef: Allen Williams
    Grew up in México, trained in Switzerland
    Formerly chef at Chamonix Restaurant
Delightful, elegant setting (inside or on covered terrace)
Located in restored *manta* factory
Attractive table settings, wooden floor and menu board
Special entrées, salads, soups, pastas and desserts
Cold drinks include beer and wine
Opened Sept'04

7. El Market Bistro

Hernández Macías #95 (between Pila Seca and Umarán)
Tel: 152-3229   Tel/Fax: 152-3140
E-mail: bistro@yahoo.com
Hrs: Daily 1-11pm, weekends until midnight
Credit cards: Amex, Master and Visa
Three owners: Alex (Mexican), Daniel (French) and Genevieve
        (French-Canadian)
Attractive patio and indoor dining with fireplace–nice ambiance
One of the best menus in town
Tasty specials prepared daily–authentic French cuisine
Attractive outdoor courtyard in the back for special events
Rotating art for sale
Opened Jan'98
Petit Bar (both sides of main entrance)
        All drinks, specialize in wine
        Fireplace and sofas on right side
        Daily happy hour 6-8pm
        Opened Aug'99

8. Chamonix

Sollano #17 (look for the red door)
Tel/Fax: 154-8363
Hrs: Tues-Sat 1-10pm, closed Sunday and Monday
Credit cards: Master and Visa
Small restaurant—indoor (with fireplace) and outdoor dining
Separate attractive bar area called Bar-Celona
Interesting menu board
        Try Vietnamese spring rolls with peanut sauce
        Excellent home-made soups
Reservations recommended
Also sell high-end decorative art
Opened Sept'01

9. Villa Santa Monica Restaurant

Baeza #22 (east side of Juárez Park)
Tel: 152-0427 and 152-0451
Hrs: Daily Breakfast 8am-12 noon
        Lunch/Dinner 1:30-10pm
Credit cards: Amex, Master and Visa
Gorgeous outdoor courtyard setting (water fountain, birds & flowers)
Tasty food; must try *gazpacho*, mushrooms with garlic and *parfait de mango*

Fresh flowers on table and cloth napkins
Sometimes closed for a wedding or special event

10. Casa Don Quijote
Restaurant Bar and Grill
Prolongación de Pila Seca #55 (3 blocks west of Zacateros)
    Look for a large tree in the middle of the street
Tel: 152-0807
Hrs: Tue-Sun 1-10pm, closed Monday
Credit cards: None
Owners: Donn and Julieta Stewart (bilingual)—son of legendary Don Stewart
Wonderful relaxing garden setting (also a covered patio)
    Outdoor kitchen and grill plus a bar
Barbeque ribs, steaks, wings, hamburgers and much more
Also beer, wine and sodas
Finger bowls available after meals
If you liked El Ranchito, you'll love this place!
Opened June'00

11. Casa Mía
Hernández Macías #88 (across from Market Bistro)
Tel: 154-7466
Hrs: Mon-Sat 12 noon-10pm, Sunday 12 noon-6pm
Owner: Isabel Cisneros
Attractive decor with wooden floor and wooden tables
Eat indoor or in small courtyard with water fountain
Sandwiches (*panetos*) and salad bar (more than 35 ingredients)
Choose your own *chapata* or baguette bread, spreads, veggies and cheese
Also soups, fondue, desserts and cold drinks (incl. beer and wine)
    Try a fruit flavored hot or cold tea
Reasonable prices
Small bar in front
Opened Sept'03

12. La Enchilada
Reloj #40-A (near Insurgentes)
Tel: 152-3684
Hrs: Daily 12 noon-8pm (bar open until 11pm)
Credit cards: None
Run by Claudia del Carpio (bilingual, college-educated and very friendly)
Small, clean, colorful eating place (also tables on second floor)
Wonderful, filling chicken or cheese *enchiladas*
    (choice of green or red sauce or *mole*)—served with
        consommé, rice and beans

Beer and *margaritas* available
A real treat and strongly recommended
Opened March'95

13. Nutri Verde Restaurant
100% Vegetarian Restaurant
Cuna de Allende #17
Tel: None
Hrs: Daily 10am-8pm
Credit Cards: None
Owner: Patricia Corpi (bilingual)
Clean eating area with small tables inside and outside
Interesting and varied menu—moderate prices
Offers a delicious daily *comida corrida* special
A variety of health drinks
Very clean—all fruits and vegetables treated
Opened Sept'03, relocated Sept'04

14. El Tomato
Vegetarian Restaurant
Mesones #62-B
Tel: 151-6057
Hrs: Mon-Sat 9am-9pm, closed Sunday
Credit Cards: None
Owner: Sra. Lourdes Harrsch (bilingual)
Attractive red and green décor with glass tables
Food is fresh and clean (fruits and vegetables are disinfected)
Comida corrida (fixed menu) changes daily
Try the spinach or tofu burger and steamed vegetable plate
AAA recommended restaurant
Opened Nov'95, relocated March'97, new owner Dec'01

15. Hacienda Los Laureles
Hidalgo #4 (outdoor courtyard)
Tel: 152-4212 or 152-5300
Hrs: Daily 1-10pm, closed Tuesday
Web page: www.haciendaloslaureles.com.mx
Credit cards: Amex, Master and Visa
Manager/Owner: Juan Lejtik (bilingual)
Beautiful restored patio with outdoor tables and umbrellas
Complete Mexican menu with full bar
    Also offers all you can eat menu
Family owns several restaurants in Querétaro
Opened Sept'02

16. El Correo
Correo #23 (across from the Post Office)
Tel: 152-4951
Hrs: Daily 8am-11pm, closed Tuesday
Credit cards: Master and Visa
Housed in a colonial building and includes a fireplace
Owners: Alvaro Zubeldía and Stephanie Bubela
Serve breakfast, lunch and dinner
Authentic Mexican cooking—a favorite for locals
Try the *caldo tlalpeño* or *tortilla* soup and *sopes de la casa*
Very reasonable prices
Full bar: excellent *margaritas*, mixed drinks, beer and wine
Opened Sept'88, new ownership May'03

17. Olé-Olé (small outside sign on façade + small hanging black bull)
Loreto #66 (next door to small tienda, 3½ blocks north of Jardín)
Tel: 152-0896
Hrs: Daily 1:30-9pm
Credit cards: None
A great experience and well worth the trip
Unique family-run restaurant—interesting atmosphere
Owner is Sr. Rafael Mendoza (Don Rafa)—one of a kind!
Limited menu as the main entrees are chicken or beef *fajitas* and
     beef, chicken or shrimp *brochetas*—large portions
For dessert try mango mousse
Full of bull fighting memorabilia—note large black *toro* in entrance
Wooden tables and chairs replaced metal ones
Background cassette music

18. Quinta Loreto Restaurant
Hotel Quinta Loreto
Calle de Loreto #15
Tel: 152-0042
Hrs: Daily 8-11am (breakfast) and 2-5pm (lunch)
Credit cards: Master and Visa
Popular daily *comida corrida* (partial order at a reduced price)
May be hard to find tucked away several blocks north of the Jardín
Very popular with hotel guests and local residents
Reputation for quality food and healthy portions
Cozy fireplace fire in winter, summertime outdoor tables on
     verandah

19. El Palacio Chino (China Palace)
Mesones #57 (at Reloj)
Tel: 154-5360
Hrs: Mon-Sat 12 noon-10pm, Sunday 12 noon-7pm
Credit cards: Amex, Master and Visa
Manager: José (bilingual)
Special *comida* Mon-Fri 12 noon-3pm—$75 *pesos*
Comfortable courtyard with fountain and tables
Good variety of tasty Chinese food
Also beer, wine and mixed drinks available
Same menu and chefs as when opened Sept'99
Take out and delivery services available
New management Feb'02

20. Restaurant 73 Bar & Café
Zacateros #73
Tel: 044-415-101-3186 (cell)
Hrs: Daily 9am-11pm, closed Tuesday
        Daily happy hour 6-8pm (2 x 1 beer and *margaritas*)
Credit cards: None
Owners: Leonardo & Teresa Paredes (bilingual)—20 yrs experience
Breakfast, lunch and dinner
Sandwiches, salads and Mexican dishes
Exceptionally reasonable prices
All kinds of drinks
Live music Fri/Sat nights, open mike Monday night
Shares space with **David Mallory Studio**
Relocated from Recreo #8, May'04

21. La Palapa
Calle Nueva #8 (behind Espino's)
Under a large yellow "Sol" beer tent
Tel: 044-415-100-6252 (cell)
Hrs: Mon-Sat 12 noon-6pm, closed Sunday
Owners: Ray Pieri and Morris Hancock
Informal, casual setting with neighborhood atmosphere
Specialize in fish or beef *tacos* plus chili dogs & burgers from the grill
Always fresh home-made carrot cake
Soft drinks and cold beer
Some of the best prices in town—very popular with locals
Newspapers and magazines to read—clean washroom in back
Opened Sept'02

22. La Fonda
Cocina Mexicana
Aldama #67½ (faces Parque Juárez)
Tel: 152-8077
Hrs: Tues-Sat 1-8pm, closed Sunday and Monday
Owner: Gabriela Green (bilingual)
Traditional home-made Mexican food
Daily specials—very reasonable prices
Formerly located Recreo #10 (upstairs from MBE)
Reopened Sept'04

23. Casa Relox
Relox #17 (½ block from Jardín)
Tel: 152-0097
Hrs: Daily 8am-11pm, closed Tuesday
    Breakfast specials 8am-12 noon
    Comida/cena buffet (drinks extra) 12 noon-6pm—$85 *pesos*
    Also can order menu items
Daily Happy Hour 5-8pm (domestic drinks)
Credit cards: Master and Visa
Owner: Juan Monroy (bilingual)
Beautifully rennovated courtyard with fountain and tables
Eating area surrounded by small *tiendas* and a bar
Opened March'02

24. El Asador Catalán
Restaurant-bar-sausage store
Road to Querétaro, km 9.5 (past Gigante)
Tel: 152-7900
Hrs: Tues-Sun 12:30-8pm, closed Monday
Credit cards: Master and Visa
Manager: Pablo Cervantes (bilingual)
Serving Catalán and Spanish food in a country setting
Offer a wide variety of sausages from their factory
Try *paella,* rabbit or a grilled meat dish
Sangria plus a good selection of beer and imported wine
Eat indoors or outdoors
Order a suckling pig for home delivery
La Barcelonesa factory outlet store (adjacent to restaurant)
    Tel: 152-0378
    Hrs: Tues-Sun 10:30am-7pm, closed Monday

25. Aquí Es México
Restaurante Fonda
Hidalgo #28
Tel: 152-0430
Hrs: Daily 8am-10pm
Must go upstairs to first floor (watch your head!)
Typical Mexican decor—open kitchen—Michoacán pottery
Run by Rogelio Gordillo, a local doctor
    Four generations of cooking experience
Piano ready to be played

℃26. Torta Mundo —
Umarán #29 (near Zacateros)
Tel: None
Hrs: Mon-Sat 10:30am-6:30pm, closed Sunday
Owners: Luis and Cleo Chavez
    Pride of ownership shows
Delicious *tortas* (sandwiches), hamburgers and *quesadillas*
Fresh squeezed fruit juices plus cold drinks
Excellent value—simply the best for the money!
Small, spotless kitchen and eating area
Opened Mar'99

ℂ27. Restaurant Lila ("lilac color")
Terraplén #2-C (near Recreo)
Tel: 044-415-101-3393 (cell)
Hrs: Daily 10am-9pm, closed Tuesday
Small, 4-table eating area
Breakfast, lunch and dinner
Juice, coffee, tea, beer and wine
Soup, salad, baguettes and hamburgers
    Also crêpes, pasta, lasagna and trout
Some of least expensive prices in town
Opened Aug'04

28. Apolo XI
Mesones #43 (upstairs)
Tel: 152-1260
Hrs: Daily 9am-7pm
Credit cards: None
Serve only *carnitas* (sliced pork loin) with onion, *salsa* and *tortillas*
Favorite of local *campesinos* (country people)—check out salt shakers

Cold drinks (try an apple flavored *refresco*)
Now eat upstairs—large covered terrace since Mar'01
Take-out orders downstairs

☾ 29. Tortitlán —
Ancha de San Antonio #75
Tel: 152-8931
Hrs: Mon-Sat 9am-9pm, Sunday 10am-6:30pm
Tortas, jugos, licuados and refrescos
Highly recommend a *torta con pollo*–inexpensive
Busy place–eat at counter or take out–also will deliver
Now has sitting area with tables
Opened in 1985, moved to nearby expanded location April'00
Also: Juárez #17 (alongside San Francisco church), Tel: 152-3376

30. Restaurant El Infierno "Doña Anita"
Mesones #23 (across from Calle Juárez)
Tel: 152-2355
Hrs: Daily 8am-10pm
Plain basic restaurant in busy part of town
Favorite of local Mexicans and budget travelers
Chicken seems to be the specialty of the house
Try a *torta con pollo* (chicken sandwich) or *consomme de pollo*
Waiter: Gerardo López (bilingual) will take good care of you
Small bar offers drinks

31. El Caribe
Juárez #23 (a larger restaurant is located at Canal #85)
Tel: 152-0893
Hrs: Daily 9am-8pm
Upstairs—very basic small restaurant with unusual *bóveda* ceiling
Seafood specials (fish and shrimp)—also *sopas* and *filetes*

32. Bocato
Deli-Expresso Restaurant
Zacateros #34-A
Tel: 152-0374
Hrs: Mon-Sat 10am-6:30pm, closed Sunday
Owner: Marco Antonio Gutiérrez (also makes large San Miguel maps)
Small restaurant with stools
Offers a large variety of cold drinks and coffees
Also breakfast, soups, sandwiches and *tacos*
Opened 1997

Evening Meal Out On The Town:

33. Casa Blanca/Gombos
Restaurant/Bar
Hidalgo #34 (near Insurgentes)
Tel: 154-6070
Hrs: Daily 1-10pm, closed Monday
Credit cards: Master and Visa
International cuisine—lunch and dinner
Owners: Fernando and Pablo Jiménez and their ten brothers
Excellent food, must try one of artistically presented desserts
Combined menus from Casa Blanca and Gombos
Relocated March'03
Also owns **Gombos** (name means one who sells buttons in Hungarian)
Col. Guadalupe
Tata Nacho #2 (corner of Canción India)
Tel: 152-8121
Hrs: Daily 1-10pm, closed Thursday
Credit cards: None
Small out of the way place—must get there by car or taxi—worth the trip
Some say the best pizza in town!
Also salad, delicious crêpes and an expanded menu—nice
    presentation of food
Beer and soft drinks (if you want wine they will go out and buy at
    a nearby *tienda*)—wine served in "Murphy" glasses
Very clean restaurant (check out kitchen and bathroom)
Rafael (one of the ten brothers) is the attentive waiter
Take out or home delivery available

34. Romano's
Italian Restaurant/Bar
Hernández Macías #93 (between Pila Seca and Umarán)
Look for the bubbles in the air out front
Tel: 152-7454
Hrs: Tues-Sat 5-11pm, closed Sunday and Monday
Credit Cards: None
Owner: Dick Weber—40 years restaurant experience
    Owned chain of Italian restaurants in 5 southern states
A taste of "little Italy" in the sauces and pastas
Open wood-burning pizza oven
Eat downstairs, on the rooftop (rez suggested) or in a new expanded
    outdoor patio in the back with a fireplace and bar
Small bar at entrance is welcoming

Attentive and friendly wait staff
The right place to go if you are hungry!
Live music on weekends
Opened June'02

35. Hecho en México
Restaurant/Bar
Ancha de San Antonio #8 (next to the Instituto)
Tel: 154-6383
Hrs: Daily 12 noon-10pm
Credit cards: Amex, Master and Visa
Proprietor: Eric Nemer—from Alabama
Two patios with cactus garden and water fountain—retractable roof
    Indoor dining as well (with fireplace)
Good selection of starters, sandwiches, salads, pasta, seafood,
    steak and chicken—try the *camote* (sweet potato) plus iced tea
Don't overlook the brownie dessert topped with ice cream (ask for extra spoons)
Nice presentation, generous portions—consistantly good!
Reasonable prices
Separate bar area
Bilingual wait staff always makes you feel like regulars
Opened Jan'02

36. Antigua Trattoria Italiana
Codo #9 (flat-iron building) and Zacateros
Tel: 152-3790
Hrs: Daily 12 noon-11pm, closed Wednesday
Credit cards: Amex, Master and Visa
Owner: Luciano Monterisi (from Tuscany region of Italy)
Ambiance is extremely pleasant—nice warm feeling
Authentic Italian food–ask for daily specials
Pasta, lasagna, pizza, fish, salads and a good selection of wine
Freshly made pasta and local grown salad fixings
Reservations suggested on weekends
Some street parking available
Opened Jan'91, new ownership Sept'03

> **Ristorante da Andrea,** Dr. Mora, km 2.5, Tel: 120-3481
>   Open Thursday-Sunday

37. Finnegans Pub/Restaurant
Formerly Amigos Restaurant
Codo #7 (also Zacateros #52)

Tel: 044-415-100-3525 (cell)
E-mail: earthpeople7@hotmail.com
Hrs: Daily 12 noon-12pm, weekends stay open later, closed Tues
Credit cards: None
Owners: Patrick Smith (Irish) and wife Alejandra
Outdoor courtyard under the shade of a large 100 year old
    jacaranda tree—gas heaters in the winter + a new roof cover
Also indoor casual dining in the bar area
Lunch and dinner—new menu offering wide variety of tasty Irish food
Must try the freshly baked desserts
Full bar—live music on weekends-Irish singing on Friday nights
Try "water of life", Guinness from Dublin
Reasonable prices
Easy parking
Opened Sept'03, reopened with new name June'04

38. El Campanario (named for the bell tower across the street)
Canal #34
Tel: 152-0775   Fax: 152-4983
Wcb page: http://unisono.net.mx/campanario
Hrs: Daily 1-11pm, closed Thursdays
Credit cards: Amex, Master and Visa
Elegant dining experience—intcrnational cuisine
11th International Diamond Star Award for Quality
Combination of great food, atmosphere and service
Separate bar area off dining area and on the roof-top
Now has air conditioning for your comfort
Guitar music in the evening on weekends

39. Harry's New Orleans Café
Formerly La Vendimia and Harry Bissetts
Hidalgo #12 (½ block from Jardín)
Tel: 152-2645   Fax: 152-3642
E-mail: harrysnoc@hotmail.com
Web page: www.harrybissetts-mexico.com
Hrs: Daily 12 noon-12 midnight
    Sat and Sun (11am-3pm)—New Orleans jazz brunch
    Steak and eggs, crab cakes, eggs benedict and shrimp and grits
Credit cards: Amex, Master and Visa
Owner: Bob Thieman from Cincinnati, Ohio
Blend of creole, cajun and Mexican cooking
Variety of fresh fish and shellfish prepared Lousiana style

Also US certified Angus beef
Enjoy the large patio bar
    Happy Hour: Mon-Fri 5-7pm
    Like a scene from "Casablanca"—nice mix of gringos & Mexicans
Rooms with a fireplace are very inviting in the winter time
    Back dining room has both a fireplace and a wooden floor
Note the shoe shine stand at the entrance (daily 1-8pm)
Check-out **Harry's Market** deli next door
New ownership and name change Dec'03
Also opened downtown Querétaro restaurant Dec'04

40. El Bacha de San Miguel

Piedras Chinas #21 (just off Salida a Querétaro by the Mirador)
Tel: 152-8110 and 152-4339
E-mail: elhr@prodigy.net.mx
Hrs: Daily 1-11pm, Sunday 1-6pm, closed Tuesday
    Happy hour: Daily 5-7pm (except Sunday)
Owner: Dr. Edgar Hoppe, wife Xochitl & daughter Heidy (bilingual)
Welcoming, warm ambiance decorated with Arabian art
    Middle Eastern music
    Panoramic city views from inside or from large outdoor patio
Credit cards: Master and Visa
Authentic Arabian specialties—chef from Syria
Tasty buffet (Wed-Sun)—cold appetizers, hot dishes including
    soup, pita bread, rich desserts and Arabian coffee
Also *a la carte* menu offering a wide variety of dishes
Plus hard to find wines and after dinner *liqueurs*—try *crema con tequila*
Special live show with dinner one a month
Also Lebanese restaurant in Querétaro since late 1970's
Special events, catering, take-out
Opened July'04

41. Tío Lucas

Restaurant/Bar
Mesones #103 (near corner H. Macías)–across from Teatro Angela Peralta
Tel/Fax: 152-4996
E-mail: tiolucassma@hotmail.com
Hrs: Daily 12 noon-12 midnight (serving lunch and dinner)
    Happy hour: Mon-Fri 6-8pm
Credit cards: Amex, Master and Visa
Max Altamirano is the friendly bilingual owner
Traditional menu—excellent beef and chicken dishes
Charming covered outdoor patio or indoor dining

Live music in evening—some of the best jazz in town (after 9pm)
Completely renovated May'04 with larger dining area
Popular with locals and tourists

42. Bugambilia

Hidalgo #42 (2½ blocks from the Jardín)
Tel: 152-0127   Fax: 154-5180
E-mail: bugam45@prodigy.net.mx
Web page: www.infosma.com/bugambilia
Hrs: Daily 12 noon-11pm
Credit cards: Master and Visa
Owner: Sra. Mercedes Arteaga
60th anniversary year (2005)
Authentic Mexican cuisine – delicious *sopa azteca, chiles en nogada*
     and *tres leches* cake
Relaxing covered courtyard in colonial elegance
Fireplace in dining room used in winter
Very good service
Evening guitar player from 7:30pm

Insider's Tip: Chiles en Nogada are a traditional favorite with the ingredients representing the red, white and green of the Mexican Flag. A seeded poblano chile (not spicy hot) is stuffed, usually with ground beef, nuts, fruit and spices and sauced with a sour cream and decorated with red pomegranate seeds and parsley. Normally served as a cold dish.

43. Nirvana

Restaurant Fusion
Hernández Macías #56-A (across from Sautto Hotel)
Tel: 150-0067   044-415-103-0188 (cell)
E-mail: abueloesc@hotmail.com
Hrs: Daily 1-10pm, closed Tuesday
Credit cards: Master and Visa
Owner: Juan Carlos Escalante Martínez (bilingual)
     Trained at Culinary Institute of America (CIA)—Hyde Park, NY
     Chef at Ibero Americana in Mexico City
Soho-style restaurant—nice decor and place settings
Serving lunch and dinner with tempting desserts
Menu board changes periodically
Suggest trying crab croquettes, fresh fish and Thai soup
Full bar serving mixed drinks, wine and beer
Opened July'01

44. Azafrán
Lounge & Design
Hernández Macías #97 (between Pila Seca and Umarán)
Tel: 152-7482   Tel/Fax: 152-7507
Hrs: Daily 11am-11pm, closed Wednesday
Credit Cards: Amex, Master and Visa
Owner/Chef: Luís Maubecín
Mediterranean fusion cooking
Dining room has a bright and classy look
        Also covered courtyard with attractive bar
All dishes low fat—desserts are sugar-free
Fresh fruits and vegetables
Recommend evening reservations
Note **El Otro Camino** showroom with contemporary home furnishings
Opened Mar'03

45. La Capilla (the chapel)
Cuna de Allende #10 (alongside La Parroquia)
Tel: 152-0698 and 154-4944   Fax: 154-4945
E-mail: capilla@unisono.net.mx
Web page: www.la-capilla.com
Hrs: Daily 1-11pm (or later), closed Tuesday
        Sunday brunch 11:30am-1:30pm (with jazz group)
        Happy Hour: Mon, Wed & Thurs 7:30-8:30pm
              With *estudiantinas* (singers)—on ground floor
Credit cards: Amex, Master and Visa
Maitre D': José Dolores Gutiérrez (bilingual & very personable)
Now run by family members since the untimely death of the
        founder, Cassandra Webb, in May'01
Reservations recommended—no children under 12 upstairs (evenings)
One of the most beautiful settings in all San Miguel - movie set ambiance
        Upstairs terrrace with indoor dining and large bar
International and Mexican cuisine
A pianist plays during lunch and dinner
        Estudiantinas sing on weekends (8-9pm)
Extraordinary location to watch the September fireworks or usher
        in the New Year

Downstairs **El Atrio de la Capilla**
        Deli plus candy (chocolates), cookies, jams and gift baskets
        Opened July'99

158

46. Casa de Sierra Nevada Restaurant

Casa de Sierra Nevada
Hospicio #35
Tel: 152-7040
Hrs: Breakfast 8-11am, Lunch 1-4pm (closed Tues) Dinner 8-11pm
Credit cards: Amex, Master and Visa
Haute cuisine
Indoor and outdoor dining
Admit only guests 16 years old and above
Good wine selection
Also **Casa de Sierra Nevada en el Parque** (El Chorro area)

Breakfast	8-11am
Lunch	1– 5pm
Dinner	7-10pm

       Menu: Mexican specialities
       Music (Thur-Sun) 2-4pm and 8-10pm

47. Casa Payo

Argentinian Grill
Zacateros #26 (corner of Pila Seca)
Tel: 152-7277
Hrs: Daily 1-11pm
Credit cards: Amex, Master and Visa
Owner: Lic. John Paul Lane (bilingual)
Beautiful indoor/outdoor dining areas—great decor!
Specialty is Argentine-style steak cooked on a charcoal grill
Try home-made grilled Argentine sausage or *empanadas* with
     chimichurri (parsley, garlic, vinegar, oil, sauce)
Share a grilled meat combo served on a hibachi
Have a drink in a sitting area around a tree and under the stars
Opened Dec'96
Manolo's Sports Bar (opened Sept'03)—to the left at entrance

48. L'Invito (the invitation)

Restaurant/bar
Ancha de San Antonio #20 (inside Instituto Allende-back
    courtyard next to art gallery)
Tel: 152-7333
E-mail: sber@unisono.net.mx
Hrs: Daily 1-11pm
     Happy Hour (2x1): Daily 7-9pm
     Mon-Fri 4-7pm, 50% off food and drinks
     20% Instituto student discount

Credit cards: Amex, Master and Visa
Italian owner: Silvia Bernardini (trilingual)
    Trained professional cooks in Italy and France before coming to México
Indoor with large bar and wood burning fireplace
Outdoor under *portal* with dramatic view of the Parroquia
Five small, very attractive dining areas
All home-made Italian food, including bread and ice cream
    Many home-made pasta choices and salads
    Also, some Mexican favorites
Takeout–can deliver for extra charge
Opened Dec'97, relocated Dec'03

49. Villa Jacaranda Restaurant
Aldama,#53 (near Parque Juárez)
Tel: 152-1015 or 152-0811
Hrs: Daily 7:30am-10:30pm
    Sunday champagne brunch 11:30am-2:30pm
Credit cards: Amex, Master and Visa
Proprietors: Don and Gloria Fenton
Distinguished Restaurants of North America (DiRoNa) Award (since'93)
Excellent food—try the homemade tomato soup, fish & chips
    wrapped in newsprint and the key lime pie!
Comfortable, quiet and relaxing setting
Inside and outdoor dining
Popular with locals

50. Bella Italia
Hernández Macías #59 (Hotel Sautto)
Tel: 152-4989
Hrs: Daily 1:30-11pm
Credit cards: Master and Visa
Paolo is the Italian proprietor
Delicious Italian food–reasonable prices
Indoor or large outdoor garden patio—dine under the stars
Fireplace used in winter months
Sometime live music in the evenings

51. La Grotta
Cuadrante #5 (around the corner of Cuna de Allende)
Tel: 152-4119
Hrs: Daily 1-11pm
Credit cards: Master and Visa
Owned by Esther and Daniel Ramírez

Small intimate, cozy setting—step down from street
Try spinach lasagne, soup and the special home-made desserts
Some of the best pizza anywhere (try blue cheese with pepperoni and olives)
A second-floor addition opened in Feb'98 doubling the number of
   tables. It has a high ceiling, French windows and fireplace.
   Only dumbwaiter in town!
Also beer, wine and mixed drinks are available

52. El Rinconcito
Refugio #7 North (residential area in Col. San Antonio)
Tel: 154-4809
Hrs: Daily 1-9pm, Sun 1-7pm, closed Tuesday
Owners are Mercedes and Michael (bilingual)
Small restaurant in front of their home
Salads, *tacos, burritos,* hamburgers plus chicken and steak dishes
Recommend shrimp and spinach *quesadillas*
   Try the house dressing
Soft drinks, beer, wine, mixed drinks, coffee, tea and desserts
Reasonable prices
Opened Feb'99

53. Bouquet
Cuadrante #34-A (west of Jesús and near H. Macías)
Tel: 154-7881
Hrs: Mon-Sat 12 noon-4pm and 6-9pm, closed Sunday
Credit cards: None
Owner/Chef: Heriberto Ramírez–trained in México City
Menu–crêpes and pastas (spaghetti and fettuccine)
   Choose own ingredients for pasta dishes
Small intimate restaurant–four tables only
Beer and wine plus soft drinks and coffee & tea
Opened Aug'99

54. El Ten Ten Pie
Cuna de Allende #21 (corner of Cuadrante)
Tel: 152-7189
Hrs: Daily 9am-12 midnight
Credit cards: None
Restaurant's name translates, "A little something to keep you on your feet"
Juan, the owner, says if you don't like the food, don't pay!
Ask to see if the *comida corrida* is still available in the evening
Tacos a specialty of the house, home-made *tortillas*

Nice background music, popular gathering place for locals
    Fun place to play cards or board games
Art work in restaurant is for sale
Restaurant has a new upscale look (Oct'99) including a bar
Reasonable prices

55. Pueblo Viejo Restaurant/Bar
Umarán #6 (just off the Jardín)
Tel: 152-4977
Hrs: Daily 8am-11pm
Credit cards: Amex, Master and Visa
Old México ambience with separate bar area—should see!
Good selection of Mexican food
Full breakfast, lunch and dinner
Home-made *tortillas* (check out *tortilla* kitchen)
Live music daily at lunch 3:30-4:30pm and at dinner 8:30-10pm
    Jazz (Fri and Sat) 10pm-12 midnight
Opened Dec'95

56. Rincón Español
Correo #29 (corner of Recreo and across from El Pegaso)
Tel: 152-2984
Hrs: Daily 1-11pm, closed Thursday
Credit cards: Master and Visa
Spanish food (*paella* is a speciality)
Flamenco dancer (full menu and 45 minute show)
    Sunday 3pm and Monday 8:45pm
    Make reservation—usually no cover charge
Live music Tues-Sat after 8pm
Note reproductions of famous Spanish painters (Picasso, Dali and
    Miro) hanging on the wall
Sushi Bar
    Entrance around the corner, Recreo #1
    Hrs: Daily 1-10pm, closed Thursday
    Opened Aug'99, relocated Dec'03

57. El Harem
Arabian Restaurant
Murillo #7 (corner of Correo)
Tel: 152-1504
Hrs: Daily 12 noon-9pm, closed Tuesday
Family run restaurant
Small restaurant with a few tables on first and second floor

Authentic Lebanese food
  Hummus, taboule, lentil soup, stuffed grape leaves, lamb
    brochette and pita bread
Since 1985, reopened in new location Feb'00

C 58. La Alborada (Dawn)
Sollano #11 (near Correo and next to bus ticket office)
Tel: 154-7728
Hrs: Mon-Thurs 6pm-2am, Fri/Sat 6pm-4am, closed Sunday
Small, local restaurant–María Angeles (Sanny) is the owner
Some of the best *pozole* (chicken, beef, or pork) around
  Also *flautas, quesadillas* and *tostadas*
Cold drinks, bottled water, beer or coffee
A popular late-night hangout
Opened May'00

Pizza

Home delivery (free)
1. **Pronto Pizza**, Héroes #1, Tel: 152-4066
2. **Buona Pizza**, 20 de Enero #38, Tel: 152-4411
3. **Domino's Pizza**, A. de San Antonio #17, Tel: 154-5300
Take-out:
1. **La Grotta**, Cuadrante #5, Tel: 152-4119
2. **Gombos**, Tata Nacho #2 (Col. Guadalupe), Tel. 152-8121
3. **Mama Mía**, Umarán #8, Tel: 152-2063
4. **Juanita's Pizza**, Orizaba #19, Tel: 154-5148
5. **Pronto Pizza**, Reloj #33-A, Tel: None

Insider's Tip: Ten inexpensive eateries that give good value and tasty food:

(58) La Alborada	(27) Restaurant Lila
(28) Apolo XI	(52) El Rinconcito
(12) La Enchilada	(54) El Ten Ten Pie
(30) El Infierno	(26) Torta Mundo
(—) Juanita's Pizza	(29) Tortitlán

Numbered as listed in Restaurant Section

Insider's Tip: Tipping—give till it hurts! The local foreigners use a minimum guideline of 10% in restaurants. Should service and/or food quality warrant, US norms of 15% at lunch and 20% at dinner could be followed.

Some of the Insider's Favorites:

28. Apolo XI	_____	*carnitas*
50. Bella Italia	_____	goat cheese salad
42. Bugambilia	_____	*chiles en nogada*
Café Jardín	_____	a cup of coffee
1. Café Parroquia	_____	*pan francés* and *conejo*
38. Campanario	_____	Archie soup
46. Casa Sierra Nevada en el Parque	_____	*margaritas*
47. Casa Payo	_____	*elote* (corn) *empanadas*
16. El Correo	_____	*sopas de la casa*
12. La Enchilada	_____	chicken *enchiladas*
33. Gombos	_____	crêpes – dinner and dessert
51. La Grotta	_____	blue cheese pizza
39. Harry's New Orleans Café	___	popcorn shrimp
35. Hecho en México	_____	sweet potato (*camote*)
49. Jacaranda	_____	fresh tomato soup
43. Nirvana	_____	Thai soup
17. Olé Olé	_____	*fajitas*
5. Pegaso	_____	chicken caesar salad
4. Posada Carmina	_____	*alcachofa* and *flan*
41. Tío Lucas	_____	caramel crepes
29. Tortitlán	_____	*torta con pollo*
9. Villa Santa Monica	_____	*gazpacho*

Numbered as listed in Restaurant Section

Some useful Spanish terms to use when visiting the local eating establishments:

breakfast	*el desayuno*	with/without	*con/sin*
lunch	*la comida*	drinks	*las bebidas*
supper	*la cena*	fruits	*las frutas*
I'm hungry	*Tengo hambre*	vegetables	*las verduras*
I'm thirsty	*Tengo sed*	meat	*la carne*
for me	*para mi*	water	*el agua*
good	*bueno*	pure water	*agua purificada*
very tasty	*muy sabroso*	milk	*la leche*
bad	*malo*	ice	*el hielo*
spoon	*la cuchara*	ice tea	*té helado*
knife	*el cuchillo*	cheers!	*¡salud!*
fork	*el tenedor*		

Would you like anything else?	*¿Algo más?*
Nothing more, thanks	*Nada más, gracias*
Would you like a drink?	*¿Algo de tomar?*
Have a good meal	*Buen provecho*
The bill, please	*La cuenta, por favor*

164

Rest Places

It's time to slow down as you are now in México! The warm, sunny weather or the 6,000 + foot altitude may be enough reason to take it easy. San Miguel offers many resting spots, so take advantage of them.

1. The Jardín

The main square in the heart of town, where many of the expatriates start their day. It might be to pick up a newspaper, pass through enroute to the Post Office, meet friends, or just sit to admire the scenery while basking in the sun. Dark green iron benches can be found on all sides of the square, shaded by perfectly groomed laurel trees. Most of the town's attractions are within walking distance. Nighttime brings out the young local people who fill the square. Sometimes on the weekends there is live music at the gazebo while *mariachis* wait under surrounding portals to be hired.

2. Jardín de San Francisco

Just one block east from the Principal Plaza at Calle San Francisco and Juárez. The Church of San Francisco is located there. A small park with benches to relax on, a fountain and a stone statue of Columbus (replaced Oct'96) on the corner. A nice alternative to the Jardín.

3. Parque Juárez

A lovely, spacious shady park located on the southern end of Recreo, Sollano or Aldama and about three blocks from the Jardín. It has walking paths, fountains, flowers, large towering trees, benches, basketball courts, playground equipment and a picnic area. White egrets can be seen flying overhead.

4. Allende Plaza (Civic Plaza) (Plaza de la Soledad)

Located near the old Mercado at the intersection of Mesones and Colegio. A large equestrian statue of General Allende can be found there. Also numerous benches for sitting but little shade can be found. Many civic functions are held here.

5. Bellas Artes

Located on Hernández Macías near Canal. A beautiful 18th century former convent has a large interior courtyard. Well-groomed gardens and a fountain make this a pleasant, cool retreat. An added attraction is the hanging art work and a patio coffee shop.

6. Instituto Allende

Located south of town on Ancha de San Antonio #20. A former *hacienda* that has a beautiful flower-filled outdoor courtyard with tables, chairs and some benches. Art and Spanish students can be seen during breaks from class.

7. Parque Guadiana
Located in Col Guadiana (south of the Instituto) between Potranca and Guadiana near Ancha de San Antonio. A small, well-kept park with a fountain and benches in a quiet residential neighborhood.

Not to be overlooked are the outdoor garden courtyards that are part of some of the better known restaurants in town as well as the Biblioteca on Insurgentes.

Schools

1. José Vasconcelos
Barrio del Obraje (north of Calzada de la Luz)
Tel/Fax: 152-1869
E-mail: escjosev@prodigy.net.mx
Director: Lic. Jesús Ledezma (bilingual)
Bilingual school (age 3 - grade 9)
Opened 1974

2. Colegio Atabal
Guarde Agujas #8—Los Frailes
Tel: 155-8248
E-mail: colegioatabal@email.com
Web page: www.geocities.com/colegioatabal
Principal: Guadalupe Méndez (bilingual)
Bilingual grades 1-6
Hrs: Mon-Fri 8am-2:30pm
Opened 1997

3. Naciones Unidas School (United Nations)
Fuentes #33 (Atascadero)
Tel: 152-5179 (school)   154-5086 (home)
Founder/teacher: María Teresa Burillo
Bilingual primary grades 1-7
Opened 1999

4. Colegio Los Charcos
Road to Dolores Hidalgo, 5 km (near Taboada turn off)
Tel: 154-7869   044-415-153-7988 (cell)
E-mail: loscharcos@hotmail.com

Web page: www.unisono.net.mx/loscharcos
Director: Lisa Wright
Waldorf inspired school
Bicultural/bilingual (pre-K thru grade 6)
Bus service available
Opened 1996

5. Instituto Bilingüe Juan Gutenberg
Off road to Dolores Hidalgo (approx 15 min from San Miguel)
Tel: 185-2000 or 185-2001
Web page: www.schooloftomorrow.com
Private & accredited school with a Christian curriculum
Grades K-12
Directors: Dan and Christine Conlon
Offers own bus service for students
Established 1982

6. Miss Victoria Robbins
School location changes
Tel: 152-0287 (home)
Home school tutoring service (English only)
Upper elementary - high school
Since 1989

Sewing

Seamstress:

1. Carmen
Aldama #11 (relocated August'98)
Sewing including mending and alterations
Very reasonable prices
Spanish speaking only

2. Casi Bowman
Los Leones
Zacateros #8 (near Umarán)
Tel: None
Hrs: Mon-Sat 10am-2pm and 4-7pm, Sunday 1-4pm
Casi is bilingual and has over 40 years' experience sewing to
    order with store material
Some mending and alterations
A few ready-made clothes plus odds and ends
Moved after many years from Calle Canal April'97

Shippers

1. La Unión
Zacateros #26-A (corner of Pila Seca)
Tel/Fax: 152-5694
E-mail: launion7@prodigy.net.mx
Hrs: Mon-Fri 10am-2pm and 4-8pm, Sat 9am-5pm
Owners: Jorge and María Eugenia Peña (both bilingual)
Offer packing supplies and packing service plus shipping
Also has warehouse for storage
Recommend that you check it out!

2. DHL International
Correo #21 (near Post Office)
Tel: 152-3564
Hrs: Mon-Fri 9am-2pm and 4-6pm, closed Sat and Sun
Manager: María Guadalupe Ortíz (bilingual)

3. Multipack
Federal Express outlet
Salida a Querétaro #117-A
Tel: 154-9271   Tel/Fax: 154-9272
Hrs: Mon-Fri 9am-2pm and 4-7pm, Sat 9am-2pm, closed Sunday
Manager: Ing. Oscar Horta González
Messages and packages
Will pick-up
Relocated Jan'03

4. Estafeta
Blvd. de la Conspiración #1000 (just past Gigante traffic circle)
Tel/Fax: 152-0700
Web page: www.estafeta.com.mx
Hrs: Mon-Fri 10am-2pm and 4-8pm, Sat 10am-2pm, closed Sun
Manager: David Cruz Salas
International and Mexican shipping
Shipments in USA via RPS
Ample parking
Will pick up
Relocated Oct'04

5. Redpack
Plaza Real del Conde (Gigante)—past twin theaters on ground floor
Tel: 154-7500 and 154-7400

Hrs: Mon-Fri 9am-2pm and 4-7pm, Sat 9am-2pm, closed Sun
National and international shipping
Since 1999

6. Maraye, S.C.
Calzada de la Luz #82 (near Reloj)
Tel: 152-6199
Hrs: Mon-Fri 9am-6pm, Sat 10am-2pm, closed Sunday
Materials for packing only
Reasonable prices
Opened January'97

Also Packing materials:
    Cajas y Empaque, Quebrada #87, Tel: 152-1254 (*casa*)

Also check Communication Centers:
    Pack 'N'Mail, Canal #42, Tel: 152-5461
    Solutions (EXPORTA), Recreo #11, Tel: 152-6152
    Border Crossing, Mesones #57 (Int), Tel: 152-2497
In addition, the **Post Office** and the next door **Mex Post** provide
shipping services (no packing) from their convenient downtown locations.

Shoe Stores/Shoe Repair

Shoe Stores:

1. Zapatería Martha
Reloj #27 (near Mesones)
Tel: 154-4702(*casa* and *taller)*
Hrs: Mon-Sat 10am-8pm, Sunday 10am-4pm
All kinds of women's shoes, including the popular official San
    Miguel sandal–aka *cocktail combat boot*–all colors
Make an effort to purchase sandals from the source as Martha's
    husband is the sole manufacturer of these shoes in San Miguel
All hand made in México
Reasonable prices
Also repair or replace elastic on sandals
In business since 1977
Other outlets: Reloj #91, Mesones #48 and Hidalgo #48

2. Vilar
Sollano #6 (also Recreo #5)
Tel: 152-3130
Hrs: Mon-Sat 10am-2pm and 4-8pm, Sun 10:30am-2:30pm
Owner: Marisa Vilar
High-class leather goods store—made-in-México shoes
Popular ladies' styles for the under 35 crowd–also men's shoes
Good stock of sizes 8 and above
Also leather handbags, jackets, vests and accessories

Women's Shoe Sizes

US	5	6	7	8	9	10	11
MEX	2	3	4	5	6	7	8

Shoe Repair:

1. El Anuj
Reparación de Calzado
Puente de Umarán #23-A (go toward the Civic Plaza and the
       Mercado. Near entrance to the market turn right on a short
       side street. This shop is back in the corner.)
Tel: 154-5924
Hrs: Mon-Sat 10am-8pm, closed Sunday
Owner: Guillermo Hernández (speaks English)
Fully equipped shop
Repairs all leather things such as jackets, belts, suitcases and
       purses, also will resole sneakers
Friendly service, nice family to do business with
Very good prices

2. Reparadora de Calzado
Casa Blanca
Callejón Blanco #29 (behind Sautto Hotel, a small street between
       Quebrada and San Antonio Abad)
Tel: None
Hrs: Mon-Sat 8:30am-7pm, closed Sunday, also closed for *comida*

3. Reparadora de Calzado
Reloj #108
Tel: 152-6488
Hrs: Mon-Sat 9am-2pm and 4-7:30pm, closed Sunday
All kinds of shoe repairs
More than 20 years' experience
Reasonable prices

Shopping

If you came to shop, you came to the right place as San Miguel won't disappoint you. Literally hundreds of shops! Just fan out in any direction from the Jardín and you can't go wrong. Make sure before it's over you hit the east/west streets of Mesones, Canal, San Francisco, Umarán, Correo and Cuadrante. North/south streets of Reloj, Hidalgo, Jesús, Hernández Macías, Zacateros and Ancha de San Antonio offer an equal opportunity. The town is known for its metal work — brass, bronze, tin and wrought-iron, for its textiles, glass products, *papier mâché*, pottery, art work and "wearable art." In general, stores are open daily from 9am-2pm and 4-7pm and half a day on Sunday. Remember, returning Americans have a US$400 duty-free allowance when entering the USA. Canadians have a C$500 duty-free allowance after being out of the country 7 days. So don't waste any more time; get out there, pound the pavements and spread the pesos around!

SHOPS FOR THE NEW MILLENNIUM:

In recent years, shops with styles and products new and unique in San Miguel have opened all over town. As the offerings in these shops tend to be very modern and different from many of the older established businesses it was decided to give them their own category. These shops are a must see, particularly for the return visitors to San Miguel who may think they have seen it all.

1. Caracol Collection
Cuadrante #30 (corner of Jesús)
Tel: 152-1617
E-mail: caracolmexico@hotmail.com
Hrs: Daily 12 noon-6pm, closed Tuesday
Credit cards: Master and Visa
Owner and collector Kathleen Mann has traveled most of the Republic to research and select high quality Mexican crafts. Caracol Collection is a broad and tasteful selection of decorative, functional objects in wood, copper, glass, ceramic, textile, palm and even feathers. Using her knowledge and discriminating eye, Kathleen presents crafts that may have generations or in some cases centuries of tradition yet are contemporary and functional. Highly recommend that you stop in to see the growing collection of fine and applied art. You will enjoy meeting and talking with the owner, who is very knowledgeable about her collection. Relocated to a larger space July'04

2. Clandestino
Zacateros #19 (near Umarán)
Tel/Fax: 152-1623
E-mail: clandestinosma@yahoo.com
Hrs: Daily 11am-7pm, Sun 11-3pm, closed Tuesday
Credit cards: Amex
Partners: Silvia Herrasti (Casa Rosada), Harris Donovan and
         Leslie Warnick (Delirio)
Three different businesses joined together in Sept'00 to create this
unusual store of eclectic, contemporary and funky furniture decor
and art. The unique compilation of items found in this store
make it difficult to describe in satisfactory terms. From small
unusual gift items, to large antique Mexican and Indian furniture,
this store is a fun, creative and interesting place to spend time
and pesos. Anyone interested in collecting Mexican *retablos*
and antique religious art will find this store a small treasure of
rare items of a quality not often found for sale.

3. Goldie
Designs & Concierge
Canal #9 (½ block from Jardín)
Tel: 154-7420
E-mail: goldiedesigns@hotmail.com
Hrs: Tues-Sat 11am-6pm (or by appointment)
Credit cards: Amex, Master and Visa
A wonderful and unique addition to San Miguel's shopping
experience. Owner and designer, Diane Goldie, has made this a
classic *boutique*, much like one would find in her home town of San
Francisco. As you enter, it is visually inviting. Many of the designs
of classic pants, jackets and blouses are hers exclusively. There are
many wonderful pieces of one-of-a-kind jewelry to choose from as
the owner has her own line. Diane will be happy to help you put
your own look together that will be suited for you and your lifestyle.
The striking artwork and home accent furnishings are also for sale
or by order. Sitting areas provide warmth and charm to relax and
chat while shopping.

4. Icpalli
Correo #43 (corner of Chiquitos)
Tel: 152-1236   Fax: 154-5483
E-mail: icpalli@cybermatsa.com.mx
Hrs: Mon-Fri 10am-6pm, Sat 10am-2pm, closed Sunday
Credit cards: Amex, Master and Visa

A move to a historic building in January 2004 continues Icpalli's reputation as one of San Miguel's leading businesses. Owner, Angélica Baca, a graduate of Guanajuato University School of Design, has sought out the best quality of *equipal* furniture and other home furnishings. You will find top of the line fabrics, window treatments, shades, blinds, light fixtures and lamps, sisal rugs and quality furniture. Angélica has an innovative design business that has a style and flair which captures the best of the past and renders it useful and beautiful in the present. This new relocated store is an exciting must-see for all who visit or live in San Miguel.

5. El Otro Camino ("the other way")
Hernández Macías #97
Tel: 152-2874   Tel/Fax:152-7507
E-mail: maubecin@prodigy.net.mx
Hrs: Daily 10am-2pm and 4-8pm, closed Wednesday
Credit cards: Amex, Master and Visa
Owner/Designer: Luís Maubecín
Aptly named The Other Way, this shop is in the forefront of modern design in San Miguel. Innovation and exceptional craftsmanship are the hallmarks of the items available in furniture, lighting and accent pieces. Pay particular attention to some of the very different uses for, and designs in, cast aluminum, often called pewter in San Miguel. Some of these items belong in your suitcases as you head home. The space has been reduced to one showroom to acommodate an equally classy restaurant called **Azafrán**.

6. Sazón
Correo #22—just past Pegaso restaurant
Tel: 154-7671
E-mail: srateresa@aol.com
Web page: www.sazonsanmiguel.com
Hrs: Mon-Sat 10am-6pm, Sunday 11am-3pm
Credit cards: Master and Visa
Owner: Teresa Jones from Minneapolis and Tucson
A great store in a new (Nov'03) exciting building. There is nothing else like this in México. You can find just about anything you need to be a great host or hostess. From the exclusively designed Mexican ceramics and handblown glass, to Provence-style linens, to a set of professional Henkel knives. The cooking school, with top of the line equipment, offers unique classes taught by local and visiting

chefs and entertaining experts. There is a market tour most Saturdays. You will be taken on a culinary adventure at San Miguel's colorful Mercado, finding and buying the best that the market has to offer. Check out their website or stop by the store for their quarterly newsletter, listing the schedule of events and classes.

Also: **EXIM,** Hidalgo #6-A, Tel. 154-5282
      Cerroblanco, Canal #21, Tel: 154-4888
      Talisman Too, San Francisco #7, Tel: 152-0438

The following are the "shopping" sub-headings:

Bath Products	Linen
Brass and Metal	Market of Artesanías
Ceramics/Tile	Masks
Crafts and Things	Miscellaneous
Furniture	Paper Products
Glass	Papier Mâché
Imports	Quilts
Jewelry	Textiles
Leather	Woven Baskets
Lighting/Candles	

Bath Products:

1. La Victoriana
Hernández Macías #72 (across from Bellas Artes)
Tel: 152-6903   Fax: 152-7003
    Toll free (in country) Tel: 01 (800) 465-8000 (orders only)
Hrs: Mon-Sat 9am-8pm, Sunday 11am-3pm
E-mail: nebula@unisono.net.mx
Owners: Helio and Alison Bastien
They make by hand all the medicines (homeopathic and botanical)
    and body products as well as children's clothing
Also jewelry, cards, linens, lace, bath products and more
A very special store!

Brass and Metal:

1. Productos Herco
Casa Cohen (note the façade of the building)
Reloj #12
Tel: 152-1434 and 152-0666

Hrs: Mon-Sat 9am-2pm and 4-7pm, closed Sunday
Bathroom and kitchen accessories
Brass, bronze, iron and aluminum bowls, basins, house numbers,
    doorknockers, drawer pulls, plus wrought-iron furniture
Family business since 1927, David and Elvira Cohen are bilingual

---
Also: **Counter Cultures**
    Recreo #11 (next to Solutions)
    Tel: 152-6409
    Copper, stone and resine sinks + custom faucets & tiles

---

2. Gaby
Artesanías y Novedades
Zacateros #33
Tel: 152-2797
Hrs: Daily 11am-3pm and 5-8:30pm, Sun 11am-3:30pm
Family business: Daughter Anna Luisa speaks English
    Dependable people to do business with
All kinds of brass and metal lighting fixtures, mirrors, frames and more
Made in San Miguel–will also custom make
Opened 1987

3. Arte en Cobre
Zacateros #55 (next to David's)
Tel: None
Hrs: Mon-Sat 10am-2pm and 4:30-7:30pm, closed Sunday
Owner: Verónica Pérez
Small shop full of copperware
    Everything comes from Santa Clara del Cobre in Michoacán
Opened June'99

4. Fun Art
Zacateros #26 (near Pila Seca)
Tel: 152-5770
Hrs: Daily 10am-2pm and 4-8pm, Thurs and Sun 10am-2pm
Owner: Salvador Ramírez
Large selection of gift items made of Mexican pewter (aluminum)
Factory: Lib. Celaya a Dolores #5 (near *glorieta*)-Tel: 154-5030
Since 1991

Also check out:
    Casa de los Milagros, Sal. a Celaya #24, Tel: 152-2224
    Herrería Rosas, Ancha de San Antonio #53, Tel: 152-3256
    Hierro a Mano, Reloj #106, Tel: 152-5190

Ceramic Tile:

1. Talavera la Hidalguense
Calle Antonio Plaza #21-A, Col. Guadalupe
> Go to end of Hidalgo, turn left, then first right on Calle Julián
> Carrillo for one block, then turn left and go two blocks

Tel: 152-3546
Hrs: Mon-Sat 10am-7pm, Sun 10am-5pm
Good selection of all kinds of *talavera*
Made in Dolores Hidalgo
Opened in 1993, relocated May'03

2. México Lindo
Arte en Cerámica
Mesones #85 (corner of Hidalgo)
Tel: 152-0730
Hrs: Daily 10:30am-2pm and 4-8:30pm, closed Tuesday
Tiles and ceramics are made in Dolores Hidalgo
Changed name/ownership Aug'97

3. Zarco Artesanías
Zamora Ríos #10-B (Col. Allende)
Tel: 154-6851
Hrs: Daily 9am-9pm
Owner Zarco speaks Spanish, English and French
Ceramic tiles, *papier mâché* and good collection of locally made
> tin products

Ask to see tin Christmas ornaments, miniature nativity scene figures
Reasonable prices
Also a hair salon
Ask about free transportation by owner
Moved April'01

Also try: **EVOS/Artesana,** H. Macías #55, Tel: 152-0813
Tepalcatt, Canal #21 (Int). Tel: None
Boutique Isis, Zacateros #29, Tel: 152-3139

If time permits, visit a master potter, **Estéban Valdéz**, at his home workshop just 15 minutes outside town. It is an opportunity to buy inexpensive clay bowls not found anywhere else. For more details, check the ***Things to Do*** chapter in this book.

> **Note:** Serious ceramic shoppers should plan a trip to Dolores
> Hidalgo and Guanajuato (see green pages in back of book)

Crafts and Things:

1. Zócalo
Hernández Macías #110 (near bend in street)
Tel: 152-0663
E-mail: info@zocalotx.com
Web page: www.zocalotx.com
Hrs: Mon-Sat 10am-2pm and 4-7pm, Sunday 10am-2pm
Owners: Rick and Debra Hall
Folk art and furnishings
Tables, chandeliers, benches, pottery, copper, candles, masks and more
Also a store in Houston, TX
Opened July'01

2. Galería Mariposa ("butterfly")
Recreo #38 (near Hospicio)
Tel: 152-4488
Hrs: Mon-Sat 10am-7pm, Sunday by appointment
Owners: Ilse Sheffield and Regina Thomas von Bohlen
Mexican folk art
Select, one-of-a-kind pieces
Work by recognized Mexican folk artists and craftsmen from
        Oaxaca, Michoacán, Colima and many other regions
Some local paintings
Opened July'02

3. Elementos
Recreo #36 (near Hospicio)
Tel: 044-415-103-5095 (cell)
E-mail: jenniferrgill@yahoo.com
Hrs: Mon-Sat 10am-2pm and 4-6pm, closed Sunday
Owner: Jennifer Gill
Sells folk and religious things, some from Tibet
Home decorations
Also antiques and iron furniture
Opened Jan'03

4. Origen
Zacateros#12
Tel: 154-8387

E-mail: origen_sma@yahoo.com.mx
Hrs: Daily 10am-8pm, closed Tuesday
Owner: Ornella Ridone from Italy
Three large rooms with decorative crafts
Furniture and creatures of the wild made from *chuspata* (a reed
    that grows in lakes in Michoacán)
Wooden frames and candle holders (copies of colonial pieces)
Artistic hangings woven and embroidered by owner
Opened Nov'01

5. Berkana
Correo #14
Tel: 152-0877
E-mail: flotario_sma@hotmail.com
Hrs: Daily 10am-8pm
Credit cards: Amex, Master and Visa
Gift items, lamps, vases and candles
Custom furniture made in state of México
Imports from Indonesia—also some paintings for sale
Craft shows and special events next door during the year
Since Jan'02, relocated Oct'03

6. Galería Savia
Jesús #12
Tel/Fax: 154-4866
Hrs: Mon-Sat 10am-2pm and 4:30-8pm, Sun 11am-3pm
Owner: Verónika (bilingual)
Popular art from México—a nice collection
Paintings from young Oaxacan artists

7. Gusano Azul
Formerly Galería del Pueblo
Loreto #24
Tel: 152-7115 (*casa*)
Hrs: Mon-Sat 10am-2pm and 4-8pm, Sun 11am-3pm
Small store
Carefully selected mix of paintings, sculptures and craft items
Opened Apr'96, relocated Oct'03

8. Casa Maxwell
Canal #14 and Umarán #3 (two entrances)
Tel: 152-0247

E-mail: maxwellm@cybermatsa.com.mx
Hrs: Mon-Fri 9am-2pm and 4-7pm, Sat 10am-2pm and 4-8pm
    Sunday 11am-3pm
Credit cards: Amex, Master and Visa
Large beautiful *casa* that stretches from Calle Canal to Umarán
A wide variety of Mexican crafts on display in numerous rooms
    and courtyards-well worth a look around
First opened 1956

9. Casa Vieja

Mesones #83 (corner of Hidalgo)
Tel: 152-1284
Hrs: Mon-Sat 10am-2pm and 4-8pm, Sun 11am-3pm, closed Thurs
Manager: Guadalupe de la Sota de Hynes
A large collection of Mexican art objects
Kitchen and dining room things, candles, religious art, linens,
    some furniture, plus antiques
Two sister stores:
    (a) **Casa Canela,** Umarán #20, Tel: 152-1880
    (b) **La Calandria,** San Francisco #5, Tel: 152-2945

10. Corazón Divino

Loreto #10-A
Tel: 152-3505
Hrs: Mon-Sat 10am-2pm and 4:30-7:30pm, closed Sunday
Owners: Odilia and Beto Domínguez
Enterprising family with a creative take on some standard items
Fun take-home gifts–reasonably priced
Everything made in San Miguel
Opened Nov'96

11. Artes de México

Calzada de la Aurora #47 (4 blocks north of Centro)
Tel/Fax: 152-0764 and 154-5951
E-mail: artesdemexicosma@hotmail.com
Hrs: Mon-Sat 9am-7pm, closed Sunday
Family owned since 1950
Managers: Marcos and Sylvia Hernández (bilingual)
Manufacturers of gift items, furniture to order, lamps (wiring and
    repairs), tin work, *equipal* and wrought iron accessories
Also packing and shipping

12. Casa Anguiano
Canal #28 at H. Macías
Tel: 152-0107
Hrs: Mon-Sat 9:30am-8:30pm, Sunday 9:30am-6:30pm
Known as the five-and-ten store—a busy place
Large inventory of Mexican arts and crafts
Also have bolts of materials

13. Casa Canal
Canal #3 (corner of Hidalgo)
Tel: 152-0479
E-mail: ksacanal@prodigy.net.mx
Web page: www.casacanal.cjb.net
Hrs: Mon-Fri 9:30am-2pm and 4-7:30pm, Thurs 9:30am-2pm
      Sat 10am-2pm and 4-8pm , Sunday 11am-2:30pm
Credit cards: Amex, Master and Visa
Sales Manager: Luís Araiza (bilingual)
Large property with many rooms and outdoor courtyard
Main line: Custom-made furniture plus lamps and house accessories,
      paintings and sculptures
Boutique (right at entrance) —made-in-México women's clothing
Since 1965

14. La Casa del Diseño ("house of design")
(formerly Casa Antigua Lamas)
Ancha de San Antonio #11-A
Tel: 152-1264
Hrs: Mon-Sat 9am-2pm and 4-8pm, Sunday 9am-2pm
Master and Visa cards accepted
Old *hacienda*—must see the two beautiful patios and small chapel
Crafts and furniture all made in San Miguel (own design)
Germán Llamas, son of the owner speaks English
5th generation in the business

15. Casa Virreyes
Canal #21 (corner H. Macías)
Tel: 152-7389
Hrs: Mon-Sat 10am-2pm and 4-8pm, Sunday 11am-4pm
      Closed Thursday
Owner: Paolo McLendon Agundis
A wide variety of products made in San Miguel
Paolo has access to owners capable of producing interesting items
      of the highest quality and craft

A great assortment of decorative items
If you don't see what you like or want, just ask
Opened Sept'96
A second store (**Casa del Angel**)
    Hernández Macías #76 (next to Chelo's)
    Tel/Fax: 152-1392

16. El Claustro
Hernández Macías #74 (interior)—across from Bellas Artes
Tel: 154-4032
Hrs: Mon-Sat 10:30am-2pm & 4-8pm, Sun 10:30am-3pm, closed Thurs
Credit cards: Amex, Master and Visa
Owners: Rafael and Luisa Villicaña Martínez (brother/sister)
Small shop of religious art
Excellent quality of workmanship—uniqueness, one-of-a-kind
Opened Dec'98

Also: **El Pegaso,** Corregidora #6, Tel: 152-1351
     7th Heaven, Sollano #13, Tel: 154-4677
     Llamas, Zacateros #11, Tel: 152-1691

Furniture:

1. CML (Casa María Luisa)
Canal #40 (corner of Zacateros)
Tel/Fax: 152-0130
E-mail: jomaxil@prodigy.net.mx
Hrs: Mon-Sat 10am-2pm & 4-8pm, Sunday 10am-4pm
Credit cards: Amex, Master and Visa
Managers: Enrique Morales and Francisco Baltista (bilingual)
Contemporary Mexican furniture and accessories
Made in San Miguel
Also some art pieces
Reopened April'01

2. Euromex
Essential Studios
Hospicio #20 (near Chiquitos)
Tel: 044-415-151-0823 (cell)   Tel/Fax: 152-6270 (*casa*)
Hrs: call and make an appointment
Owner: Abram Corts (from Holland)
Custom-made furniture, European styling, local production
Also interior design
Opened Dec'00

3. Davila Antiques
Recreo #13
Tel: 154-7022
Hrs: Daily 10am-7pm, closed Monday
Credit cards: Amex, Master and Visa
Beautiful old colonial building, several rooms
Owners: Gustavo and Martha Davila and Miguel Francisco
     (bilingual and from México City)
Mexican antique furniture, bronze reproductions and Mexican paintings
Opened Nov'99, moved June'02

4. Arlequín
Loreto #7
Tel: 152-1620
Hrs: Mon-Sat 9am-8pm, Sunday 9:30am-7pm
Owner: Fidel Gordillo (bilingual) delightful and fun to work with
Wooden colonial furniture off the floor or special order
     Tables, chairs, desks and chests
     Custom finishing available
Ceramics, glass and pottery available
Reasonable prices

5. Casas Coloniales
Canal #36 (corner of Zacateros)
Tel: 152-0286 and 154-5731
E-mail: vidargas@unisono.net.mx
Hrs: Mon-Sat 9:30am-2pm and 4-7:30pm, closed Sunday
Owner: Dotty Vidargas—many years in San Miguel
Interior design store
     Furniture, lamps and rugs
     Also fabrics, bedspreads, curtains and pillows
Some Gorky González and Santa Rosa ceramics
In business more than 30 years

6. Artesano de la Bayoneta
Callejon de la Bayoneta #6 (near La Vida Bar/Restaurant)
Tel: 152-6450
Building or remodeling
All kinds of custom-made wooden furniture at fair prices
Owner: Simon Desgagnes (speaks English, French and Spanish)
Free estimates

7. Maestro Benjamín
Ben Becerra
Orizaba #5 (north side, street numbers not in sequence)
Tel: None
Hrs: Mon-Fri 9am-5pm, Sat 9am-12 noon
Cabinet maker–master carpenter specializing in fine furniture
Also walking canes of noble woods
> Keeps an inventory of fine, hand-made wooden canes for men and women

---

Also:
  Icpalli, Correo #43, Tel: 152-1236
  Artes de México, Calzada de la Aurora #47, Tel: 152-0764
  El Otro Camino, H. Macías #97, Tel: 152-2874
  Casa Canal, Canal #3, Tel: 152-0479
  Casa y Campo, Recreo #98. Tel: 152-6748
  La Vie de Chateau, Organos #29, Tel: 154-4076
      Alejandro Cruz—by appointment only

And:
  DeWa, Calzada de la Aurora s/n, Tel: 152-5481
  EVOS/Artesana, H. Macías #55, Tel: 152-0813
  Casa María José, Umarán #21, Tel: 152-2182
  Christopher Fallon Design, Cal.de la Aurora s/n, Tel: 154-5075

Insider's Tip: For chair caning or repairs, you might check in front of Pegaso Restaurant on Corregidora. Periodically a young man sets up shop on the sidewalk, usually in the morning, but at no set time.

Glass:

1. La Casa del Vidrio
Correo #11 (also upstairs)
Tel/Fax: 152-0102
Hrs: Mon-Sat 11am-2pm and 4:30-8pm, Sun 11am-3pm
San Miguel glass factory outlet (Guajuye)
Worldwide export—15+ years in business
Glass products, candles, iron, tin and aluminum things
40% sale during the month of August on all glass items
Owner/Factory Manager: Juan José Alvarez (bilingual)
See **Things To Do** chapter about glass factory tour
Also: Ferreti, Calzada de la Estación, Tel: 152-5858
      Factory outlet–Hrs: Mon-Sat 10am-6pm

2. Vitrales Exclusivos de San Miguel
Calzada de la Luz #8 (near of Calzada de la Presa)
Tel/Fax: 154-5292
Hrs: Mon-Fri 9am-5pm, Saturday 9am-4pm
Owners: Gustavo Gómez Sánchez (bilingual)
Award-winning craftsmen—everything made with care and
    exceptional quality
Specialize in stained glass windows and lighting fixtures, tin work
Custom orders—some jobs in USA
Eighteen years working in stained glass—Also teaches classes
Opened Nov'95

3. Artesa
Canal #32
Tel: 152-2477
Hrs: Mon-Sat 10am-2:30pm and 4:30-8pm, Sun 10am-3pm
Master and Visa cards accepted
Decorative glass/brass boxes (different colors)–made locally
Also mirrors and picture frames

Also:
  Basia Glassworks, Col. San Antonio, Tel: 154-5645
  Casa Virreyes, Canal #21, Tel: 152-7389
  Casa Pérez, Pila Seca #17, Tel: 152-3321

Imports:

1. La Calaca
Mesones #93
Tel: 152-3954
Hrs: Mon-Sat 11am-2pm and 4-6:30pm, closed Sunday
Owner: Evita Avery (bilingual), fourth-generation resident of México
Folk (*arte popular*) and ceremonial art from different parts of
    México, Peru and Guatemala
Masks, *retablos*, pottery, hand-woven materials, folk furniture and
    ethnic jewelry
Ask about the Day of the Dead things
Since 1987

2. Ono
Plaza Principal #20-A (faces Jardín)
Tel: 152-1366
Hrs: Mon-Sat 9am-8pm, Sunday 10am-8pm
All major credit cards

Five stores managed by owner Evelyne (bilingual) and h
   Jaime Goded, a respected local artist—his brightly
   wooden sculptures, furniture and puzzles are for sal
Imaginative and educational toys
Textiles from Chiapas, India and Guatemala
Four sister stores:

(a) **Habanera,** Portal Guadalupe #10 (east side of Jardín),
   Tel: 152-1311—gifts including Cuban, Mexican and
   European cigars plus custom wooden humidors-first class store

(b) **Galería Goded,** San Francisco #11
   Tel: 152-0074—space exclusively for exhibition of recent
   works by Jaime Goded, includes drawings, paintings,
   wooden and ceramic sculpture and objects of art.

(c) **El Nuevo Mundo,** San Francisco #17 (corner of
   Corregidora) Tel: 152-6180—well-displayed collection of
   craft items—a good place to do business! Popular with locals
   and tourists

(d) **Piaf,** Correo #6, Tel: 154-5186—women's underwear and
   nightclothes

Also: **Galería Tesoros,** Recreo #8-B, Tel: 154-5880

Jewelry:

1. Joyería París
Umarán #8 (next to Pueblo Viejo Restaurant)
Tel: 152-2637
Hrs: Mon-Sat 10am-2pm and 4-8pm, Sunday 11am-3pm
Credit cards: Amex, Master and Visa
Owner: Dr. Luís Manuel Dorantes (dentist) – from Querétaro
Family-run business—4 stores in Querétaro
Interesting selection, including gold, and prices are fair
A second store is inside same building by the restaurant

2. El Topacio
Umarán #12 (near Jesús)
Tel: 152-4979
Hrs: Mon-Sat 9am-2pm and 4-8pm, Sun 10am-2pm
All sterling silver—good prices
Since 1966

3. Candela
Joyería de Plata
Cuna de Allende #3 (adjacent to La Fragua)

Tel: 154-5701
Hrs: Sunday-Thurs 10:30am-8pm, Fri and Sat 10:30am-11pm
Credit cards: Master and Visa
Owner: Gerardo Ehrlich (bilingual)
Two rooms with attractive display cases
All silver jewelry made in México City-new designs arrive each month
Competitive prices
Opened Sept'99
Also: **Candela,** Correo #17, Tel: 152-2933
      Gema, Cuna de Allende #7, Tel: 152-8170

4. Galería Casiopea
Juan Ordoñez
Jesús #20
Tel: 152-5543
Hrs: Mon-Sat 10am-2pm and 5-8pm, Sunday 10am-2pm
Exclusive designs in silver, one-of-a-kind and wholesale
Interesting display cases
Workshop in back on premises
Also sells art work
Since 1993

5. Cerroblanco
Canal #21 (Plaza Colonial–interior)
Tel/Fax: 154-4888
E-mail: katepepe@unisono.net.mx
Other outlet:
      Canal #17 (men's jewelry), Tel: 152-0502
Hrs: Mon-Sat 11am-2pm and 5-8pm, closed Sunday
Old family business—Irma and Rosa María (bilingual) sisters
Exclusive designs of fine jewelry in silver and gold
Specializing in semiprecious and precious stones
Since 1940
Relocated Feb'98

6. Ambar
Jesús #21-B
Tel/Fax: 154-4058
Hrs: Tues-Sat 10am-2pm and 5-7pm, Sun 10am-4pm, closed Mon
Designer: Thomas le Noir (trilingual)
Jewelry in gold and silver—amber (gold, red, congac and green)
    from Chiapas
Very impressive collection

186

First class operation–all work guaranteed
Many satisfied customers–will custom design
In business since 1995, retail shop opened Dec'01

7. Patricia's Jewelry (Xóchitl)

Artesanías Market (stall left of Hotel Quinta Loreto entrance)
Tel: 120-3443   044-415-149-2920 (cell)
E-mail: tanzanitepc@yahoo.com.mx
Hrs: Daily 11am-5pm, closed Tuesday
Handmade 100% sterling silver jewelry/unique designs
Large rings at affordable prices
Work with natural stones from different parts of México
    Best to buy what is in stock
Family business–Patricia Cordova and husband Jaime speak English
Make appointment to display jewelry for your parties

8. Galería de Marianne Johansson

Hidalgo #4 (Interior)—across the street from American Express
Tel: 154-4110   and   154-8934
Hrs: Daily 11am-6pm, closed Tuesday
Custom-designed jewelry
Unique, one-of-a-kind silver rings with semi-precious stones
Also works with ebony, mammoth ivory, red amber, Mexican fire
    opal, sterling silver and 18k gold
Has own cutters
Collects rare precious stones
Represented at the prestigious Nedra Matteucci Gallery in Santa Fe, NM
Featured on national TV programs like "Good Morning America"
English spoken
Relocated Nov'04

9. Azul & Plata

Cuna de Allende #15 (interior)
Tel: 154-8192
Hrs: Daily 10:30am-2pm and 3:30-7pm, closed Tuesday
Credit cards: Master and Visa
Owner: Yadira Ibarra (bilingual)
Jewelry designs by leading Mexican and international designers
Impressive small shop
Mostly silver items
Opened Sept'01

10. Platería Guerrero
Ignacio (Nacho) Guerrero Pérez
Plaza Real del Conde (Gigante)–just outside of town
      Ground floor (across from Café la Plaza)
Tel: None
Hrs: Mon-Sat 9am-2pm and 4-7:30pm, closed Sunday
Exclusive designs in silver—also special orders
Showroom—very good prices!
Taller upstairs
Since 1982

11. Darla
Recreo, s/n (corner of Correo)
Tel: 154-5550
Hrs: Daily 10am-3pm and 4-7pm
First class store
Darla Nordstrom from Boston-over 20 years in México
Mostly sterling silver items
One-of-a-kind limited editions–dramatic!
Also unique evening handbags and accessories
Imported women's clothing from France and USA
Opened Dec'00

12. El Zafiro Joyería
Insurgentes #73-A (near H. Macías)– note blue and yellow building
Tel: 152-3499
Hrs: Mon-Sat 9am-2:30pm and 4-8pm, closed Sunday
José Serafín, the owner, has been in the business since 1973
Special designs in gold or silver
Also repairs and does silver plating
Reasonable prices

13. Nuevo México
Aparicio #1 (upper end of Mesones)–*taller* location
      Retail store: Zacateros #23
Tel/Fax: 152-4510
Hrs: Mon-Fri 9am-6pm, Sat 9am-2pm, closed Sunday
Owner: Julio Miguel Pérez (blingual)
Navajo style crafts
Alpaca concha belts of many designs
Quality craftmanship and attention to detail
Will custom make (also in sterling)
Opened 1985

14. Joyería David
Zacateros #53
Tel: 152-0056   Fax: 152-3100
Hrs: Mon-Sat 9am-7pm, closed Sunday
Large display room—huge selection
Sterling silver and gold — discounts for cash payments
Prices based on prevailing international silver market
Since 1963
Centro store: **El Globo,** Correo #4, Tel: None
Also: Zacateros #11 and #13 (corner of Umarán), Tel: 152-3100
        Zacateros #23-A, Tel: 152-3446

15. Beckmann Showroom
Hernández Macías s/n (across from #114 and near bend in road)
Also: H. Macías #105 (special collection) ring bell (Carmen speaks English)
Tel: 152-1613 and 152-0112
Hrs: Mon-Sat 9am-2pm and 4-7:30pm, closed Sunday
Gold and silver jewelry
Credit cards: Amex and Visa
Note prices are in US dollars
Long time business in San Miguel

16. "A Mano" Joyería
Hernández Macías #116 (at the "elbow")
Tel: 152-6078
E-mail: jmbamano@hotmail.com
Hrs: Mon-Sat 10am-7pm, Sunday 10am-2pm
Owner: José Mario Bustamante
Make your own jewelry—pay by materials used
Necklaces, bracelets and earrings
Good selection of silver, amber, coral, pearls and beads-all from México
Some custom-designed jewelry for sale
Ask about classes
Opened Oct'03, moved June'04

Also: 7th Heaven, Sollano #13, Tel: 154-4677
        Rene Courtney, Santa Cruz #3 (Aldea), Tel: 154-4804
        Girasol Boutique, San Francisco #11, Tel: 152-2724

Note: By the way, if you are taking a day trip to Querétaro
and are interested in opals you may want to check out
Lapidaría Ramírez, Pino Suárez #98 Centro, Tel: (442)212-1642

| Leather: |

1. The Leather Shop (La Tienda de la Piel)
Umarán #1 (across from Mama Mia)
Tel/Fax: 152-8679
E-mail: leatherpiel@prodigy.net.mx
Hrs: Daily 10am-8pm (they don't close for lunch)
Credit cards: Amex, Master and Visa
Owners: Alma and Jesús Iturralde (Georgetown grad who speaks
        English, Spanish, French and Italian)
First-class store–quality leather goods (imported and national leather)
        Jackets, bags, wallets, belts, briefcases, etc.
Also Ecuadorian-made Panama straw hats
Plus custom-made silver jewelry, sandals, masks and crosses
Opened Dec'97, relocated May'03

2. Corium
Moda Piel
Reloj #17
Tel: 152-3035
Hrs: Daily 10am-3pm and 5-8pm, closed Tuesday
First-class leather goods (bags, belts, wallets, boots, jackets and
        backpacks) also watches
All made in León and Guadalajara (México)
Sister store (**Baccara**) located at Hidalgo #9 (corner of Mesones)
        Tel: 152-0062
Also stores in Guanajuato and Tequisquiapan

3. Vilar
Sollano #6 (also Recreo #5)
Tel: 152-3130
Hrs: Mon-Sat 10am-2pm and 4-8pm, Sunday 10:30am-2:30pm
Owner: Marisa Vilar
Made in México jackets, bags, shoes and belts
Also imported neckties

4. Artesanías Búfalo
Zacateros #23-B
Tel: 152-1052 and 152-2271
Hrs: Mon- Sat 10am-2pm and 4-8pm, Sunday 10am-2pm
Wallets, purses, vests and belts
Opened for business 1978

| Also: **La Colombina 30/30,** San Francisco #30, Tel: 152-0504 |

Lighting/Candles:

1. Diseño y Vitral
Zacateros #49 (corner of Pila Seca)
Tel/Fax: 152-4879
Hrs: Mon-Sat 9am-2pm and 4-8pm, Sunday 10am-4pm
Good selection of stained glass lamps (many are Tiffany
    reproductions)–made in San Miguel
Also candles, frames and other glass items
Relocated Nov'97
Second store and *taller,* Fracc. La Lejona, Tel: 152-7490

2. La Luminaria
Reloj #41-A
Tel: 152-7780
Hrs: Mon-Sat 10:30am-2pm and 4-8pm, Sunday 10:30am-3pm
Credit cards: Master and Visa
Family business–owners: Eduardo Juárez and Teresa Ortega
Nice collection of locally-made lamps and lighting fixtures
Opened Sept'97

Also check out :
  El Otro Camino, H. Macías #97, Tel: 152-2874
  Stilo, Calzada de la Luz #16, Tel: 152-2660
  Maja, Mesones #60, Tel:154-6150
  Gaby, Zacateros #33, Tel: 152-2797, for metal "star"
    lighting fixtures
  Casa Roberto, Fracc. La Lejona, Tel: 152-8620, imported
    light fixtures, ceiling fans and gas heaters
  Casa de Luz, Umarán 24-A, Tel: 044-415-101-7590 (cell)

Candle Places:

1. La Nueva Lucha
General Store
Juárez #2 (SW corner of Mesones)
Tel: 152-1401
Largest selection of beeswax candles–most are hanging from ceiling

2. López Funeral Home
Mesones #47
Tel: 152-0208
Different size candles (*velas*)

3. Temporary Booths (November Day of the Dead festivities)
Civic Plaza
Beeswax candles in pure white

4. Zócalo
Hernández Macías #110
Tel: 152-0663
Good selection of made-in-México candles

Linen:

1. La Alfonsina
Hidalgo #36 (corner of Insurgentes)
Tel: 152-1429 and 152-1572
Hrs: Mon-Sat 9:30am-2pm and 4-7pm, Sunday 10am-3pm
Ready-made or custom tablecloths, napkins and clothing
Beautiful embroidery work

2. La Bottega di Casa
Umarán #26
Tel: 152-2748
E-mail: labottegadicasa@hotmail.com
Hrs: Daily 10am-7pm, closed Tuesday
Owner: Patrizia Trevisiol (Italian) - trilingual
Mostly Italian linens (towels, sheets, tablecloths & pillow cases)
Sell Italian/USA fabrics by the meter
Beautiful embroidery done by Mexican women
Good selection of burnished clay (tiles, candle holders, etc)
Own customed designed *talavera*
Opened Feb'03
Second location: Fábrica La Aurora, Calzada de la Aurora, Tel: None

Also: **Dulces Sueños** (Yolanda), Col. Guadalupe, Tel: 154-4713

Market of Artesanías:

Artesanos of San Miguel
Plaza Lanatón (entrance from Loreto or the *Mercado*)
Tel: 152-2844
Hrs: Mon-Sat 10am-2pm and 4-7pm, Sun 10am-4:30pm
Various vendors of local crafts; glass, brass, woolen cloth, *papier
      mâché* and masks
Silver jewelry with some of the best prices in town

Masks:

**Tonatiu Metztli (S
Cerrada Manan
Col. Allende
Tel: 152-24
E-mail: xikury
Owner: Inti Guz.
Father, Jorge, had b
Masks from México, C

Also: **Casa de la Cuesta,**
    The Leather Shop, Um.
    Border Antiques, Prol. Cue.
    Lavandería la Famosa, Correo

Shopping

3. Sierra Madre
Correo #12-A (jus
Tel: 154-7312
E-mail: smsma@
Hrs: Daily 9a
Credit cards:
Owner: Sra.
Attractive s
with
Post card
Purchas
One of
Also

4. U
Ca
T

Miscellaneous:

1. El Arrecife
San Pedro #18 (corner Umarán)—no outside sign
Tel: 152-5921
Hrs: Mon-Sat 9:30am-2pm and 4-8pm
Owner: Javier Hernández (bilingual)—25 years experience
All kinds of tropical fish (fresh and salt water)
Aquariums and related equipment
Some birds
Can order other special animals (with permits)
Opened Dec'02

2. Puzzlemania
Recreo #12
Tel: 152-5891 (*casa*/workshop)
E-mail: quetzalv@prodigy.net.mx
Hrs: Daily 9am-8pm, Tuesday 2-8pm, Sunday 11am-5pm
Owner: Elena Sarvide (bilingual)
Quality, hand-made, colorful wooden puzzles
Simple to intricate ones, which are framed
Made from recycled wood and painted with an airbrush
Order a custom-made puzzle of your name
Great kid's gifts
Ask about a workshop tour

off the Jardín)

prodigy.net.mx
1-9pm
Amex, Master and Visa
Lorea San Martín (bilingual)
tore offers a good selection of tee-shirts and posters
ature themes
, books, puzzles and more
s support various conservation projects
30 such stores in México
cybercafé

urich (Means seashell in Mayan)
hal #34-A (next to El Campanario Restaurant)
el: None
Hrs: Daily 10:30am-2pm and 4:30-8pm, Sun 10:30am-3pm, closed Wed
Owner: Laura Reyes (bilingual)
All sorts of seashells and conchs such as nautilius, starfish & abalones
Some jewelry crafted from coral, pearls and conchs
Most shells come from the Philippines
Also some agates, geodes, amethyst stones
Opened July'04

Paper Products:

Plásticos "Castañeda"
Mesones #66 (near Hidalgo)
Tel: 152-0757
Hrs: Mon-Sat 9:30am-2pm and 4:30-8pm, closed Sunday
Owner: Verónica Castañeda Cano
All kinds of paper products: tablecloths, flags, flowers, party supplies
Also rolls of colored plastic
Plus stationery supplies and copy machine
Other locations: Canal #162 and Insurgentes #45

Also: **Marca de Agua,** paper products sold at **Terra,**
Cuadrante #6, Tel: 152-7754

Papier Mâché:

La Unica
Originales Papel Mâché
Portal Guadalupe #4 (east side of Jardín)
Tel: 152-3866
Hrs: Daily 10am-8pm
All kinds of bright colored *papier mâché* items
Made in San Miguel
Owner: Pedro Cruz

Insiders Tip: You can buy the popular, colorful *papier mâché* chickens at Casa Mason (Aldama #17). They are often on display in the front window of the house (Mon-Sat). They are made by Rosa Hernández, the maid.

Quilts:

Victoria's Chest
Tinajitas #24 (Col. San Antonio)
Tel: 152-4176 (*casa*)
Hrs: By appointment
Professional textile artist: Lilia Galeana (bilingual)
Quilts, pillows, wall hangings, dolls, and women's wearable art
Custom orders welcome
Quilting classes available

Textiles:

Bolts of material:
       Casa Anguiano, Canal #28, Tel: 152-0107
       Magnolia, Recreo #2, Tel: 154-5705
       Frida, Recreo #24, Tel: 154-8322

Woven Baskets:

1. La Casa
Pepe Llanos #10 (one block street between Mesones and Insurgentes)
Tel: 152-1027
Hrs: Daily 10am-7pm
Luz Espinosa, a delightful owner—worth a visit to meet her
Started business in 1934
Shop is overflowing with baskets, wood products and ceramics

2. Jarciería
Mesones #36 (faces Plaza Allende)
Tel: None
Hrs: Daily 10am-7pm
Antonia Soto is the proprietor
Small interesting shop full of wooden items and baskets

Insider's Tip: Basket salesmen work the streets around the Jardín in Centro. Prices are negotiable.

Look under the listings below for additional shops and stores:
Antique shops	**Carpets**
Art Galleries	**Clothing Stores**
Book stores	**Hat Shops**

Helpful shopping words and phrases:

What time are you open?	*¿A qué hora abren ustedes?*
What are your hours?	*¿Cuál es el horario de servicio?*
What day are you closed?	*¿Qué día cierra?*
open	*abierto*
closed	*cerrado*
How much does it cost?	*¿Cuánto cuesta?*
it's expensive	*es caro*
cheaper	*más barato*
discount	*descuento*
Made in México	*Hecho en México*
I want	*Quiero*
I like	*Me gusta*
I don't like	*No me gusta*
How many?	*Cuántos*
new/old	*nuevo/viejo*

Spanish Schools

1. Warren Hardy Spanish
San Rafael #6 (across from San Juan de Dios church)
Tel/Fax: 154-4017 (9am-12 noon)   Tel: 152-4728 (afternoons)
E-mail: info@warrenhardy.com
Web page: www.warrenhardy.com

• Warren Hardy internationally recognized teacher, author and
     instructional innovator
• He teaches every class with his team of native facilitators
• Learning system includes workbooks, flashcards and CD/cassettes
• Study materials are effective for independent study
Students work in pairs and use flashcards
     This method is fun and gives great results
     Very popular with local foreigners and visitors
Drop-ins welcome
Pay by the class or by the course
In San Miguel since 1990

2. Academia Hispano Americana (AMA)

Mesones #4
Tel: 152-0349 and 152-4349   Fax: 152-2333
E-mail: info@ahaspeakspanish.com
Web page: www.ahaspeakspanish.com
Director: Paulina Hawkins Masip (May'02)
Beautiful 18th century colonial house with patio and garden
13 classrooms
First school in town to specialize in teaching Spanish as a foreign
     language (since 1959)
Year-round total immersion program, levels 1-5
     Also one on one program, levels 1-5
Experienced native Spanish speaking teachers
Earn an official diploma in Spanish as a second language
     Accredited by the Ministry of Education State of Guuanajuato
Afternoon courses in Mexican history and culture
Home stays with Mexican families

3. Instituto Allende

Ancha de San Antonio #20
Tel: 152-0190   Fax: 152-4538
E-mail: iallende@instituto-allende.edu.mx
Web page: www.instituto-allende.edu.mx
Latin America's oldest and largest school of arts and language for
     English speaking students—year-round instruction
Campus former palace of 17th century Counts of Canal
All instructors are Mexican nationals with teacher training
Beginning, intermediate and advanced students are welcome
One, two, four or six hours a day classes (conversational or intensive)
Courses relating to Mexican history and culture taught in English

Also field trips and lectures
Member of International Association of Language Centers
One-on-one classes pair the student with a single instructor

4. Centro Bilingüe
Correo #46 (near Barranca)
Tel: 152-5400 or 152-6316
E-mail: centrobilingue@yahoo.com
Web page: www.geocities.com/centrobilingue
Director: Sara Hernández Murillo (bilingual)
Five classrooms plus large outdoor courtyard
Intensive and semi-intensive courses
Adults/teenagers/children—many referrals
Day camp during summer, Christmas or Spring breaks
Private lessons in Spanish for educators
Great flexibility—will tailor a class for you
Opened April'98, relocated Nov'01

5. Centro Mexicano de Lengua y Cultura de San Miguel
Director: Josefina Hernández
Orizaba #15 (Col. San Antonio)
Tel/Fax: 152-0763
Web page: www.infosma.com/centromexicano
Seven classrooms around an open patio
Conversation and grammar classes, group or private
Students most welcome at all levels–classes limited to 5 students
All teachers are bilingual and in tune with individual needs
Special courses for teachers and children in the summertime
Also English classes at reasonable rates

6. Instituto de Habla Hispana
Calzada de la Luz #25 (north end of Reloj)
Tel: 152-0713   Fax: 152-1535
E-mail: info@mexicospanish.com
Web page: www.mexicospanish.com
Directors: Attilio and Angelica Tonelli
Year 'round instruction–relaxing setting
Small group (ten or less) using lesson book
Four week session
    80 hours in classroom
    40 hours of discussion groups and walking tours
    Minimum enrollment is one week
Opened Nov'96

7. Spanish For You
Formerly Inter-Idiomas
20 de Enero Sur #42, Col. San Antonio
Tel: 152-4115
E-mail: spanish4u@prodigy.net.mx
Web page: www.spanish4u.com
Director: Gerald Baker
Graduate bilingual instructors-small group size of three
Since 1980

Tutors:

1. Antonieta Espinosa Deanda
One-on-one Spanish
Tel: 044-415-101-3247 (cell)
E-mail: esda2003@yahoo.com
A popular tutor with a busy schedule

2. Marisela Patterson
Promotion of Mexican Culture (PMC)
Hidalgo # 16/18 (near Mesones)
Tel: 152-1630 and 154-5312
Private lessons
Teaching since 1968

3. Maru Paulin
Private Spanish lessons
Tel: 044-415-100-0949 (cell)
E-mail: marupaulin@hotmail.com
All levels conversation, grammar and writing
Former teacher at Instituto Allende
Will arrange a convenient location
Since 1987

4. María Teresa Frazee
Col. Olimpo
Tel: 152-4310
One-on-one or small group
Convenient location
Short-term or long-term
Teaching since 1987

There are many excellent and interesting people who freelance as language tutors. Listed above are just a few of them. For additional names, check with the schools, ATENCIóN newspaper or the community bulletin boards.

<u>Conversation Class:</u>

1. Conversaciones con Amigos
Biblioteca courtyard patio
Tuesday and Thursday 5-6:30pm
Practice your Spanish and English with other eager students
Small fee requested

Stationery Stores

1. La Esmeralda Mercería
Juárez #3 (east of Jardín de San Francisco)
Tel: 152-1396
Hrs: Mon-Sat 10am-2pm and 4:15-8pm, Sun 10am-2pm
Owner: Lupe (bilingual)—always smiling and ready to help
A good selection of stationery products
Same location since 1926

2. El Iris Mercería y Papelería
San Francisco #16
Tel: 152-0738
Hrs: Mon-Fri 8am-2pm and 4-8pm, Sat 10am-2pm and 4-7pm
     Sunday 10am-3pm
Paper, notebooks and cards
Good selection of gift wrapping paper
Will put spiral binding on your guidebook (for about US$2)
Copy machine

3. Centro Papelero de San Miguel
Ancha de San Antonio #55
Tel: 152-1937
Hrs: Mon-Fri 9am-2:30pm and 4-8pm, Sat 9am-12 noon
Complete selection of stationery supplies
Also printer cartridges
Will deliver
Also located at: Insurgentes #134-A, Juárez #25 and
     Calzada de la Aurora #18-A

Also check out the small stationery stores around town.

> **Insider's Tip: One can call Office Depot in Querétaro (01-800-910-0000 toll free) and order office supplies. The store offers free delivery to San Miguel.**

Card Shops:

1. Casa de Papel
Mesones #57 (Interior)—China Palace Restaurant (corner of Reloj)
Tel: 154-5187   044-415-100-5302 (cell)
E-mail: bevgray@unisono.net.mx
Hrs: Mon-Sat 10am-8pm, Sunday 10am-6pm
Owner: Beverly Gray
Best selection of imported cards in town
Some cards created by local artists
Cards for all occasions (birthdays, anniversaries, etc)
Stationery, writing pens, gift wrap, napkins, bridge sets and more
Some selected books
Opened July'03

> **Also** check out:
> **La Tienda,** Biblioteca, Insurgentes #25, Tel: 152-0293
> **Berkana,** Correo #14, Tel: 152-0877

Storage

1. Security Storage
Tel/Fax: 152-4299
E-mail: nesti@unisono.net.mx
Call Paula Nesti for details
Secure storage — nothing too small or too large
Rent individual lockers (approx 40 cu/ft)—min. charge US$10 per mo
Expanded warehouse space (dry and secure)
Since 1994

2. Mibosa (mini *bodega* of San Miguel)
Salida a Celaya #52 (between Pemex and Corona distributor)
Tel: 152-1842, 152-1636 and 152-1917
E-mail: c21bueno@prodigy.net.mx
Owner: Armando Bueno (American)
Locked secure units are 4x8x8 ft.—also bulk open space
Since 1995

Supermarket/Markets

1. Gigante
Plaza Real del Conde
Road to Querétaro (2 km SE from Centro)
Tel: 152-4047
Hrs: Daily 9am-9pm
Large chain of 130 + supermarkets in México
Customer service counter at entrance
Large meat, produce, milk products and deli sections
Also a good selection of household items, cosmetics, clothing,
　　　spirits and fresh tortillas
Added a bakery and pharmacy (30% discount on medicines)
Some luggage/suitcases for sale
Sale items on the weekends
Must travel 10 minutes by car, taxi or bus from Centro
Banamex branch inside store near checkout
　　　Check cashing, exchange plus one ATM machine

Markets (covered):

1. Mercado Ignacio Ramírez
Go east on Mesones at Plaza Allende (large equestrian statue)
　　　turn left on Colegio and proceed one block, the market will
　　　be visible on the left
Built in 1970
Large produce and meat section plus flowers (fresh on Thursday
　　　afternoon), key stand, dry goods and small eating counters
Hrs: Daily 9am-9pm

2. Mercado de San Juan de Dios
Go west on Canal four blocks to San Antonio Abad, turn right and
　　　then left on Indio Triste for one block (near former Tuesday
　　　market area)
Opened April 1992–very clean
Note red brick that separates interior stalls
Produce, meat, chicken, flowers, kitchen items, dry goods and food *tiendas*
Hrs: Daily 9am-8pm

Also check out: ***Grocery Stores***

Markets (open):

1. Tuesday Market (Tianguis del Martes)
Salida a Querétaro (east of Gigante and the Bomberos buildings
    and adjoining the Municipal Stadium)
Hrs: 8am-4pm (It pays to shop early!)
Vendors set up temporary stalls and displays on a large new site
    built by the Public Works Department (Sept'96)
Usually crowded so beware of pickpockets (keep valuables at home)
Good selection of fresh produce
Plus everything imaginable; household items, clothing (new or
    used), radios, cassettes, hardware things and much more
Prices are negotiable at some stands
Good idea to bring a shopping bag
Best way to get there is by bus ($4 *pesos*)
    Buses marked "Gigante" and/or "Placita" leave from the east
    side of the Civic Plaza or the east side of the Jardín de San
    Francisco. The ride takes approximately 10 minutes
Also one can get there by taxi ($20 *pesos*) or by car
    (plenty of parking)

2. Sunday Market (Tianguis)
Callejón de San Antonio (out past Walter Weber's tennis courts
    and adjacent San Antonio church)
Hrs: 8am-2pm (Sunday only)
Small scale "Tuesday Market" with some of the same vendors
Very good selection of fruits and vegetables

Telephone

TELMEX
Salida a Celaya #56 (corner of Calle Guadalupe just before Corona bldg)
Tel: 152-5222 and 152-2331
Hrs: Mon-Fri 8am-2pm, closed weekends and holidays
Pay bills, file complaints, etc. (You can also pay bills at any bank
    or telegraph office—Correo #16)
Manager: Ramiro Rodríguez (bilingual)
Customer service: Gustavo Soltero (bilingual) and
    Ismael Valderaha (bilingual)
Moved office Dec'03

TELMEX switched to seven-digit local dialing on June 26, 1999. In San Miguel **TELMEX** has a new switching system and tone dialing and can now offer call waiting, call forwarding, caller ID and conference calling. In addition, local telephone customers can choose their long distance telephone company (i.e., AT&T, MCI, MARCATEL and others).

Direct internet service provider (Apr'99)
  –call 01 (800) 123-2222 (toll free) for details
  –call 01 (800) 123-3456 (toll free) for Prodigy Internet or Infinitum Prodigy Internet

How to telephone long distance:

WITHIN MEXICO: Direct dial
01 + area code + local numbers
50 % discount from 7pm-7am Mon-Fri & Sun and all day Sat
If you have a phone, call 01-800-123-2900 and subscribe to **LADA Unica** (additional long distance savings) at no cost
  Any day–any time: $1.47 *pesos* + IVA per minute
  No other discount program applies

As of Nov 17, 2001, all area codes (*ladas*) in México changed as México has gone to ten-digit dialing. México City (55), Guadalajara (33) and Monterrey (81) have eight-digit local numbers plus two-digit area codes. All other cities will have seven-digit local numbers plus a three-digit area code as noted below.

Ajijic/Chapala	376	Nuevo Loredo	867
Cancún	998	Oaxaca	951
Celaya	461	Puebla	222
Dolores Hidalgo	418	Puerta Vallarta	322
Guanajuato	473	Querétaro	442
León	477	San Luis Potosí	444
Morelia	443	San Miguel	415

020 National calls, operator assisted, collect calls
030 Time
040 Directory Assistance–national
050 Repairs

OUTSIDE MEXICO: Direct dial

To USA/Canada: Dial 001 + area code + local numbers
33% discount Mon-Fri 7pm-7am & Sun and all day Sat
    (Does not include Alaska or Hawaii)
If you have a phone, call 01 (800) 123-2900 and subscribe to **LADA**
    Unica (additional long distance savings) at no cost
        Any day–any time: USA $4.57 *pesos* + IVA per minute
                Canada $5.71 *pesos* + IVA per minute
    No other discount program applies
Lada Favorito (one special number in the USA)–Nov'01
    Call 01 (800) 123-2001 to subscribe
    $3 *pesos* + IVA per minute–any day any time
To the rest of the world: dial 00+country code+area code+number
090 International operator, for operator assisted calls (English)

Useful time comparisons between San Miguel and USA

East Coast	+ 1hr
Central	same
West Coast	–2 hrs

México observes daylight savings time (DST).
First introduced April-October '96

ProCommDirect discount long distance program. Any phone, any time. To USA 35 cents per minute and USA to México 17 cents per minute. Can access all US 800 numbers. Sign up on the Internet: sales@mextel.net or call 01-800-234-0206 (leave a message)

Dial toll-free:

AT&T 001 (800) 462-4240   MCI 001 (800) 674-7000
         Sprint 001 (800) 877-8000

San Miguel de Allende direct dial **from** USA
011-52-415 + seven local numbers

Insider's Tip: For the best rates for international phone calls try; Net@ San Miguel cybercafé, Aldama #60. The rates are $2 *pesos* per/minute. Calls are made through a computer using a telephone.

JU*A*RDE ("who are they?")
Directory of San Miguel residents—since 1960
Updated yearly (in the Fall), published in December
Cost: US$13 or *peso* equivalent
Call Bob Fangue, Tel: 152-0638
Sold at the Biblioteca, Libros el Tecolote and Lagundi book
	stores, La Conexión and Border Crossings

TELMEX
Other US and Canada toll-free numbers dial 001-880 and the
	number (instead of 1-800)
Cost will be $8 *pesos* per minute + IVA

> You can purchase a phone debit card ($50 or $100 *pesos*) to
> be used in designated telephones in México. The card can be
> purchased at the TELMEX office (Salida a Celaya #56)
> and many other marked stores in town. Designated
> LADATEL telephones are located at the west side Jardín
> portal, San Francisco Hotel, inside the Presidencia, Hotel
> Quinta Loreto, Post Office, Instituto, Jardín de San Francisco
> and many other locations. The charge is $1 *peso* for a three-minute
> local call, which includes 800 toll-free numbers and operator
> services. In México, coin pay phones are being phased out.

LADATEL: (Operator Assisted)

1. La Caseta de Pepe
Sollano #4
Tel: 152-6061 and 152-6001
Hrs: Daily 8am-9:30pm
Operated assisted calls worldwide—payment in cash
Customers talk in one of ten private booths

2. Multicom (communication multi-services)
Correo #3 (Parroquia side of Sollano)
Tel: 152-1579   and   152-6368
E-mail: multicom000@yahoo.com
Hrs: Mon-Sat 10am-3pm and 4:30-7pm
Owner: Lic. Ana Lilia Buendía (bilingual)
Cell phones for sale or rent
Buy prepaid telephone cards (private, public or cell)
Subscribe to telephone service for national or international long
	distance at economical rates + other services available
Opened Nov'01

Tennis Courts

1. Walter Weber's
Callejón de San Antonio #12
Tel: 152-0659
Three private clay courts
Court rental per hour—very reasonable
Lessons available
Bathroom, but no showers at the courts
Walter died Dec'03, now run by his son Walter, Jr.

2. Mauricio Chauvet
Hotel Aldea
Calle Ancha de San Antonio s/n (across from the Instituto)
Tel: 152-1022
E-mail: tenisma@mexmexmex.com
Web page: mexmexmex.com/tenisma
Two clay courts
Tennis pro (some English spoken)
Daily 8am-7pm
    Mornings–adults (lessons)   Afternoons–children (clinics)
Weekends
    Sat 8am-2pm (lessons/clinics)–afternoon rentals
    Sunday court rentals
Restrooms and soda machine
Hotel restaurant plus swimming pool (small fee when not busy)

3. Hotel Aristos
Calle del Cardo #2 (across from St. Paul's church)
Tel: 152-0392
Two hard-surfaced courts–poor condition
Non-guest court rental

4. Hotel Real de Minas
Calle Ancha de San Antonio s/n
Tel: 152-2626
Two new hard-surfaced courts–excellent condition
Hourly fee for non-guests

5. Malanquín Country Club
Road to Celaya (2 kms south from Centro)
Tel: 152-0516
Hrs: Tues-Sun 8am-6pm, closed Monday
4 clay tennis courts
Guest membership (one day) tennis

Theater

Teatro Angela Peralta
Mesones at Hernández Macías (down the street from Bellas Artes)
Theater was built in 1873 (130th anniversary in 2003)
At the time, soprano Angela Peralta was the reigning Queen of Opera
She opened the new theater and later it was named after her
Now run by the Federal government
Stop by to see the mural, "Homage to the Arts" in the main lobby,
    by professor Carmen Cereceda, which was dedicated Oct'03
Three seating areas:
    Orchestra (*luneta*), First balcony (*palcos*), Second balcony (*galería*)
Numerous events are held throughout the year, including the
    August Chamber Music Festival (founded in 1979)
      E-mail: fesmusic@chambermusicmexico.org
      Web page: www.chambermusicmexico.org
    November International Jazz Festival
      Web page: www.jazz-sma.com
See the ATENCIóN for specific dates and times

Also: **El Sindicato** (El Recreo), Recreo #4
Teatro del Pueblo, Calle Stirling Dickinson #28

In addition, lectures, plays and playreadings are held at smaller theaters located at the Bellas Artes auditorium, Teatro Santa Anna at the Biblioteca, Instituto Allende, Villa Jacaranda, Sindicato (Recreo #4), as well as the Parish Hall at St. Paul's church. All activities are listed in the ATENCIóN Arts & Culture supplement.

Things to Do

Listed below are things to do when not shopping, eating or night clubbing. All are affordable and some are free.

1. Just sit in the town's beautiful central square, the Jardín. No better place to relax and take it all in. Watch both the locals and gringos of this unique town in action.

2. Take a 3-hour trip to San Miguel surroundings, a benefit for Centro de Crecimiento (school for rehabilitation of handicapped children). The English speaking tour departs Saturday at 10:30am from the Jardín. The price is approximately US$15 and a ten-trip ticket can be bought at a discount. A great way to entertain houseguests.

3. Visit **Los Pocitos,** the orchid gardens at the home of Stirling Dickinson (second American to settle here), Santo Domingo #38 (east on Correo and continue up the hill). View the largest private collection of orchids in México. Open from 10am-5pm Tues-Fri, Sat 10-2pm (closed Sun & Mon). A small admission charge (US$1). Located on the ruins of a former tannery. Note new side entrance. Remember, not all times of the year will you see orchids in bloom. Stirling, a treasured citizen and friend of all, lived in San Miguel 61 years, died in a solo car accident on 29 October, 1998, at age 87. Now managed by Nina Gama of Cante. A bust of the late Stirling Dickinson stands at the corner of Ancha de San Antonio and the new Stirling Dickinson Street (alongside the Hotel Real de Minas). It was dedicated on October 29, 1999.

4. If you don't do anything else, take the Sunday **House and Garden Tour.** It leaves via bus from the Biblioteca at 12 noon for a 2-hour tour of three of San Miguel's finest homes. See what is "behind the walls." You may be introduced to *bóveda* brick domed ceilings and rooftop *cúpulas*. Now over 300 homes in inventory. The tours are a voluntary project sponsored by the library for the educational benefit of the youth of San Miguel. Tickets are US$15 or *peso* equivalent and go on sale Sunday morning at 11am. Come early to enjoy the festive atmosphere in the outdoor courtyard with live Mexican music. Also an opportunity to meet some of the volunteers, visit with other people going on the tour and buy cards and books to support the Library. Discounts given for groups of ten or more.

5. Walking tour of San Miguel is sponsored by Patronato Pro-Niños. Proceeds provide medical care for underprivileged children of San Miguel. Tours leave from in front of the Parroquia on Monday, Wednesday and Friday at 10am and lasts a couple hours. A *peso* donation of approximately US$10 is requested. Check "Ongoing Events Calendar" in the ATENCIóN to confirm tour schedules. Private or special arrangements can be made for groups of five or more. Call 154-4353 or 152-7796.

6. Visit **Guajuye,** the local *vidrio* (glass) factory, located at Lupita #2 (approx ½ km west of the bus station). Witness the art of glass blowing. Call Tel: 152-7033 (factory telephone numbers are 30-34) one or two days in advance to make a Wed, Thurs or Friday morning (10:30am) factory tour reservation. Ask for an English-speaking guide who will explain everything in about ½ hour from a single location inside the factory. No picture taking allowed. Factory-made glass products are for sale in a retail outlet across the street on Cal. de la Estación. The store is open Monday to Saturday 10am-6pm.

7. Take a walk in the **Centro Historic District.** Any direction you go from the Jardín will be a rewarding experience. You will be walking on narrow cobblestone streets and equally narrow sidewalks (Note that locals always walk on the shady side). Enjoy the numerous beautiful water fountains that were restored to working order in the summer of 1997. Pass Spanish-style *haciendas* with high walls and massive doors. You will see scarlet bougainvillea cascading over stone walls and in the spring, blooming purple *jacaranda.* The walls are white or pastel shades of faded pink, orange, green and blue. A great photo op! In addition, you will be treated to the special sounds of San Miguel. The ubiquitous church bells and firecrackers, school bands rehearsing, dogs barking and roosters crowing, as well as the distinctive metal clanging of a passing garbage truck or the high pitched horn of a fresh milk delivery pickup truck.

One such walk from the Jardín might take you east on Correo two blocks to Recreo. Turn right and walk several blocks south, past the Plaza de Toros, to the end. You will now be at **El Chorro** where in the mornings women scrub clothes in outdoor tubs. Continue your trek east uphill through the Waterworks and past a small chapel and then a steep climb to a main road called Salida a Querétaro. Now head north (left) a short distance before coming to the *"mirador"* for a fantastic panoramic view of San Miguel and beyond. Afterwards, take any downhill side street and return to Centro.

Insider's Tip: Public rest rooms (*sanitarios públicos*) are few and far between. One is located half a block from the Jardín on Cuna de Allende, across from Posada Carmina—cost $2 pesos. Another one is located at the Biblioteca at Insurgentes #25. The bathrooms are located in the back between the courtyard and Café Santa Ana. Of course, all hotels and restaurants have facilities for their guests.

8. Hike up to the **Botanic Garden,** on the outskirts of town. The **Jardín Botánico Conservation Area,** which opened in July 1991, covers a total area of approximately 250 acres. It is made up of the Jardín Botánico, Parque Las Colonias and Parque el Charco del Ingenio (roughly translated as "the devil's water hole"). The area includes a canyon, a small lake, an ancient dam and numerous hiking trails. The terrain supports many types of bushes, trees, wild flowers and cacti.

The **Jardín Botánico** consists of approximately two hectares and is managed by Cante. It has a collection of some 826 different species of cacti and succulents. The entrance fee is modest and it is open daily from sunrise to sunset.

The **Parque Las Colonias** consists of approximately 36 hectares and is a city-owned recreation area. It includes a nursery with some 30,000 plants for sale. Also, it has six miles of hiking trails and the park can be used for picnics, games, bicycling and camping. The entrance fee is very modest and the park is open daily.

The third area, **Parque el Charco del Ingenio** (since 1998) is run independently by César Arias. It consists of approximately 63 hectares of preservation land and has approximately six miles of hiking trails. The entrance fee is modest and the park is open from sunrise to sunset. The office is located in Jesús #32, Tel: 154-4715.

The directions from the Jardín are:

Go north one block to Mesones

Turn right, continue east, crossing Nuñez. Mesones becomes Aparicio. Continue east, winding left (pass two streets on right)

Turn right (third street) on Calle del Tecolote (marked in black letters on building)

Go uphill (east) and turn right at first intersection (Calle de San José) and continue uphill to edge of nice houses (Los Balcones)

Turn left on Montitlán, continuing up steep hill past all houses.

Go past Privada de Montilán sign on left and more houses, staying on Prolong. Montitlán. Soon you will come to a gate and a sign, El Charco del Ingenio. If gate is locked, continue 1/4 mile along path to main gate. Entrance fee is $20 *pesos.*

Allow 30 minutes — bring a hat, H_2O and a friend

A word of caution. If you have any health problems, take a taxi. Also keep in mind that late afternoon during the rainy season (May-Oct) would not be a good time to go hiking.

Cante, founded 1987, is a non-profit organization that promotes conservation and is located in a national historic monument at Mesones #71 (Tel: 152-4015, E-mail: canteac@gto1.telmex.net.mx). Federico Gama (trilingual) is the director. Today Cante also manages Los Pocitos (Stirling Dickinson's orchid gardens) at Santo Domingo #38 in Atascadero. The greenhouses and plant collection were donated to Cante in 1993.

9. Hop a bus and take a day trip to nearby **Querétaro** (a very clean colonial city with interesting parks, museums, shops and cafés), **Dolores Hidalgo** (a historic town known for its *talavera* factories) or **Guanajuato** (a charming old silver mining city with its unique underground roadway, winding narrow streets, plazas, churches and a university). See green **Addendum.**

10. Take a 10 minute ride out of town on the road (Rt 51) to Dolores Hidalgo. Stop at a *carnita* restaurant called **La Cruz del Perdón,** on the left, and near the Taboada hot springs. It is open only on the weekends. Well worth the mid-day trip, as a whole pig is cooked on the premises in a large vat near the entrance. The sliced pork loin (*lomo* and *costillas*) is very tasty and is served with homemade *tortillas, guacamole,* and *salsa.* Quite rustic with small plastic tables in a country setting. Also, the *cerveza* is cold! It is easy to flag down a bus on the main road heading back to town.

11. After a few days you might be ready to visit the **Taboada** public hot springs (**Agua Mágica**). It is only a 15-minute ride from Centro on the road to Dolores Hidalgo. The easiest way to get out there is by car or taxi (negotiate a price first). Located well off the main road which may be a problem when heading home. There are three outdoor pools, one which is olympic size and good for doing laps. It does have some grassed picnic areas, palm trees plus changing rooms. Open daily from 9am-6pm, except Tuesday when it is closed. Weekends can be crowded. The best day to go is Wednesday after the water has been changed on Tuesday. The cost is about US$3 per person. Remember to take a towel! If you feel adventurous, take a bus marked "Nigromante," for about $5 *pesos*, to the Taboada hot springs turn-off. The Santa Verónica pool is nearby or you could take a rather lengthy walk in to the Taboada public hot springs. In San Miguel, pick up the bus at the bus stop on Insurgentes near the Oratorio Church.

Nearby is the Hotel Hacienda Taboada (Tel: 152-0850 and 152-0888, Fax: 152-1798, E-mail: htaboada@starnet.net.mx) which has several pools (112° F) and is well-groomed and maintained. One must buy a rather expensive lunch (approximately US$30 excluding drinks) before gaining entry. The pool hours are 9am-6:30pm and is closed Wednesday.

On the highway there are three other places. The nearby **Santa Verónica** has one large outdoor pool (plus two small pools with warmer water), but more cement and less grass. They have tables with umbrellas. You will be surprised to see a fronton court on the grounds. The hours are 9am-5pm. Friday it is closed while the water is changed. The advantage is that it is located alongside the main road where one can catch a bus back to town. Another place, about three miles from the Taboada turnoff, is the **Escondido Spa**, a series of thermal indoor and outdoor pools. It is open daily from 8am-6pm and costs about US$5 (children half price). During the week only four pools are open. Check out the lotus ponds. Changing rooms, showers and toilets plus soft drinks and chips are available. Very clean and a good place just to relax. A little further on the Dolores road, also on the left, is **La Gruta.** A clean, peaceful natural hot water spa with a small pool, tunnel and indoor cave. It is run by Sra. Flor de María Pérez who can be reached at 185-2099. It is open daily from 8am-6pm. Cost is about US$5 per person. Private parties (from 5pm-12 midnight) can be arranged. Complete facilities plus a small restaurant with snacks and cold drinks. Enjoy! You can reach both **Escondido** and **La Gruta** by bus from San Miguel. Go to Calz. de la Luz (end of Loreto St. and then turn right) and look for a yellow bus (marked Santuario) with a friendly driver, Teofilo. It leaves San Miguel every day (except Thursday) at 8am, 10am, 12 noon, 2pm and 4pm. The 25 minute ride costs $6 *pesos*. The bus also goes to Atotonilco.

12. Visit or tour the Sanctuary of **Atotonilco** (Indian word for a place of hot waters) some 7 miles north of San Miguel off the road to Dolores Hidalgo. It is a very important religious and historical shrine in México. The church was built in the mid-18th century by Father Alfaro and was dedicated to Jesus of Nazareth. Inside one will see the many poems and frescoes painted on the walls and ceilings of the shrine and its chapels. In 1810 it was the site where Father Hidalgo stopped during his march to San Miguel to pick up the standard of the Virgin of Guadalupe. Also the place where Ignacio Allende was married. Atotonilco attracts thousands of pilgrims annually. It is listed as a World Heritage site by the United Nations.

13. Take a drive or a tour to the ghost mining town of **Pozos** (northeast of San Miguel). By car it is 40 minutes (take the Salida a Querétaro road out of town past Gigante and the jail, left on Dr. Mora until you cross Route #57, then left on road to San Luis de la Paz). The first hotel in town is the **Hotel Casa Mexicana** on the main square. It has been completely renovated and offers seven upscale rooms, a restaurant and an art gallery which promotes international artists. Gourmet meals are prepared daily and are highly recommended. Owner Teresa Martínez, is bilingual and on hand to greet you. While there check out **Emporio Pozos** (exclusive leather and wrought iron furniture, ceramics and rugs.) Call Tel: 01 (442) 293-0014 or E-mail: pozosmex@yahoo.com for reservations (Web page: www.casamexicanahotel.com). Next door is a second equally impressive hotel called **Casa Montana**, run by Susan Montana (Tel: 01 (442) 293-0032, 293-0033 and 293-0034). It has five guest rooms plus a restaurant and bar. It officially opened in June'00. Other galleries worth checking out are **Galería Maya Productions**, run by John Osmond an Australian sculptor

Tel: 01 (442) 293-0052, **Arte Studio** and **Los Famosos de Pozos** café/restaurant and bar, Hidalgo #10B, Tel: 01 (442) 293-0112, run by an American and San Miguel artist Dan Rueffert and one run by Mónica and Mario Sánchez, located across Plaza Zaragoza, which exhibits pre-hispanic musical instruments, Tel: 01 (442) 293-0045. Several other artists and photographers (Geoff Winningham, Janice Freeman and Bill Lieberman) also show their work in town. Allow time to explore the town center and countryside with many silent ruins, underground mine shafts and tunnels. A camera is a must as this is a real photo op! For additional information, contact the State Tourism Office located at the Jardín in San Miguel (Tel: 152-6565). Pozos' web page: www.mineraldepozos.com

14. Maestro Estéban Valdéz, at age 75, is a self-taught master potter and folk artist whose work has been included in the Smithsonian collection. A visit to Rancho Las Flores is a unique opportunity to see both the creator of the charming clay bowls and the primitive lifestyle of a family in the campo. The *maestro*'s pieces are all under 50 *pesos* which makes them extremely affordable to folk art collectors as well as giving visitors to his home and workshop an opportunity to help this hard-working family. A morning trip to Rancho Las Flores is well worth the small effort involved to set it up. It is suggested that unless your Spanish and driving/navigating skills are excellent you arrange a visit with Angélica (Tel: 152-6305) or a driver of your choice. You should also include a visit to a nearby brick factory.

15. For the adventurer, take a **hot air ballon ride** over or around San Miguel. Jay Kimball, from Napa Valley, CA is the licensed/certified pilot. He has 4, 6 or 8 passenger gondolas and the one-hour flight departs at sunrise. On *terra firma* he can be reached at Recreo #68, Tel: 152-6735 or E-mail: kimballflight@hotmail.com.mx. The cost is US$150 per person, which includes breakfast upon landing. Inquire about other adventure tours to the beaches and pyramids.

Insider's Tip: Some organized summer programs for kids:
1. Centro Mexicano de Lengua or Centro Bilingüe
      Spanish and art classes
2. Malanquín Country Club
      Sports, art and field trips (mid-July to mid-August)
3. Instituto Allende
      Creative summer fun (ages 5-11; starts late June for 6 wks)
4. Coyote Canyon Adventures
      Summer adventure horseback riding and camping

Tortilla Factories

1. Tortilla de Maíz ("corn")
Reloj #68
Tel: 152-1265
Hrs: Daily 7:30am-5pm
Owner: Roberto (friendly, speaks a little English)
Sold by weight: $6 *pesos* per kilo (approx 32 *tortillas*)

2. Tortillas de Harina ("flour")
Burritacos
Mesones #69-A
Tel: 152-3222
Hrs: Mon-Sat 10:30am-6pm, closed Sunday
Celina is the friendly manager/owner
Whole wheat *tortillas* Tuesday and Thursday
A package of ten costs $3 *pesos*
Inside is a small, busy lunch counter
Cold drinks available

3. Tortilla La Entretenida
Murillo #13 (between Correo and San Francisco)
Tel: None
Hrs: Daily 7am-5pm
Tortillas de maíz
Cost: ½ kilo for $3 *pesos*

> **Insider's Tip: If you are new to San Miguel and Spanish, it's fun to walk up to a *tortilla* counter, with a *peso* and a smile and receive 6-8 wonderfully, hot fresh *tortillas* and a smile. It's painless!**

Transportation

Private Vehicles:

In San Miguel it isn't necessary to have a car. It is easy to get around town on foot (you see more plus the exercise is beneficial to all). Public transportation (buses and cabs) is still quite reasonable and readily available. By leaving your car at home you don't have to worry about its security or expenses such as gasoline, insurance and parking or the wear and tear from driving on the cobblestone streets.

Look for a green sign which indicates lead-free (*magna sin*) gasoline
        Current price $6.28 *pesos* per liter (March'05)
    A red sign indicates a new Premium (*sin plomo*) gasoline
        Current price $7.45 *pesos* per liter (March'05)
The price will increase 1 or 2 *centavos* per month
Make sure dial is set to zero before the attendant starts pumping!

PEMEX (Government-run gas station)
There are now a number of stations in the San Miguel area. One is
    located on Salida a Querétaro (near Gigante—open daily
    10am-9pm) and others are on Salida a Celaya, Calzada de la
    Estación at the Libramiento (open 24 hours), the road to
    Querétaro past Gigante and by the *glorieta* south of town.

Conversion Chart			
Gallons	Liters	Liters	Gallons
1	3.79	10	2.64
		20	5.28
5	18.93	30	7.93
10	37.85	40	10.57
		50	13.21
15	56.78	60	15.85
		70	18.49
20	75.71	80	21.13

If you should drive in México City or the 28 surrounding
communities, remember to note the last number of your license plate.
Whether you have foreign or Mexican plates there is one weekday
each week when you cannot drive. If you do not comply, the fine is
stiff! The day is determined by the last digit of your plate:

Mon	5-6	Thur	1-2
Tues	7-8	Fri	9-0
Wed	3-4		

Taxis:

Taxis are readily available as there are approximately 300
registered taxis in San Miguel. Most drivers are quite pleasant and
some speak English. Local taxis do not have meters. The normal flat
fare in the Centro area is about US$2. The fare to outlying areas is more

216

and should be negotiated before starting. The new rates allow the driver to charge more per ride after 10pm at night. It is **not customary to tip** cab drivers. In the event a taxi driver insists on a higher than legal rate, pay the rate demanded but write down the taxi number and note the particulars of the trip. Then telephone 152-0164 (the state *Delegación de Tránsito*) or visit the state *tránsito* office, Correo #26, 2nd floor (Chief Antonio Ramírez) to complain that you have been overcharged. There is a good chance the taxi driver and owner will be penalized. Taxi stands are located on the east side of the Jardín, south side of the Civic Plaza and at Central de Autobuses (bus station). If you need to call a taxi, be prepared to pay double. Several numbers to call for this 24-hour service are listed below:

Tel: 152-5993 or 152-4086
044-415-103-2961 (cell)

In San Miguel the state official taxi color is apple-green & white.

Servicio Mixto de Taxi is the name of a taxi that transports people and/or freight. They are small trucks (*camionetas*) and yellow in color. Call Tel: 152-2635 to request one or go to a taxi stand (*sitio*) at Mesones and Juárez and with luck you will find one there. San Miguel has some thirty.

Cars/Vans for Hire:

Cars or vans can be hired for rides to neighboring towns or airports. A number of companies and individuals offer this service. Reservations must be made in advance.

1. Angélica Transportation and Tours
Purísima #4   Col. San Antonio
Tel/Fax: 152-6305   044-415-153-5067 (cell)
E-mail: angelica@unisono.net.mx
Web page: www.angelicatours.com
Family business–Angélica speaks English, ask for Mario!
Airport trips or tours–24-hour service
Different types of vehicles (sedan or Suburban)
Licensed and insured–very reliable
Reasonable rates–varies depending on vehicle type and number of passengers
Competitive airport shuttle rates at peak times

2. Teocalli Tours and Transportation
Refugio Norte #4, Col. San Antonio
Tel: 154-7339   044-415-101-5953 (cell)
E-mail: paulguerin@yahoo.com
Web page: www.tours-in-mexico.com
Owner: Paul Guerin (bilingual)
7-passenger air-conditioned van
Airport runs, shopping excursions plus day trips from San Miguel
Flat rate: US$90 León airport, US$225 México City
Flexible custom tours (US$25 per hour)
    Informative with emphasis on historical perspective
    Guide has traveled México extensively since 1963
Excursions to Pátzcuaro, monarch butterfly sanctuaries, surreal
    ruins of Englishman Edward James or the fascinating ghost
    mining town of Pozos

3.Rafa Tourist Tours
Col. Guadalupe
Tel: 152-7196   044-415-149-8463 (cell)
E-mail: rafatours@hotmail.com
Rafael Tovar (bilingual)
Organized tours or airport transportation—hourly rates or by the day
Car or Suburban
Graduate of Federal Tour Guide course

4. Viajes de San Miguel
Sollano #4 (inside courtyard in back corner)
Tel: 152-2832 and 152-2537   Fax: 152-2538
    Emergency shuttle Tel: 154-6287
E-mail: info@viajessanmiguel.com
Web page: www.viajessanmiguel.com
Hrs: Mon-Fri 9am-7pm, Sat 10am-2:30pm
Also a tour operator for colonial cities

Daily airport shuttle service offered by **Viajes de San Miguel**

México City Int'l Airport	Leon Int'l Airport
Van/First class bus	Van to airport 24 hours daily
24 hours daily	US$27 per person (each way)
US$50 per person	Daily pickup and return
(Special price for three or	Groups-special van price
more people booking together)	US$2 Senior discount
Also private service available	

---

5. Promotion of Mexican Culture (PMC)
Formerly Travel Institute
Hidalgo #16 (near Mesones)
Tel: 152-1630 or 154-5312   Tel/Fax: 152-0121
E-mail: info@pmexc.com
Web page: www.pmexc.com
Hrs: Mon-Sat 9am-7pm, closed Sunday
San Miguel's oldest bilingual tour service
A van with a bilingual driver is available (up to 5/6 passengers)
Insured and licensed tour operator
Airport trips plus other destinations upon request—call for rates
Relocated Jun'03

6. And you thought you'd seen everything . . .
Apdo #928
Tel/Fax: 152-0849   044-415-153-5944 (cell)
E-mail: tours@helenekahn.com
Web page: www.helenekahn.com
Personalized tours for lovers of México
Guide: Helene Kahn
     Background in art history and antiques
     35 years' traveling in México
Walking tours of San Miguel scheduled at your convenience
Motoring trips throughout historic Bajío area
     Focus on history, art, architecture and folkart
     Tours are small and private (can accommodate large groups
       with advanced notice)
     Interior designers and buyers taken to the sources to save
       time and money
Vehicles fully insured

7. Reyna Polanco Tours
Cri Cri #25 (Col. Guadalupe)
Tel: 152-4193   044-415-153-6684 (cell)
E-mail: sydyreyna@yahoo.com
Web page: www.infosma.com/polanco
Car or van, 1-8 passengers
Day or night to León airport and nearby towns
On time, safe and insured, 24-hour service
English spoken
Call for rates

8. Tours México Colonial
Portal Allende #4 (upstairs from Café del Jardín)—Centro
Tel/Fax: 152-5794
E-mail: tour@toursanmiguel.com
Web page: www.toursanmiguel.com
Hrs: Mon-Fri 9am-2pm and 4-7pm, Sat and Sun 9am-3pm
Owner: Jaime Olalde (bilingual)
Local tours, day trips and overnight excursions
　　Daily tours to Guanajuato, Querétaro and Dolores, etc.
　　Excursions to México City, Pátzcuaro, Zacatecas, etc.
　　Bilingual guides
　　Groups no larger than eight people
Also airport transport in a comfortable surburban

9. Leandro Tours
Montes de Oca #1, Centro
Tel: 152-0155 (leave message)　　　　044-415-153-3594 (cell)
E-mail: leandrotours@hotmail.com
Leandro Delgado (bilingual)—professional guide
Small car or 7-passenger air-conditioned van
Airport shuttles and personalized field trips to surrounding towns
Over ten years' experience–very personable and knowledgeable
Reasonable rates

10. Fernando Ibarra (bilingual)
Cinco de Mayo, Col. Allende
Tel: 152-3934
Private car—up to 4 passengers
　　Dolores Hidalgo　　　　US$ 65 per car
　　Querétaro (dropoff/tour)　US$ 50/$100 per car
　　León Airport　　　　　US$ 65 per car
　　Guanajuato (8 hour tour)　US$ 120 per car
　　México City Airport　　US$175 per car

11. American Express Viajes Vertiz Travel Agency
Hidalgo #1-A
Tel: 152-1856 or 152-1695　Fax: 152-0499
E-mail: info@viajesvertiz.com
Two vans available with a limit of six passengers each
　　León Airport　　　　　US$ 95 per van
　　México City Airport　　US$170 per van

12. Itzcuinapan Tours & Transportation
Tel: 152-3873   Fax: 152-0872   044-415-151-3611 (cell)
E-mail: patyw@unisono.net.mx
Web page: http://gomez_tour.tripod.com
Antonio Gómez Hernández (bilingual)—more than 8 years experience
   "Mi pais es su pais" (my country is your country)
Sedan or Suburban
Airport transportation
Local tours plus overnight to Zacatecas, Pátzcuaro, Monarch
   butterfly sanctuary, Teotihuacán pyramids and Sierra Gorda

13. Liliane Maya
Villas del Parque
Tel: 152-3098
E-mail: lcerutti@lycos.com
Tours of the beautiful chapels, all within 15 miles of town
Designed for people sensitive to nature (photographers, artists, etc.)
Spend a day with the outgoing and personable guide
   Liliane speaks English, Spanish and French
Your car or hers (1-4 people)
Optional picnic or swim at a hot spring

14. Aventuras San Miguel
Aldma #1-A
Tel: 152-6406   044-415-153-5489 (cell)
E-mail: aventurasma@yahoo.com
Hrs: Mon-Fri 10am-2pm and 4:30-7pm, Sat 10am-2pm, closed Sun
Owner/tour guide: Antonio Canales (bilingual)
Tours to nearby cities—day or overnight
Mountain biking, horseback riding and camping
Airport trips and San Miguel tours
Since Aug'94, relocated Dec'03

15. Sol y Luna
Hospicio #10
Tel: 154-8599   044-415-103-4112 (cell)
E-mail: reynaldo_vazquez_tours@yahoo.com.mx
Web page: www.solylunatours.com
Hrs: Mon-Fri 9am-7pm, Sat 10am-5pm, Sun 12 noon-5pm
Owner: Reynaldo Vázquez (bilingual) and Katherine
Tours, transportation and rentals
Horseback riding, bicycle tours, kayaking, camping and more

More than 10 years experience
Opened new office Nov'03
Also rentals, translation services and babysitters
2nd office: Correo #41, Tel: 152-1922

Others: **Dali Amaro**, Tours, Tel: 044-415-100-3046 (cell)
　　　Juan Vázquez Transportation/Tours, Tel: 152-4173
　　　Kurt Tours/Transportation, Tel: 154-7250
　　　Nopal Tours, Horacio Miguel, Tel: 152-7932
　　　Mario's Transportation, Tel: 152-5614
　　　Francisco Santiago, Tel: 044-415-103-8974 (cell)

Buses (In Town):

Buses run all day on prescribed routes and the fare is about $4 *pesos*. All buses leave from Calle Colegio (east side of Civic Plaza). Following are some routes and designated bus stops.

1. Gigante–Placita–La Luz
　　Civic Plaza or Jardín de San Francisco
　　Calle San Francisco (east)
　　Pedro Vargas
　　Salida a Querétaro

2. Central (bus station)**–Estación** (RR station)
　　Civic Plaza
　　Insurgentes near Hidalgo
　　Las Monjas (Canal at Zacateros)
　　Canal (west)

3. Central (bus station)**–Malanquín**
　　Civic Plaza
　　Insurgentes near Hidalgo
　　Las Monjas (Canal at Zacateros)
　　Canal (west)
　　Libramiento (Hospital de la Fé)

4. San Antonio
　　Civic Plaza
　　Insurgentes near Hidalgo
　　Umarán at Zacateros
　　Zacateros (south)
　　Ancha de San Antonio (Instituto)-Orizaba (Col. San Antonio)

5. Unidad DPVA
Civic Plaza
Insurgentes near Hidalgo
Umarán at Zacateros
Zacateros (south)
Ancha de San Antonio (Guadiana)
Salida a Celaya (Country Club and Los Frailes)

6. Cinco de Mayo–Col. Allende
Civic Plaza
Insurgentes near Hidalgo
Umarán at Zacateros
Zacateros (south)
Ancha de San Antonio (Guadiana)

7. San Luis Rey
Civic Plaza
Insurgentes near Hidalgo
Hernández Macías (north)
Calzada de la Aurora

Buses (Out of Town):

Central de Autobuses (bus station) is located 1½ km west on Calle Canal. The two major lines that service the area are Flecha Amarilla (yellow arrow) and Herradura de Plata (silver horseshoe). Bus departures are frequent and there are three classes of buses (luxury, first class and second class) which offer reasonable fares.

Luxury/first class buses are modern, comfortable, clean and usually have TV monitors to show video movies. Herradura de Plata seems to be very well run and offers courteous service. Flecha Amarilla's security has been known to be lax. You must always be alert and careful with luggage and it is best never to leave it unattended.

Following are the first class bus schedules, which of course, are subject to change at any time. The cost is about US$19 each way. Be prepared for future price increases. Primera Plus tickets can be paid by credit card.

San Miguel-México City (3½-4 hour trip)

Primera Plus (Flecha Amarilla) Tel: 152-7323
Departures: 9:30am and 4pm, Sunday add 5pm
Also buses to **Guanajuato,** León and Guadalajara leave at
    7:30am, 9:45am, 12:45pm (Gto only) 5:30pm and 7:50pm
    Return first class bus from Gto: 1:30pm, 3pm, 5:15pm and 7:20pm

The trip to Guanajuato takes 1½ hours and costs approx. US$7
> Return second class buses run at other times

Guadalajara takes 5 hours and cost approx. US$30

Pegasso Plus (Herradura de Plata) Tel: 152-0725
> Departures: 6am and 1pm, Sunday 4:30pm

**The destination in México City is the Terminal de Autobuses
del Norte (North bus station)**

México City-San Miguel (3½-4 hour trip)

Primera Plus (Flecha Amarilla)
> Daily departures 7am, 11:15am and 5:40pm

Pegasso Plus (Herradura de Plata)
> Daily departures: 3:45pm and 11pm

Primera Plus (Flecha Amarilla) has an in-town ticket/
reservation office at Sollano #11 (near Calle Correo)
Tel: 152-5043
Office Hrs: Mon-Sat 9am-5pm, closed Sunday
Check travel agencies also for bus ticket purchases

A third line, **ETN**, in early 1995 inaugurated a luxury service to
México City.

The current schedule is:
> Depart San Miguel daily 7am, 12 noon, 3pm and 6pm (Sun no 7am trip)
> Depart México City 10:05am, 12:30pm, 4:30pm and 6:20pm
> Two daily departures to Guadalajara via Guanajuato departs
> San Miguel 8:45am and 4:15pm–about US$34 (US$9 to Gto)

After some six years all ETN buses now depart and return to the
Central de Autobuses (bus station) located west of Centro on
lower Calle Canal. The 3½-4 hour trip may stop in Querétaro
if enough seats are empty. All buses have only 24 reclining
seats with leg supports plus a bathroom. In addition, they
offer free cold soft drinks and sandwiches.

Tickets cost about US$22 (about US$6 to Querétaro) and may be
purchased at the bus station–Tel: 152-6407 and **Promotion
of Mexican Culture**–Hidalgo #16–Tel: 152-1630
Prices and schedules are subject to change at any time.

Seat reservations can be made up to 15 days in advance with payment

224

Aero Plus first class bus has service to México City International Airport **(Gate D area)** from Querétaro (first take a 50-minute 2nd class bus ride or taxi from San Miguel). The three-hour bus ride costs about US$19 and tickets are purchased at the Querétaro bus station (Tel: 01 (442) 211-4001). The current schedule and price are subject to change at any time without notice.

Querétaro – México City Airport (Departure Times)		México City Airport – Querétaro (Departure Times)	
2 am	10:30 am	7 am	4 pm
3 am	11:30 am	8:30 am	4:45 pm
3:30 am	12:30 pm	10 am	5:30 pm
4:30 am	1:30 pm	11 am	6:15 pm
5:30 am	2:30 pm	12 noon	7 pm
6:30 am	3:15 pm	1 pm	7:45 pm
7:30 am	4 pm	1:45 pm	8:30 pm
8:30 am	5 pm	2:30 pm	9:15 pm
9:30 am	6 pm	3:15 pm	10 pm

> Direct **Aero Plus** bus service between San Miguel – México City airport and San Miguel – León airport has been discontinued (Dec'96).

Autobuses Americanos
Tel: 154-8233
First-class bus departure daily at 6pm, many stops enroute
USA stops:
    Laredo, TX approximately US$55–13-hour trip–return at 7:30pm
    San Antonio US$68, Houston US$79, Dallas US$87
Trips to Austin, Texas or Dallas from Querétaro or San Luis Potosí
From Houston–also connections to Chicago
Tickets can be purchased two weeks in advance at the bus station
Querétaro bus station Tel: 01(442) 229-0003

Transportes San Miguel
Behind Plaza Real del Conde (Gigante)
Tel: 154-7540 and 152-5637
    Dallas, TX (214) 946-2022 (Bruno is the owner)
    Toll Free (USA) 1-877-846-2022
Office Hrs: Daily 9am-7:30pm
    Small lounge with TV and bathroom
Private bus company

    Buses include bathroom plus video movies
    Non-stop to the Texas border—best to travel weekdays
    Also take small packages
San Miguel departures: Daily 6pm from back of Gigante
    Dallas, TX plus other Texas cities enroute
Competitive prices (approx. US$50)—Senior discount (age 60) less US$20
Return from Dallas—Daily departure at 7pm
    Upon San Miguel arrival, don't leave bags unattended

Estrella Blanca (Transportes del Norte) Tel: 152-2237 first class bus (cost approx US$51) leaves daily at 7pm for Nuevo Laredo, México via Monterrey. The trip takes approx. 12 hours.

Flecha Amarilla has a second class bus (cost about US$11) from San Miguel to San Luis Potosí. The trip takes approx. 4 hours and goes via Dolores Hidalgo and San Felipe. The current schedule is:

SMA – SLP		SLP – SMA	
7:40 am	3:20 pm	6 am	4 pm
8:55 am	5:50 pm	8 am	6 pm
11:15 pm	6:30 pm	10 am	8 pm
12:25 pm		12 noon	10 pm
		2 pm	

It might be faster to take a second class bus to Querétaro and then a first class bus to San Luis Potosí.

Airlines:

León (town of Silao)–near Guanajuato
International airport (BJX)
Flights less frequent and a little more expensive
American Airlines and Continental fly from Dallas and Houston
Mexicana and Aeroméxico Airlines fly from US west coast
1½ hour private car/van or taxi ride to San Miguel

> Most airline tickets purchased outside México include the departure and visitor's tax. Visitors (not FM-3 holders) who purchase airline tickets locally must pay in cash a visitor's tax (US$21 or *peso* equivalent) at the time of departure at the airport.

México City
International airport (MEX)
United, American, Continental, Delta and Canadian airlines all fly
    to México City

3½ to 4 hour bus or van ride to San Miguel
> There are a number of first-class direct buses (Aero Plus)
> from the airport to Querétaro–then take a taxi or
> second-class bus to San Miguel

Aeromar–Aeroméxico (VW)–(domestic airport)
> Tel: 01 (55) 5627-0207 or 01 (442) 224-1333
> **México City-Querétaro:**
> > 2:45-3:30pm   5-5:45pm   8:45-9:30pm
>
> **Querétaro-México City:**
> > 6-6:45am   10-10:45am   3:45-4:30pm
> > > One way–approx US$90

Trains (*FFCC*):

The train station (Tel: 152-0007) is located approximately 1km west of the bus station. Trains are not very reliable and often run late, if at all. Presently no passenger trains run to the border. Since 1997 TFM, a private company, operates the line and freight is the main business of the railroad.

Travel Agencies

1. Viajes de San Miguel
Sollano #4 (inside courtyard in the back corner)
Tel: 152-2832 and 152-2537   Fax 152-2538
> Emergency Tel: 154-6287
E-mail: info@viajessanmiguel.com
Web page: www.viajessanmiguel.com
Hrs: Mon-Fri 9am-7pm, Sat 10am-2:30pm, closed Sunday
Credit cards: Amex, Master and Visa
Partners: Luís Antonio and Detlev (English, Spanish & German spoken)
Ticket sales for international and domestic flights
Daily shuttle service to and from airports
Tour operator for colonial cities
Hotel reservations (special rates in México)
In business since 1987, new ownership 1996

2. Viajes Vertiz (American Express Travel Service)
Hidalgo #1-A (½ block from Jardín)
Tel: 152-1856 and 152-1695   Fax: 152-0499
E-mail: info@viajesvertiz.com

Hrs: Mon-Fri 9am-2pm and 4-6:30pm, Sat 10am-2pm, closed Sun
Manager/owner: Malinda Vertiz (bilingual)
Connected to Sabre Travel Information Network
Airline tickets, tours and cruises
Airport van shuttle service available (for a fee)
Sell American Express travelers' checks (US$ or *pesos*)
Receive moneygrams from all over the world–same day service

3. Promotion of Mexican Culture (PMC)
Hidalgo #16 (near Mesones)
Tel: 152-1630 or 154-5312   Tel/Fax: 152-0121
E-mail: info@pmexc.com
Web page: www.pmexc.com
Hrs: Mon-Sat 9am-7pm, closed Sunday
Owner: Marisela Patterson (bilingual)
English-speaking staff
Ask about local tours (SMA and surrounding area), shopping trips
    to Querétaro and transportation to airports
No airline ticket sales—sells first-class bus tickets
Sells maestro Estéban Valdéz' hand-made pottery made in his village
Opened in 1986 (formerly called Travel Institute), relocated Jun'03

Toll-free airline offices in Mexico:

1. Air Canada	01-800-719-2827
2. American Airlines	01-800-362-7000/800-904-6000
3. America West	001-800-235-9292 (USA)
4. Continental Airlines	01-800-900-5000
5. Delta Airlines	01-800-902-2100
6. United Airlines	01-800-003-0700
7. Aeroméxico Airlines	01-800-021-4010
8. Mexicana Airlines	01-800-502-2000

Mexico's Ministry of Tourism (SECTUR) toll-free number
in USA and web site for information and brochures:
1-800-44-México
www.visitmexico.com

Utility Companies

1. Comisión Federal de Electricidad
Regional San Miguel de Allende
Zona Celaya División Bajo
Callejón de Loreto #13
Tel: 152-0004
Hrs: Mon-Fri 8am-3:30pm, closed weekends and holidays
   (8am-1pm payment only)
Place to pay monthly electric bills (Note: you can pay at an
   automatic machine in the lobby)
Can also pay at local bank for a small fee

2. Gas Inem, SA de CV (Gas Express)
Carretera Celaya, km 48 (near Los Frailes)
Tel: 152-7777 and 152-6465   Emerg Tel: 152-0228
Hrs: Mon-Fri 8:30am-4pm, Sat 8:30am-1pm
Call to request gas LP, must pay at time of delivery
Under new management

Also: **Termo Gas,** Umarán #20-A, Tel: 152-2272
Gas Noel, Fracc. La Lejona, Tel: 154-8383

3. SAPASMA (Sistema de Agua Potable y Alcantarillado SMA)
Ancha de San Antonio #81 (below Oxxo store and around back)
Tel: 152-4429 and 152-4641
Hrs: Payments Mon-Fri 8:30am-2pm
     Services Mon-Fri 8am-3pm, Sat/Sun 9am-3pm (tel only)
Director: Arq. Armando Rivera Salas
Customer Service: Hidalia López (bilingual)
Some office personnel speak English
Place to pay water bills
More than 15,000 individual water meters in San Miguel

4. Tele Cable
Salida a Celaya, km1 (just past Ford agency)
Tel: 152-1942 and 152-3442   Fax: 152-1145
Hrs: Mon-Fri 8:30am-2pm and 4:30-5:30pm, Sat 9am-2pm
     Closed Sunday (open Sundays at Gigante Plaza)
General Manager: Lic. Ricardo Trejo
Basic monthly charge approximately US$20 (installation extra)
Includes 39 channels (channels and fees can change without notice)
Additional channels extra charge plus box deposit
10,000 subscribers, 25% are English speaking

Relocated to a large, new office and studio–Sept'99
Now offers a high-speed cable Internet service called cyberm@tsa
Sub-office:
  Located at Plaza Real del Conde (ground floor)
  Tel: 152-7755
  Hrs: Daily 10:30am-4:30pm (including Sunday)

Look for a privately published free fortnight cable TV guide.

Antenna TV—Just a few Mexican stations

Satellite dish—Now quite popular in San Miguel
Celaya distributor: Enrique Rivera (bilingual) Tel: 01(461)145-3269
Buy Satellite Orbit or Direct TV magazine locally for monthly
  programming and listing of optional channel packages available

5. Radio Station (XESQ-1280 Khz)
Sollano #4 (inside courtyard, office upstairs in the back)
Tel: 152-0227 and 152-0799   Fax: 152-0803
E-mail: radiosanmiguelsa@prodigy.net.mx
Hours on air: Daily 6am-10pm
Don Manuel Zavala Zavala—announcer since 1961
Spanish only
Music, news, interviews and public service announcements
An important link for the people living in the remote ranches outside
  town. Mexican relatives in the USA send letters and money to
  the radio station. Free announcements are made on the radio at
  6:45 am so people know that messages or money are waiting for them.

6. Radio Station (EXA FM 105.9)
MultiMundo Corporation (total 10 stations in México)
Plaza Real del Conde (AB#10)—upstairs
Tel: 152-6661   Fax: 152-6999
E-mail: multisan@prodigy.net.mx
Hours: Daily 6am-12 midnight
Station 30,000 watts
Spanish only
Music
Started in 1994, renamed Jun'03

> If you should happen to lose something (i.e., camera, glasses, etc.) during your visit report it at once to the police station (Plaza Principal #10) as well as the radio station. Fill out a report with the bilingual receptionist in the radio station office (upstairs in the back). Select the times for it to go out on the airways (best times are during the 7:30am and 2:45pm news) and pay $45 *pesos* + IVA for each announcement. Remember to offer an attractive reward and with luck it will be returned directly to you. Many locals, including taxi drivers, listen to the radio regularly. Try – it works!

7. TELMEX
Salida a Celaya #56 (relocated Dec'03)
Tel: 152-5222 and 152-2331
Hrs: Mon-Fri 8am-2pm, closed weekends and holidays
Pay monthly phone bills, file complaints, etc.
Can also pay bill with Master or Visa card
     Payment can be made at the telegraph office
          (Correo #16)–next to MexPost
          Hrs: Mon-Fri 9am-6pm, Sat/Sun 9am-12 noon

You can also pay at a local bank for a small fee

*Additional information listed separately under *Telephone*

Veterinarians/S.P.A./Grooming

1. Dr. Edgardo R. Vázquez Olmos M.V.Z.
The Wendy Johnson Memorial Clinica de Animales (Nov'00)
Mesones #5 (across from Academia)
Tel: 152-6273 and 154-4785 Emer/Night: 152-1275
Hrs: Mon-Fri 9am-2pm and 4-7pm, Sat 9am-12 noon
Bilingual vet
Cats and dogs, also short-term boarding
Also an Animal Hospital
     State-of-art equipment
     Surgery and hospitalization, laboratory and radiology
Affiliate member of American Animal Hospital Association
Full line of regular and prescription foods
Also grooming

2. Dr. Robert Merrill Márquez
Pedro Páramo #67 (Col. El Mirador)
Tel: 152-2901
E-mail: dmerrill@prodigy.net.mx
Completely bilingual, will make house calls
Small animal (dogs, cats and birds) surgery
Dog and cat boarding
Dog Grooming
Will transport animals to USA
Practicing since 1983

3. Dr. Rolando Téllez Hoyos
Veterinaria de San Miguel
Mesones #14 (past Civic Plaza)–relocated July'98
Tel/Fax: 152-1698 and 152-2657
Hrs: Mon-Sat 9am-2:30pm and 4-8:15pm, Sun 10am-2pm
Dog and cat food plus much more
Since 1983

4. Pet Vet
Plaza Real del Conde (Gigante)
Pet store and clinic next to each other (near Gigante exit)
Tel: 152-4276   Emerg Tel: 152-4463 (*casa*)
Hrs: Mon-Sat 10am-2pm and 4-8pm, Sunday 11am-6pm (store only)
Dra. Alma Ruth Miranda Valenzuela, MVZ (bilingual)
Store sells dog, cat, bird and fish accessories
Clinic for hospitalization plus kennels and training
Open 1992

5. Tato and Lore (canine coiffeurs)
Prol. de Pila Seca #2 (corner of 20 de Enero)
Tel: 154-7063
Hrs: Mon-Fri 9am-4pm, Sat 9am-2pm, closed Sunday
Owners Juan Carlos (formerly with Dr. Vázquez) and Lore
Bathing and grooming—dogs and cats only
          Also ear and gland cleaning plus nail trimming
Ample parking
Open Nov'00, relocated July'04

6. Magic Pets
Umarán #64-A (west of Quebrada)
Tel/Fax: 152-1344
E-mail: milagrosverdeja@yahoo.com.mx

232

Hrs: Mon-Fri 11am-2pm and 5-8pm, Sat 11am-5pm, closed Sun
Owner: Milagros Verdeja Vázquez
Pet accessory store (dogs, cats and fish)
Cat and dog food (Royal Canine and Diamond)
Also grooming, boarding and sale of pedigree dogs
Open July'00

7. Olimpia Miranda
Tel: 152-3768
Grooming—same day pickup and delivery
Knowledgeable and gentle with animals
Trained to show dogs

8. Amigos Caninos ("canine friends")
Virreyes #11, Col. Los Frailes
Tel: 154-4182
E-mail: sueinsma@unisono.net.mx
Partners: Sue Gearhart, María Alicia Ruiz and Dr. Poncho Segura
Dog training (protection, show and obedience)
Grooming, home care, boarding—also cats
Since July'04 (formerly First Class Kennels)

9. Charlotte Peltz Dog Trainer
Diligencias #5 (Atascadero)
Tel: 152-2494
E-mail: charpeltz@cybermatsa.com.mx
Basic canine obedience course
Private or group dog training available all year
Bilingual classes
25 years' experience with animals
Look for her column in the ATENCIóN

10. S.P.A. (Sociedad Protectora de Animales, AC)
Los Pinos #7 (small street across from bus station)
Tel: 152-6124
Hrs: Mon-Fri 10am-2pm
Good selection of dogs and cats to adopt
Free anti-rabies vaccinations every Friday 8-10am

Video Rentals

1. Video Centro
Hernández Macías #12 (close to Calzada de la Luz)
Tel: 152-4348
Hrs: Mon-Fri 10am-3pm and 4-9pm, Sat/Sun 10am-9pm
Owner: Manuel González Laguna
Free membership
More than 5,000 selections—all in English
Prices range US$2—$2.50, depending if catalog, super hit or DVD
Since 1986, relocated 1996

2. Video Fuentes
San Francisco #24 (up the street from Juárez intersection)
Tel: None
Hrs: Mon-Sat 10am-9pm, Sun 10am-8pm
Owner: Sra. María Fuentes
English movies with Spanish subtitles
Good selection–new movies weekly
Very good prices
Since 1988

3. Blockbuster Video
Ancha de San Antonio #17-A (opposite side from Instituto)
Tel: 152-7580
Hrs: Daily 10am-11pm (weekends close at 12 midnight)
Manager: Oscar Arturo Hurtado
No membership fee
More than 3,000 selections–90% in English with Spanish subtitles
Prices start at about US$2 (different for new, old or kids)
Rent VCR's (about US$6) for five days, also Nintendo and Play Station
Opened July'99

Volunteer Organizations

Some of the local non-profit community organizations are listed below. For a more complete listing, check a booklet called "Community Services" (1994) at the Biblioteca office. If you have time or money these organizations are worthy of your support. Get involved–call today!

1. ALMA
Home for the elderly of San Miguel
Tel: 152-2866 or 152-7210

2. Audubon Society of San Miguel
A bicultural organization working to preserve and restore the
    natural ecosystem of the San Miguel area.
Tel: 152-1678 and 152-2985

3. Biblioteca Pública
Tel: 152-0293
    Library volunteers always welcome
    ATENCIóN San Miguel newspaper
    Computer Center
    House and Garden Tour
    English classes for school kids

4. C.A.S.A.
Medical, social service and family planning for needy families
    (teens and poor)
Tel: 154-6090 and 154-6060

5. Casa Hogar Don Bosco
Cares for girls without parents or abandoned
Tel: 152-1195

6. Centro de Crecimiento
Rehabilitation and child development for Mexican children
    with impairments
Tel: 152-0318

7. DIF (Desarrollo Integral de la Familia)
Director/President: Patricia Morán
Municipal family help program
Tel: 152-3380 and 152-0910

8. FAI
Works in rural communities to improve children's environment
    and quality of life
Retail store/office: Hidalgo #13
    Hrs: Mon-Fri 9am - 2pm and 4-6pm, Sat 10am - 2pm
Tel/Fax: 152-3686 and 152-0897
E-mail: faigto@prodigy.net.mx
Web page: www.faigto.com

9. Feed the Hungry San Miguel de Allende
Providing a nutritious hot meal to more than 3,000 children a day.
    23 kitchens provide the food that makes possible children's
health, education and future. A non-profit charity tax
deductible in the USA and México.
Executive Director: Tony Adlerbert   Dep Exec Director: Mary Murrell
Tel: 152-2402
Mail: Border Crossings, Mesones #57 (Interior)
E-mail: contact@feedthehungrysma.org
Web page: www.feedthehungrysma.org

10. Hogar de los Angeles
Free Christian day care center and shelter for children six months
    to five years for parents who work in the community
Tel: 154-5512 (Donna Quathamer)
E-mail: casangeles_sma@hotmail.com
Web page: www.casadelosangeles.org

11. Lions International
Provides eye care for needy people
Tel: 152-3563, 152-3408

12. Los Amigos de Mexiquito
Orphaned, abused or abandoned boys
Tel: 152-5082

13. IREE
Educates and rehabilitates children with physical and learning
    disabilities
Tel: 152-0913

14. Mujeres en Cambio ("women in change")
Provides support for disadvantaged women in the surrounding
    rural communities
Tel: 152-2435, 152-0935 or 154-5899

15. Patronato Pro Niños
Provides medical and dental care to needy children in the San
    Miguel area. One can volunteer to work with the children or
    some special social events.
Tel: 152-7796
E-mail: info@patronatoproninos.com

16. San Miguel Education Foundation (SMEF)
A tax-exempt, non-profit, charitable foundation for the benefit of
    San Miguel
Tel: 152-7447
E-mail: smef@smefmx.com
Web page: http://www.smefmx.com

17.San Miguel School of English
Provides low-cost English classes for Mexican adults
Tel: 152-1232

18. Save the Laja (Salvemos al Río Laja, AC)
The goal is to increase San Miguel's water supply by river restoration
Tel: 152-0158
Director: Aishling Tully

19. S.O.M.E. (So Others May Eat)
Feeds some 100 elderly men and women from the *campo* every
    Wednesday at 1:45pm at the Parroquia
Tel: 152-1302 or 152-2786 (the Lim family and friends)

20. TAU
Provides assistance to elderly poor
Tel: 152-1398

Watch Repair

1. Relojería Rosas
Mesones #34
Tel: 152-1030
Hrs: Daily 10am-2:30pm and 5-8:30pm, Fri and Sun 10am-2:30pm
Owner: Sr. Martín Rosas speaks some English, very pleasant
Watch repair, bands and engraving

2. Relojería Raúl
Orizaba #16 (near Calle 20 Enero)
Tel: 152-0568
Hrs: Mon-Sat 9am-8pm, Sun 9am-2pm
Owner: Raúl Vázquez Gómez
30 years in business
Watch and clock repair (including antique ones)
Sells watches, clocks, bands and some jewelry
All kinds of small batteries

Water (Bottled)

1. Ciel Agua Purificada
Formerly Risco
Salida a Celaya, km2 (across from Malanquín CC)
Tel: 154-5060
Hrs: Mon-Sat 7am-6pm, closed Sunday
Supervisor: Abél Avila
Owned by Coca Cola
Five gallon (19 *litros*) bottled water (about US$1.50)
Free home delivery

2. Junghanns
Carr. a Celaya #8—Fracc. La Lejona
Tel: 152-8886
Hrs: Mon-Fri 8am-6pm, Sat 8am-3pm
Manager: Juan Carlos Balderas Lugo
German technology
Five gallon (19 litros) bottled water (about US$1.50)
Free same day home delivery

3. Santorini
Salida a Querétaro #143
Tel: 152-0960
Hours: Mon-Sat 8am-6pm, closed Sunday
Manager: Ricardo Barcenas Ugalda
Owned by Pepsi Cola
Five gallon bottles of water (with handle)
Delivered at competitive price

4. TECMAN
Formerly Aqua Nova (July'00)
Enrique García Domínguez #8 – Fracc. La Lejona
Tel: 152-4972 or 152-6046
Hrs: Mon-Sat 7am-6pm, closed Sunday
Free delivery service
Five gallon (19 ltrs) bottled water—inexpensive (about US$1.50)
All water made in San Miguel
Ultrapurified water—reverse osmosis

Printed by: Imprecolor Industrial, S.A. de C.V.

Calle 2, No. 37-A

Fracc. Ind. Benito Juárez, Querétaro, Qro.

NOTES

Hotel La Abadia   36°
                    5 min - centro
                690 (01) 473 732 2464

Hacienda de Marquos   550

Posada Santa Fe   940

Hotel Real de Minas Guanajuato 995

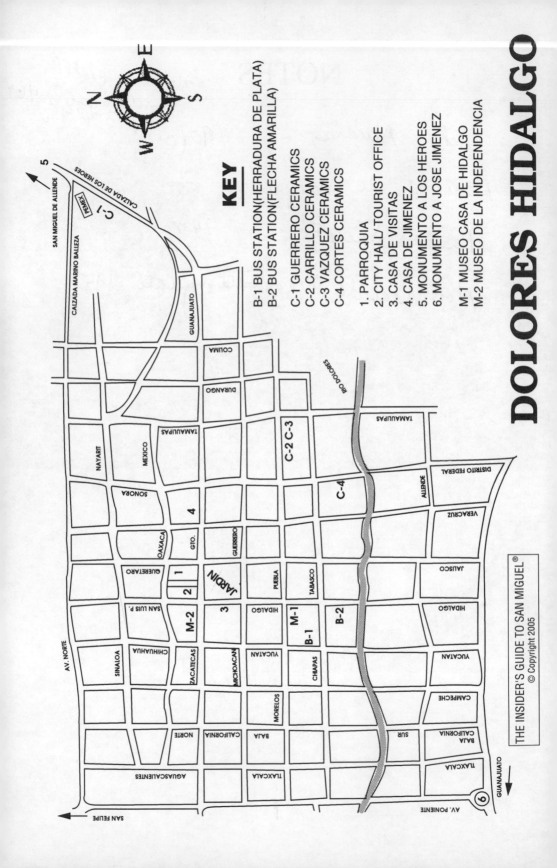

DOLORES HIDALGO

KEY

B-1 BUS STATION(HERRADURA DE PLATA)
B-2 BUS STATION(FLECHA AMARILLA)

C-1 GUERRERO CERAMICS
C-2 CARRILLO CERAMICS
C-3 VAZQUEZ CERAMICS
C-4 CORTES CERAMICS

1. PARROQUIA
2. CITY HALL / TOURIST OFFICE
3. CASA DE VISITAS
4. CASA DE JIMENEZ
5. MONUMENTO A LOS HEROES
6. MONUMENTO A JOSE JIMENEZ

M-1 MUSEO CASA DE HIDALGO
M-2 MUSEO DE LA INDEPENDENCIA

THE INSIDER'S GUIDE TO SAN MIGUEL®
© Copyright 2005

Dolores Hidalgo

(doh-LOH-rehs   ee-DAHL-goh)
Population: Approximately 40,000
Elevation: 6,517 feet
Distance from San Miguel: 43 km (27 miles)
Telephone Area Code: 418

The town was founded in 1568 on the site of an Otomí Indian settlement called Cocomacán (place where turtle doves are hunted). In the 1800s, after several name changes, it became known as Dolores Hidalgo and in 1948 the town was officially given the title of "Cradle of Independence." This is where the Mexican independence movement began in earnest in 1810.

Under the leadership of Father Miguel Hidalgo y Costilla the cry of independence (*Grito de Dolores*) was issued on 16 September, 1810. Eventually México gained independence from Spain in 1821. This important event in the country's history is ceremoniously reenacted each year on the 15th of September at 11pm in Dolores as well as throughout México.

Today, Father Hidalgo is one of México's most admired heroes, second only to Benito Juárez in the number of streets, plazas and statues named after him. Dolores is more than just an historical town, it has acquired an international reputation for its ceramics and pottery.

In addition, Dolores is the birthplace (and final resting place) of the famed singer/composer of *mariachi* music, José Alfredo Jiménez (1926-1973).

As you approach the town on the road from San Miguel, you will note a huge monument in the middle of the road dedicated to the heroes of the independence movement: Hidalgo, Allende, Aldama and Morelos. The monument was built in 1960 on the 150th anniversary of this important date in Mexican history.

Ceramic Workshops

1. Juan F. Guerrero Vajillas
Calzada de los Héroes s/n (past entrance to town on right side of
      road, across the street from an old 4-story mill)
Tel: 182-0305   Fax: 182-0961
Hrs: Daily 9am-7pm
Showroom immediately to right of entrance

241

Complete sets of dishes—high quality
Father of the owner is one of the pioneers of this kind of ceramic
Large workshop area in back
Export around the world

2. Carrillo Vertix Hermanos
(Alfredo, Oscar and Gustavo all speak English)
Puebla #54
Tel: 182-0122   Fax: 182-2596
Hrs: Mon-Fri 9am-6pm, Sat 9am-3pm, Sun 11am-2pm
Large showroom of tiles and sinks
Lowest prices

3. Juan Vázquez
Puebla #56 and #58 (next door to Carrillo)
Tel: 182-0630   Fax: 182-0630
Hrs: Mon-Sat 8am-8pm, Sunday 10am-3pm
Owner speaks English
Large showroom space in several rooms
Huge selection at reasonable prices
Workshop in back

4. Azulejos Talavera Cortés
Calle Distrito Federal #8
Tel: 182-0900   Fax: 182-1252
Hrs: Mon-Fri 8am-4:30pm, Sat 8am-2pm, closed Sunday
Largest ceramic operation in Dolores—several locations
Workshop area upstairs
Good quality—more expensive

Also: **De Talavera**, Puebla #60 (corner of Tamaulipas) Tel: 182-0749
       Good selection, nice folks (Juan Manuel Martínez)

At all of the workshops you can observe the craftspeople at work. Also, keep in mind there are many handicraft stores throughout the town where bargains are waiting for you.

Furniture Stores

1. Muebles y Decoraciones
Calzada de los Héroes km 3.5 (road from San Miguel)
Tel: 182-2195
Hrs: Mon-Sat 8am-7pm, Sunday 10am-5pm
Cedar and pine furniture made to order
Workshop on the premises

2. Bazar el Portón (means "large door")
Calzada de Los Héroes km 3.5
Outside of town (the two stores are only 300 meters apart)

Tel: 182-2229   Fax: 182-0894
Hrs: Mon-Sat 8am-6pm, Sunday 10am-4pm
Huge store with lots of wooden objects out front
Cedar, pine and mahogany furniture made to order
Large workshop in back
Will ship

Hotels

1. Posada Cocomacán Hotel
Plaza Principal #4 (east side)
Tel: 182-0018
Good location and nice courtyard
36 rooms with bath and wood parquet floors
Recently renovated
Ask if Benito Juárez stayed there over a hundred years ago
Most travelers will return to San Miguel for lodging, as Dolores
    is an easy day trip

Also: **Las Campanas Hotel,** Guerrero #15, Tel: 182-0427

Museums

1. Museo Casa de Hidalgo
Corner of Hidalgo and Morelos (one block south of Jardín)
Hrs: Tues-Sat 10am-5:45pm, Sun 10am-4:30pm, closed Mon
Admission: About US$2, free for children under 13 and seniors
    Sunday—free for everyone
Beautiful colonial home which dates from 1779
Father Miguel Hidalgo lived there prior to 1810 uprising
Houses furniture, documents of the independence movement and
    many items relating to the life of Father Hidalgo

2. Museo de la Independencia ✓ 2/8/06 excellent
Zacatecas #6 (½ block west of Jardín)
Hrs: Fri-Wed 9am-5pm, closed Thursday
Admission: Less than US$1
Director: José Ignacio Aguilar (speaks some English)
Built in 18th century and formerly a prison
Plenty of information on independence movement
Exhibition of Guanajuato State handicrafts and José Alfredo
    Jiménez (famous local composer and singer) exhibit
Small craft shop
Worth a visit

Plaza Principal

The **Parroquia de Nuestra Señora de los Dolores** (Our Lady of Sorrows Parish Church), where Father Hidalgo issued the *Grito*, is on the north side of the park. It was constructed in the 18th century with a façade of rose-colored quarry stone. The inside is fairly plain. To the left of the church is the **Presidencia Municipal** (City Hall) with two colorful murals on the independence theme. This is also called Casa de Abasolo where insurgent hero Mariano Abasolo was born in 1784.

On the west side of the park is the **Casa de Visitas** (Visitors' House), which was originally built as the government's sub-delegate house in 1786. Now it is where visiting Mexican presidents (traditionally they come to give the cry of independence in their last year in office) and other dignitaries stay.

In the Plaza (also known as the Jardín) is a large bronze statue of Hidalgo. On weekends the plaza is especially crowded with locals and vendors. Homemade ice cream, which comes in a variety of unusual flavors, is a special treat. One man, Victorino González works the southeast corner of the Jardín where his father, who died in 1994, worked for 86 years!

[handwritten: Vanilla w/ prunes, cafe nuts, chocolate, avocado, tequila, nicev?]

Restaurants

1. El Carruaje Restaurant Bar and Grill ✓ *[handwritten: great breakfast]*
Formerly the El Patio Restaurant
Plaza Principal #8 (east side)
Tel: 182-0474
Hrs: Daily 8am-10:30pm
Decent food at reasonable prices
Order from the menu
Very Mexican atmosphere

2. El Rodeo Restaurant/Bar
Calzada Mariano Balleza (corner of Calle Dolores Hidalgo)
    On bus route and near entrance to city from San Miguel
Tel: 182-2484
Hrs: Daily 12:30-9pm
Owner: Juan Antonio Ibara (former butcher)
Restaurant has five separate rooms around a garden courtyard
No menu—fresh beef only (plus soup)
Waiter brings cuts of meat to table for your selection
It is cooked on a barbecue grill

Café del Jardín, 37
Café del Sol, 38
Café Etc, 40, **57**
Café Montenegro, 40
Café San Francisco, 107
Cafecito, El, 22, **37**
Cajas y Empaque, 169
Calaca, La, 184
Calandria, La, 179
Callejón del Beso, 256
Camacho, Armando, 64
Campanario, El, 26, **155**
Campanas, Las, Hotel, 243
Canadian Embassy, 2
Canales Equestrian Center, 96
Candela, 185
Cantadora, **4,** 130
Cante, 211
Cantina La Coronela, 29
Capelo, 248
Capilla, La, Restaurant, 158
Cappuccino's, 39
Caracol Collection, 171
Carbajo, Lic María, 118
Carey's Especialidades, 80
Caribe, El, 152
Carmen Seamstress, 167
Carmina Suites/Apts, **4,** 107
Carnicería Cervantes, 122
Carnicería La Paloma, 122
Carnicería San Miguel, 123
Carnitas Vicente, 245
Carreta, La, 82
Carrillo Vertix Hermanos, 242
Carruaje, El, Rest, 244
Casa Anguiano, **180,** 195
Casa Armida, 4
Casa Blanca, 153
Casa Bonita, 141
Casa Calderoni, 31
Casa Canal, 52, **180**, 183
Casa Canela, 179
Casa Carmen, 108
Casa Cervantes, 6
Casa Cohen, 10
Casa de Artesanías, 251
Casa de Café, La, 40
Casa de Huéspedes, 112
Casa de Papel, 201
Casa de la Cuesta, **30,** 193
Casa de las Manrique, 249
Casa de Liza en el Parque, **29**
Casa de Los Milagros, 175
Casa de los Perros, 9
Casa de Luz, 191
Casa de Reina B&B, 34
Casa de Sierra Nevada, **100,** 159
Casa de SN en el Parque, 26, **101,** 159
Casa de Visitas, 244
Casa del Angel, 181

Casa del Conde, 253
Casa del Diseño, 180
Casa del Mayorazgo de Canal, 9
Casa del Vidrio, La, 183
Casa Diana, 34
Casa Don Quijote, 146
Casa Estrella, 250
Casa Granada, 30
Casa Hogar Don Bosco, 235
Casa Kloster, 250
Casa, La , 195
Casa María José, 183
Casa Maxwell, 178
Casa Mía, 146
Casa Montana, 213
Casa Olvera, 113
Casa Payo, 159
Casa Pérez, 184
Casa Puesta del Sol, 32
Casa Quetzal, 33
Casa Relox, 150
Casa Roberto, 191
Casa Schuck, 30
Casa Valadez, 254
Casa Vieja, 179
Casa Virreyes, **180**, 184
Casas Coloniales, **138**, 182
Casas Elegantes, 139
Casa y Campo, 183
Caseta, La de Pepe, 206
Casita Feliz, La, 22
Casitas, Las, 7
Castillón, Manuel, 72
Cava, La, 67
Cementos Apasco, 90
Central de Autobuses, 223
Centro Bilingüe, 198
Centro de Crecimiento, 235
Centro Médico del Potosí, **99,** 124
Centro Mexicano de Lengua, 198
Centro Papelero, 61, **200**
Century 21 Parroquia, 138
Cerrajería Ceballos, 90
Cerroblanco, 174, **186**
Cervantino, 257
Challancin, Victoria, 63
Chamonix Restaurant, 145
Chapel of Loreto, 46
Chauvet, Mauricio, 207
Chef María, 62
Chelo's, Farmacia, 56, **73**
China Palace, 149
Chorro, El, **117**, 210
Ciel Agua Purificada, 238
Cine/Bar, 48
Cineclub Bellas Artes, 49
Cinemas Gemelos, 48
Cinemateca Santa Ana, 49
Civic Plaza, 165
Civil Court, 77

Clandestino, 172
Clínica Automotríz, 42
Club 27, 66
CML, 181
COFOCE, 79
Colección Cuatro Vientos, 4
Colegio Atabal, 166
Colegio Los Charcos, 166
Colibrí, El, 20, **35**
Colmena Panadería, La, 22
Colombina 30/30, La, **91**, 190
Colonial Real Estate, 136
Comisión Federal de Electricidad, 229
Community Loan Closet, 99
Computer Center, **59**, 61
Concepción, La, 46
Conexión, La, **53**, 56, 60, 133
Cono, El, Restaurant, 245
Continental Airlines, 228
Conversaciones con Amigos, 200
Copi Jusa, 64
Copias Artículos de Ingeniería, 64
Corazón Divino, 179
Corium, 190
Correo, El, Restaurant, 148
Cortés Azulejos Talavera, 242
Cos-Az, **4**, 41
COTUR, 257
Counter Cultures, 175
Courtney, Renee, 189
Coyote Canyon Adventures, 96
Cranston, Toller, 13
Cruz del Perdón, La, 212
Cuba Vieja, La, 29
Cucaracha, La, 29
Curves, 85
Cutting Garden, the, 87
Cyberm@tsa, 57
Cybernet, 59

D
Darla, 52, **188**
Dávila Antiques, 182
Dawit, Margarette Studio, 17
Delfín, El, 245
DHL International, 168
Deserve, 126
De Talavera, 242
DeWa, 183
Dicambios, 125
DIF, 235
Diligencia, La, 3
Diseño.i, 60
Diseño y Vitral, 191
DIVA, 50
Divina, La, 121
Dobarganes, Dr Fidel, 71
Dolphy Ice Cream, 114
Domino's Pizza, 163
Don Pedro Ferretería, 89

Dos Casas, 31
DuBois, Patsy, 62
Dulcería Loreto, 82
Dulces Sueños, 192
Durable Medical, 98

E
El Asador Catalán, 150
El Caporal, 29
El Claustro, 181
El Harem, 162
El Pato, 19
Electroserc, 61, **134**
Electrosistemas Hepco, 75
Elektra, 126
Elías, Dra Laura, 68
Embajadoras Market, 251
Elementos, 177
Emergency Hot Line, 77 & yellow map
Emporio Pozos, 213
En Forma Aerobics Studio, 84
Enchilada, La, 146
Ensueños de San Miguel, Los, 140
Equipos y Sistemas, 60
Escondido Spa, 212
Escuela Gallery, La 14
Esencia, La, 61
Esmeralda Mercería, La, 200
Espinosa, Antonieta, 199
Espino's, **79**, 122
Estación Internet, 58
Estafeta, 168
Estetica Unisex Bandala, 89
Esteto Clínica, 88, **93**
Estrada, Javier, 128
Estrella Blanca Bus, 226
Estudiantinas, 256
Estudio Aparicio #4, 18
Estudio Gardner, 16
Estudio 46, 16
Estudio Victor Heady, 16
ETN Bus, 224
Euromex, 181
Europea, La, 121
EVOS/Artesana, 176, 183
Ex-hacienda San Gabriel de la Barrera, 256
EXIM, 174
Express Laundry, 116

F
FAI, 235
Fallon, Christopher Design, **51**, 183
Famosos de Pozos, Los, 214
Farmacia Guadalajara, 73
Farmacia Guanajuato, 74
Farmacia Homeopatica, 74
Farmacia Humac, 74
Farmapronto, 74
Feed the Hungry, 236
Felguera, La, Restaurant, 144

Ferre-Plomería, 75
Ferretería Cedelco, 89
Ferretería Torres, 91
Ferreti, 183
Finestra Caffé, La, 39
Finnegan's Pub, 154
Flavors of the Sun, 63
Flecha Amarilla, **223**, 226, 258
Floriade, 129
Fonda, La, 150
Food Factory, 144
Ford (RAMSA), 44
Fortuna, 20
Foto Americana, 131
Foto Bazar, 52
Foto Estudio San Miguel, 132
Foto Fácil, 131
Fotografía, La, 131
Fotografía Iris Profesional, 131
Fragua, La, 28
Frazee, María Teresa, 199
Frida, 195
Friedeberg, Pedro Museo/Galería, 12
Fun Art, 175

G
Gaby, **175**, 191
Galarza, 64
Galería Atenea, 11
Galería Casiopea, 186
Galería de Arte Fotográfico, 12
Galería de Cerámica, 11
Galería de la O, 13
Galería dos Culturas, 11
Galería Goded, 185
Galería Izamal, 13
Galería Mallory, 17
Galería Mariposa, 177
Galería Maya Productions, 213
Galería Pérgola, 10
Galería San Miguel, 10
Galería Savia, 178
Galería Sollano 50, 15
Galería Tesoros, 185
Gallo, El, Restaurant, 255
García, Lic Jorge, 118
García, Patty, 78
Gas Inem, 229
Gas Noel, 229
Gassler, Larry, 61
Gem Museum, 253
Gema, 186
Genesis Tienda Naturista, 143
Gigante, 74, 122, **202**
Girasol Boutique Willa Mina, **50**, 189
Glass Factory (Guajuye), 209
Globo, El, 189
GM (Webb Motors), 44
Godinez Paint Shop, 44
Goldie, 50, **172**

Gombos, **153**, 163
Gómez, Rangel, 18
González, ChaCha, 64
González, Gorky, 248
González Servicio, 43
Grito, El, 66
Grotta, La, **160**, 163
Grupo Nacional Provincial, 124
Gruta, La, Spa, 213
Guerin, Paul, 218
Guerrero, Juan, 241
Gusano Azul, 178
Gutenberg School, Juan, 167

H
Habanera, 185
Hacienda de las Flores, 104
Hacienda de Marfil, 253
Hacienda Los Laureles, 147
Hacienda Oficina Federal, 77
Hacienda y Crédito Público, 77
Harry's Market, **67**, 156
Harry's Restaurant/Café, 27, **155**
Hat Shop, 91
Hayes, Jack, Studio, 15
Heaven, 7th, **181**, 189
Hecho en México, 154
Helados Holanda, 56, **114**
Herald newspaper, 129
HERHER, 140
Hernández, Eduardo, 41
Hernández, Oscar, 41
Hernández, Rosa, 195
Herreria Rosas, 175
Hierro a Mano, 175
Hierro Comercial, 90
History of San Miguel Museum, 127
Hogar de los Angeles, 236
Hola Rent A Car, 42
Holly's Comfort Food, 63
Horse Boarding, 97
Horseback Riding, 96
Horse Tours, 96
Hospital Angeles del Pedregal, 100
Hospital Angeles de Qro, 99
Hospital Civil, 97
Hospital de la Fé, 70, **97**, 115
Hospital de Nuestra Señora de la Salud, 99
Hostal Alcatráz, 113
Hot Air Ballon, 214
Hotel Arcada, 110
Hotel Aristos, **109**, 207
Hotel Casa Linda, 103
Hotel Casa Mexicana, 213
Hotel Casa Rosada, 104
Hotel Castillo, 249
Hotel d'Allende, 112
Hotel El Caracol, 107
Hotel La Casa de Café, 112
Hotel Los Insurgentes, 111

Hotel Sautto, 111
House and Garden Tour, 209
House of Good Spirits, 250
House of the Inquisitor, 10
HSBC Bank, 25
Huéspedes Feliz, 112

I
Ibarra, Fernando, 220
Icpalli, **172**, 183
Immigration Office, 78
Indonesian Catering, 63
Infierno, El, 152
Imprenta Lasser, 64
Indigo Galería, 13
Instituto Allende, **14**, 56, 165, 197
Instituto Habla Hispana, 198
Intercam, 125
Internet Fácil, 59
IREE, 236
Iris Mercería y Papelería, 200
Itzcuinapan Tours & Transportation, 221

J
Jarciería, 196
Jardín, El, 165
Jardín de Don Quijote B&B, 33
Jardín de San Francisco, 165
Jardín Unión, **256**, 258
Jasmine, 92
Jehovah's Witnesses, 48
Jewish Community, 48
Johansson, Marianne, Galería, 187
Jonuco Eléctrico, El, 74
Josefa, 4
Joyería, a Mano, 189
Joyería David, 189
Joyería Paris, 185
Juanita's Pizza, 163
Juárez, Lupita, 130
Juárez, Mónica, 92
Junghanns, 238

K
Kahn, Helene, 219
Keller, Keith, La Escuela, 14
Kastenbaum Gallery, 13
Key Stand, 91
Kike's Super Mercado, 80
Kunsthaus Santa Fé, 13
Kurt Tours, 222

L
La Fragua, 28
La Loma, Rancho, 97
LABSAM, 115
LADATEL, 206
Lagundi, 19, **20**, 35
Lan-Art, 41
Lapidaria Ramírez, 189

Lara, 90
Las Colonias, 130
Lavamágico, 116
Lavandería Ana, 117
Lavandería Automática de SM, 116
Lavandería el Reloj, 116
Lavandería Franco, 116
Lavandería la Famosa, 193
Lavinia's Framing, 20
Lawrence, Sue, 85
Lawson, Mary, 71
L.D.S. (Mormon), 48
Leandro Tours, 220
Leather Shop, 52, 91, **190**, 193
Libros el Tecolote, **35**
Life Path Retreats, 87
Limerick Pub, 28
L'Invito, 29, **159**
Lions International, 236
Llamas, 181
Lloyd's, 25
Lobo Gym, 82
López, Enrique Classroom, 18
López Funeral Home, 191
Luminaria, La, 191

M
Macro Corpovino, 122
Maestro Benjamín, 183
Magic Pets, 232
Magnolia, 195
Maja, 191
Malanquín Country Club, **65**, 207
Mama Mía, 29, **66**, 163
Manantial, 7
Manolo's Sports Bar, **28**, 159
Mansión del Bosque, 107
Mansión Virreyes, 110
Marabu Framing, 20
Maraye, 169
Marcia's Boutique, 51
Marc Obras, 21
Margarita, La, Real Estate, 138
Mariachi Los Camperos, 128
Marín Estetica, 88
Mario's Transportation, 222
Market Bistro, 145
Martha's Sandals, 169
Martínez, Dr, Jorge, 70
Martínez, Juan Francisco, 61
Maya, Liliane Tours, 221
Mayólica Santa Rosa, 248
Medical Air Services, 125
Meditation Center, 86
Mensajería Local, 55
Menutre, 81
Mercado de San Juan de Dios, 202
Mercado Hidalgo, 251
Mercado, 130, **202**
Merrill, Dr, Robert, 232

Mexicana Airlines, 228
México Advisor, **118**, 135
México Lindo, 176
Mexiquito, 236
Mexisano, 64, **67**
MexPost, 133
Meyenberg, E, Lic, 118
Mezzaluna, La, 81
Mibosa, 201
Mini Lab Processing, 132
Miranda, Olimpia, 233
Monex, 126
Monterrubio, Dr, Gabriel, 71
Montes, Liz, 84
Moola Bandha Yoga Shala, 86
Morada Hotel, La, 109
Moroccan Imports, 41
Motel de las Embajadoras, 249
Moto Rent, 42
Muebles y Decoraciones, 242
Mujeres en Cambio, 236
Multicom, 206
Multipack, 168
Municipal Court, 77
Municipal Tourist Office, 76
Musas-Café Italian, Las, 39
Museo Casa de Hidalgo, 243
Museo de Arte, 253
Museo de Arte Popular, 127
Museo de la Independencia, 243
Museo de las Momias, 252
Museo Diego Rivera, 251
Museo Iconográfico del Quijote, 252

N
Naciones Unidas School, 166
Nagle, Joan, 85
Net@ San Miguel Cybercafé, 58, 205
Night Kitchen, The, 63
Nirvana, 157
Nopal Tours, 222
Nueva Lucha, La, 191
Nuevo Mexico, 188
Nutri Verde Restaurant, 147
Nutri Yogurt, 115
Nuevo Mundo, El, 185

O
Oficinas del Gobierno del Estado, 77
Ojo de Venado, 253
Olé-Olé, 148
Ono, 184
Optica Jess & Karen, 131
Optica San Miguel, 130
Oratorio, 46
Origen, 177
Ortega, Sergio, 72
Ortopedia Ortíz, 98
Osman, Ed Estudio, 16
Otro Camino, El, 158, **173**, 183, 191

P
Pack 'N' Mail, **55**, 56, 133, 169
Palapa, La, 149
Panadería El Maple, 23
Panadería La Espiga, 23
Panadería la Purísima, 23
Panadería Malena, 23
Pancho & Leftys, 66
Panteón Municipal, 44
Parador de San Sebastian, 111
Parador Hotel San Javier, 249
Pariente, 43
Parque el Charrco del Ingenio, 211
Parque Guadiana, 166
Parque Juárez, 165
Parque Las Colonias, 211
Parroquia de Nuestra Sra de Dolores, 244
Parroquia, La, 45
Patricia, 92
Patrica's Jewelry, 187
Patronato Pro Niños, 209, **236**
Patterson, Marisela (tutor), 199
Patton Ins Group, 125
Paulín, Maru, 199
Pegaso, El, 64, **144**, 181
Pegasso Plus, 224
Peltz, Charlotte, 233
PEMEX, 216
Peralta Automotríz, 43
Piña, Oscar, 72
Perfil Publicitario, 55
Petit Bar, El, 29, **145**
Petit Four, **22**, 40, 82
Pet Vet, 232
Photo Super 30, 56, **131**
Piaf, 52, **185**
Pila, La, 41, **117**
Pinguis, El, 255
Pípila, El, **10**, 256
Pípila Peluquería, El, 88
Plásticos Castañeda, 194
Platería Guerrero, 188
Plaza de la Paz, 259
Plaza de Toros Oriente, 36
Pocitos, Los, 208
Police Station, 76
Policía Judicial, 77
Pollería Zaragoza, 123
Pollo y Huevo, 123
Posada Carmina, **106**, 143
Posada Cocomacán, 243
Posada de la Aldea, 108
Posada (hotel) de las Monjas, 110
Posada la Ermita, 110
Posada Santa Fé, **249**, 254
Posada Villa Martha, 7
Post Office, 79, **132**
Pozos, 213
Premier, House Rentals, 139
Premium Home Healthcare Providers, 73

Presa de la Olla, 256
Presidencia Municipal, 75
Primera Plus Bus, **223**, 258
Princesa, La, 65
Procomm Direct, 205
Productos Herco, 174
PROFECO, 79
Promotion Mex Culture, 54, 60, 219, 224, **228**
Pronto Pizza, 163
Pueblo Viejo Restaurant, 143, **162**
Puertecita Boutique'Otel, 102
Punto G, 58
Puzzlemania, 193

Q
Quinta Loreto, **108**, 148

R
Rabern, Rosa María, 71
Radio Servicio Vega, 133
Radio Shack, 132
Radio Station XESQ, 230
Radio Station Stereo FM106, 230
Radio TV San Rafael, 134
Rafa Tourist Tours, 218
Ramiro's Club, 82
Rancho La Loma, 97
RE/MAX Colonial, 136
Real de Minas Hotel, **106**, 207
Real Estate San Miguel, 138
Red Cross Ambulance, 98
Redpack, 168
Relojería Raúl, 237
Relojería Rosas, 237
Reparadora de Calzado, 170
Restaurant 73, 17, 149
Restaurant Lila, 151
Reyna's Cooking Class, 62
Reyna Polanco Tours, 219
Rhea's Massage, 93
Rinconcito, El, 161
Rincón de Don Tomás, 38
Rincón Español, 162
Ring, El, 66
Ristorante da Andrea, 154
Rivera, Alejandro, 18
Rivera, Enrique, 230
Robbins, Miss, Victoria, 167
Roberts, Judith Colección, 51
Rodeo, El, Restaurant, 244
Romano's, 153
Ruffert, Daniel, 15

S
Sagert, Edina, 15
Sala de Belleza Carmela, 88
Sala de Belleza Evangee, 88
Sala Quetzal, 119

Salón & Spa de Robert, **87**, 93
Salud, La, 46
San Agustín Café, 38
San Antonio Church, 47
San Carlos Fotografía, 132
San Francisco Church, 46
San Francisco Hotel, 107
San Francisco Laboratorio, 115
San Juan de Dios, 47
San Miguel Education Foundation, 237
San Miguel Health & Fitness Center, 83
San Miguel House Rentals, 139
San Miguel Properties, 137
San Miguel Management, 140
San Miguel School of English, 237
San Miguel Sports Center, 83
Santa Clara, 60, **115**
Santa Mónica Hotel, **101**, 145
Santa Verónica, 212
Santiago, Francisco, 222
Santo Domingo Sports Club, 84
Santorini, 238
Santuario Hotel, El, 106
SAPASMA, 229
Save the Laja, 237
Sazón, 62, **173**
SECTUR, 228
Security Storage, 201
Segunda Llamada, 52
Select Real Estate, 136
Sensual Chocolatiers, 82
Servicio de Banquetes, **63**, 141
Servicio Mixto de Taxi, 217
Serfín-Santander, 24
Sierra Madre, 194
Sierra Nevada Spa, 91
Siesta, La, 113
Simms, Lisa, 16
Sindicato, El, 208
Sistemas Integrales, 61
Sky Med Int'l, 125
Social Security (IMSS) Hospital, 97
Sol y Luna, 34, 141, **221**
Solutions, **54**, 133, 169
S.O.M.E., 237
Sorin, Linda, 72
Soto, Lic Salvador, 117
Sours, Edwin, 61
S.P.A., 233
Spanish For You, 199
St. Paul's Anglican Church, **47**, 99
Stilo, 191
Studio Pilates, 88
Sunday Market, 203
Super Limpio, 41
Super San Francisco II, 80
Susazón, 81
Sushi Bar, 162

T

Taboada, 212
Talavera Hidalguense, 176
Talisman Too, **49**, 174
Tasca de los Santos, 254
Tato y Lore, 232
TAU, 237
Taxis (San Miguel), 216
Taylor, Dra, Juliana, 70
Teatro Angela Peralta, 208
Teatro del Pueblo, 208
Teatro Juárez (Gto), 259
Tecman, 238
Tejeda, Dra, Guadalupe, 69
Tele Cable, 229
Téllez, Dr, Rolando, 232
TELMEX, 56, **203**, 231
Templo de la Compañía, 258
Ten Ten Pie, 161
Tenorio, 23
Teocalli Tours and Transportation, 218
Tepalcatt, 176
Termo Gas, 229
Terra, **130**, 194
Terrazas, Las, 5
Thiel, Ana, Studio/Showroom, 18
Tiempos, 4
Tienda Allegro, 127
Tienda, La, 120, **201**
Tinta y Papel, 19, **35**
Tío Lucas, 26, **156**
Tlapalería y Ferretería, 89
Tocador, El, 52
Tomate, El, 80
Tomato, El, 147
Tonatiu Metztli, 193
Topacio, El, 185
Torta Mundo, 151
Tortilla de Maíz, 215
Tortillas de Harina, 215
Tortilla, La, Entretenida, 215
Tortitlán, 152
Tourist Office, State, 78
Tours México Colonial, 220
Trains, 227
Tránsito Estado, 77
Tránsito Municipal, 76
Tránsito y Transporte, 77
Transportes del Norte, 226
Transportes San Miguel, 225
Trattoria Del Gallo, 254
Tres Casitas, 5
Truco 7, 255
Tuesday Market, 130, **203**
Twenty Four Hour Association, 44
U
Unica, La, 195
Unión, La, 168
Unisex Beauty Salon, 72, **88**
Unísono Net, 56

Unitarian/Universalist, 47
United Airlines, 228
Uurich, 194

V

Vacation Homes San Miguel, 140
Valadéz, Estéban, 176, **214**
Valle, María de, 92
Vargas, Dr, Jorge, 68
Vasconcelos, José, 166
Vázquez, Dr. Edgardo, 231
Vázquez, Juan, 242
Vázquez Tours, Juan, 222
Ventana, La, 40
Vera, Dr, Alfonso, 69
Viajes de San Miguel, 218, **227**
Viajes Vertiz, 220, **227**
Victoriana, La, 174
Victoria's Chest, 195
Vida, La, 27
Vidargas, Dotty, 138
Video Centro, 234
Video Fuentes, 234
Video Geminis, 64
Vidriería La Muñeca, 21
Vie de Chateau, La, 183
Vilar, 170, **190**
Villa Jacaranda, **105**, 160
Villa Mirasol, 33
Villa Rivera, Hotel, 102
Villa Scorpio B&B, 32
Villa Xichú, 5
Vinos y Licores, 122
Vinos y Licores Don Quijote, 121
Vista Hermosa Taboada, Hotel, 113
Vista Real Hotel & Restaurant, 103
Vitrales Exclusivos, 184
Viveros Paraíso, 129
Viveros Primavera, 129
Volcán, El, 90

W

Walking Tour San Miguel, 209
Warren Hardy Spanish, 196
Weber, Walter, Tennis, 207

Y

Yamaha Scooters, 42
Yoga at Bellas Artes, 87
Yoga with Norman, 86
Yucca, La, 130

Z

Zacateros 81-B, 12
Zafiro Joyería, 188
Zandunga, La, 40
Zapatería Martha, 169
Zarco Atesanías, 88, **176**
Zavala, Lic, Roberto, 118
Zócalo, **177**, 192

About the Author ...

The author grew up outside of Buffalo in Snyder, New York. In 1959 he graduated from Bowling Green State University with a degree in business administration and went on to serve as a lieutenant with the US Navy in the Far East. Upon leaving active service, the author lived and worked in the Philippines, Hong Kong, Korea and Japan. While living in Asia, he was involved in a similar publication, *The Gentlemen's Guide to Hong Kon*g. Returning to the USA Dean lived in Honolulu, Torrance, California and Amherst, Massachusetts while raising his son Anil.

Dean first set foot in San Miguel de Allende, arriving by train from Mexico City, in November 1990. After a five-month stay the author returned once more for a two-month visit before becoming a permanent resident of Mexico in September 1993. The author has lived in San Miguel every month of the year, gaining a real feel for and understanding of the town and the people. He can often be seen with backpack and sombrero on the streets of San Miguel gathering material for the next edition. Don't hesitate to introduce yourself and get your book autographed.

To see colored pictures of San Miguel visit:
http://insidersma.tripod.com